British Foreign Policy Under Thatcher

British Foreign Policy Under Thatcher

edited by

Peter Byrd
University of Warwick

Philip Allan/St Martin's Press

First published 1988 by

PHILIP ALLAN PUBLISHERS LIMITED
MARKET PLACE
DEDDINGTON
OXFORD OX5 4SE

First published in the USA 1988 by

St Martin's Press, Incorporated
175 Fifth Avenue
New York
NY 10010

British Library Cataloguing in Publication Data

British foreign policy under Thatcher.
    1. Great Britain. Foreign relations.
    Policies of government, 1979–1987
    I. Byrd, Peter
    327.41

ISBN 0–86003–401–1
ISBN 0–86003–701–0 (pbk)

Library of Congress Cataloging in Publication Data

British foreign policy under Thatcher.
    Includes index.
    1. Great Britain--Foreign relations--1945- .
    2. Thatcher, Margaret. I. Byrd, Peter.
    DA589.8.B78 1988   327.41   88–26380

ISBN 0–312–02526–2

Typeset in 11/12 Garamond by Photoprint, Torquay
Printed and bound in Great Britain at A. Wheaton & Co. Ltd, Exeter

Contents

Contributors

David Allen is Senior Lecturer in European Studies, University of
Loughborough
James Barber is Master of Hatfield College, University of Durham
Jim Bulpitt is Reader in Politics, University of Warwick
Peter Byrd is Lecturer in Politics, University of Warwick
Michael Clarke is Lecturer in Politics, University of Newcastle
Walter Little is Lecturer in Politics and Latin American Studies,
University of Liverpool
Sir Anthony Parsons is Research Fellow, University of Exeter and
was formerly Ambassador to Iran, Permanent Representative to
the United Nations and Special Adviser to the Prime Minister
Gerald Segal is Lecturer in Politics, University of Bristol
Michael Smith is Senior Lecturer in International Relations,
Coventry Polytechnic

Introduction

PETER BYRD

Foreign policy remains a relatively unknown area of the three Thatcher governments. It is hardly surprising that most attention has concentrated on the radical domestic policies of the government since the Thatcher 'project' has demanded a complete restatement of the priorities of government towards British society. However the foreign policy of the governments is certainly worth studying and raises a number of interesting questions.

From the perspective of the student of foreign policy, the first question to ask almost invariably concerns continuity and change – to what extent is a commitment to radical change transferable into the foreign-policy sector, where it will conflict with the inertia of existing commitments and forces over which the government may in practice exercise only limited control? It is clear from the essays in this volume that the government did have radical ideas for the foreign-policy sector which it saw as complementing its domestic programme – the 'Right Approach' at home and the 'Resolute Approach' abroad. This approach to foreign policy was highly ideological, eschewing the more traditionalist and pragmatic assumptions of its predecessors. Mrs Thatcher was strongly identified with the adoption of this approach, so that the essays explore two perennially important themes in foreign policy – the role of ideology and the importance of the individual attempting to impose herself on an established institutional framework.

It follows that foreign policy has, as in most arenas of domestic policy, raised a question mark over the institutional adequacy of existing government departments, with their strongly entrenched codes of behaviour and departmental preferences (the 'official mind'), to carry out radical change. In the case of Mrs Thatcher, irritation has been directed most publicly and consistently at the Foreign and Commonwealth Office, portrayed as a sort of 'enemy within', which argues the case of foreign governments rather than strongly pursuing British national interests. The tension created by this impatience was expressed most vividly in Lord Carrington's remark, after his resignation from government, about the short-comings of Mrs Thatcher's style of 'megaphone diplomacy'. Most of the essays reveal the conflict between the Prime Minister's radical intentions and the constraining power of both her own bureaucracy and external forces. However, while in 1979 Mrs Thatcher was a novice at diplomacy and defence, armed only with radical ideals, by 1988 she had become the most experienced Western statesman; in all other countries with which she had to deal there have been major changes of government. Moreover, while in 1979 Mrs Thatcher was a radical, challenging a consensus entrenched at home and in many other Western governments, by 1988 she can claim to be widely imitated and emulated. The disciplines of the market have become the established wisdom not only in Britain, where the opposition parties have been forced to redraw party programmes in order to embrace the popularity of the market, but also abroad, where 'Thatcherism' is practised (or at least preached) both in Western societies and in many Communist and Third World regimes. Ideology has also helped restructure the overseas aid programme. The value of foreign aid has been reduced and its distribution shifted to reflect general foreign-policy objectives and British commercial interests. The separate Ministry of Overseas Development was abolished and placed within the Foreign and Commonwealth Office.

Nevertheless, the arguments for continuity in foreign policy are strong. In the chapters on the Soviet Union, the Middle East, the Far East and Pacific, and the United States, the elements of continuity appear very strong. There are changes, of course, in presentation, rhetoric and aspiration. New Right ideology, a good deal of it imported from the United States, has not only inspired a good deal of the government's domestic programme but has also helped revive the 'special relationship' with a similarly inspired American government. Nevertheless in foreign policy outputs these changes appear, after eight years, to have been marginal rather than decisive. Clarke introduces into his chapter two contrasting themes in Thatcherite ideology on foreign policy: one is the commitment to unilateral strength, fervent anti-Communism and a rather crude defence of national interests in the language of patriotism; the second is a 'Churchillian' theme of negotiation from strength combined with a far-sighted commitment to the importance of balance of power and an acceptance of the need for reassurance and security for potentially hostile states. These two tendencies within Thatcherite foreign policy coexist uneasily in an unstable balance although, over time, the Churchillian tendency has tended to dominate.

Other themes emerge alongside the ideological. One is the continuity of policy imposed by declining power and declining ability to pursue a foreign policy independently from allied states. As Parsons argues, declining power may also produce declining interests so that, in the Middle East, British policy has been relatively inactive because the scope of British power and interests is simply less than ever before – or at least less than since the Battle of the Nile! Similar constraints on unilateral policy are noted in the chapters on the United States, southern Africa and the Soviet Union.

When Britain chooses to act politically it needs support from other states and that support also constitutes a constraint and a framework for concerted action rather than independent action, as in the attempt to influence the negotiations between the United States and the Soviet Union on nuclear disarmament, the approach to South Africa, and the resolution of the Palestinian problem. All indicate action concerted with allies, primarily European allies within Nato or the European Community (EC). 'Europeanisation' of both British domestic politics and British foreign policy were, in the early 1980s, familiar themes. We have heard less of them recently but there is no doubt that in foreign policy the EC represents an institution of fundamental importance. The development of the EC and, in more narrowly strategic policy, of a loose European gathering of Nato members (sometimes meeting within the framework of the Western European Union), coincides with the displacement of the Commonwealth as an institution for managing

British interests. Only in the chapter on southern Africa does the Commonwealth emerge, and there as a rather ineffective constraint on the government rather than a support.

Two possible exceptions to the 'rule' of declining power and interests are noted in the book. The unexpected case concerns East Asia and the Pacific. Here Segal analyses a renaissance of British interests and a revival of activity. However, the return to the region has been as a commercial and economic actor and not as a strategic or political actor. Indeed, the agreement with China to end the British role in Hong Kong has probably facilitated the growth of Britain's role in the region as a normal state, rather than, as hitherto, having to act as a power with special interests which could complicate commercial or economic relations. Certainly, in this region the Commonwealth no longer appears an important component of British policy. The more striking exception to a picture of a declining global role is, of course, the Falklands. Little's chapter avoids going over the familiar ground of the background to the 1982 Argentine invasion, although it is clearly important in terms of the present argument to note that the background consisted of negotiations with Argentina to cede sovereignty in return for a lease-back to guarantee the Falkland Islanders' traditional way of life. Indeed the outbreak of the war may have been occasioned in part by the decision of the Ministry of Defence to withdraw the naval presence in the South Atlantic as an economy measure in order to help sustain the primary commitments to Nato. Perhaps paradoxically in the light of Mrs Thatcher's view of the Foreign and Commonwealth Office as a department geared to representing the interests of foreigners rather than of Britain, the FCO had strongly resisted this withdrawal on the grounds that such a decision would send the wrong diplomatic signal to Buenos Aires.

Mrs Thatcher has been decisive in shaping policy since the 1982 war. The possibility of a negotiated settlement with Argentina on the status of the Falklands, or even the normalisation of relations, has undoubtedly been reduced by her determination to uphold the gains of 1982. This decision has had diplomatic consequences, but on the whole these have been surprisingly small and the government has been able quite easily to live with the weakly articulated international opposition to Britain's position. The government has also, after a difficult period, brought the defence costs of the Falklands commitment under control, as Byrd shows in the chapter on defence. Notwithstanding the direction of British policy up to the Argentine invasion, the Falklands case since 1982 remains the clearest example of the influence of Mrs Thatcher on the making of policy and of her ability to exercise a personal stamp on policy over and above the influence of the bureaucracy.

The geographical organisation of the chapters indicates the scope of policy and the range of issues since 1979. Certain themes emerge which transcend a regional perspective, most notably the management of the international economy and the impact of international economic developments on Britain's 'open polity'. Smith's chapter discusses the crucial American dimension to the economic problem and Allen's the European dimension, while Bulpitt emphasises the international and open nature of the British economy from his domestic perspective. All the chapters assume a link between external policy and the domestic system. Barber's chapter emphasises the pluralistic nature of group involvement on southern Africa, but at the same time he contrasts group involvement with electoral apathy. Byrd's chapter on defence is more strongly orientated inwards and considers defence as a policy arena bridging domestic and external policy.

Foreign policy is politicised and the government's handling of it reflects political priorities. The negotiation of the Anglo-Irish Treaty of 1985 illustrates the linkages between foreign and domestic policy. British relations with Ireland are in fact considered most appropriately within the context of domestic politics; policy is dominated by the pressing need to normalise the situation in Northern Ireland, isolating and containing the Provisional IRA while drawing the nationalist/Catholic and loyalist/Protestant communities towards some sort of minimal consensus on the government of the province. Normalising the situation, the government decided, called for the assistance of the Irish government, which enjoys close relations with moderate Catholic opinion in the North. At the same time external pressures, particularly from the United States and the European Community states, which were echoed within government by the Foreign Office and to a lesser extent the Ministry of Defence, pointed strongly in the direction of the dual goal of normalisation in the province and a *rapprochement* with Dublin.

Bulpitt is primarily interested in domestic politics, and this leads him to adopt a fundamentally different perspective. Although he concedes that policy may reveal a considerable continuity with the pre-1979 period, he analyses foreign policy as part of a broader strategy of 'party statecraft'. Winning the party game is, he argues, the essence of politics and foreign policy offers opportunities for this party statecraft; indeed the constraints upon policy, emphasised by the other authors in the volume, can be turned, in Bulpitt's perspective, into such opportunities. This argument is in fact a version of the classical thesis about the 'primacy of domestic politics'. It is certainly relevant to Bulpitt's thesis, and indeed to all the authors, that although there are marked continuities of policy with the pre-1979 period the political context has changed. After a decade of détente, the 1980s have been a dangerous era of superpower confrontation, and of the continuing decline in the benign assumptions about international economic interdependence that began with the oil crises of 1973/4. Whether viewed from an internal or from an external policy perspective, foreign policy under Thatcher has been 'high politics'. There is a paradox here: the content of foreign policy has not changed dramatically since 1979, but the external environment has become more challenging while at the same time the domestic consensus on foreign and defence policy has weakened. Foreign policy has thus taken on a new domestic political significance and become an important tool in the game of party politics, yet without the content of policy shifting more than marginally.

Foreign policy, for Bulpitt then, has domestic consequences and acts as an instrument of party statecraft. Yet despite the successes of foreign policy in this period – in Zimbabwe, Ireland, and the Falklands, in the shaping of the EC budget, and with the United States, the Soviet Union and, to a lesser extent, Hong Kong – the government has not enjoyed a smooth ride at home. The first years of the Thatcher governments were characterised by ministerial instability. In 1979 the ministerial team was strikingly non-Thatcherite: Lord Carrington as Foreign Secretary, Sir Ian Gilmour as Lord Privy Seal or deputy foreign secretary with a place in Cabinet; Francis Pym as Defence Secretary. Each became critics of the government's general strategy for managing the economy and upholders of an older version of one-nation Toryism. In January 1981 Pym was demoted to Leader of the House of Commons and John Nott, who was much closer to Mrs Thatcher, appointed in his place. In September 1981 Gilmour was sacked and replaced by a loyalist, Humphrey Atkins. Following the Falklands débâcle of March 1982, Carrington and Atkins resigned and Nott was only kept from resigning by persuasion. Pym was brought back from exile to run the Foreign Office and to restore confidence, the second Cabinet post being abolished. In January 1983 Nott resigned after seeing through the Falklands War and the immediate postwar arrangements, which included a concession over the size of the surface naval fleet despite Nott's original reforming zeal to rationalise the defence effort. Michael Heseltine was appointed to Defence with a specific mandate to win over public opinion to the government's defence policy, which had come under severe attack from the Campaign for Nuclear Disarmament and was in some respects generally unpopular. Following the 1983 general election the ministerial team was more stable. Pym was immediately replaced by Sir Geoffrey Howe, who has retained the post. Heseltine resigned from the government in January 1986 during the Westland crisis, along with his adversary in the crisis Leon Brittan. Heseltine was replaced by Sir George Younger, a less flamboyant minister who had enjoyed success at the Scottish Office, and Howe and Younger have since 1986 given a steadier leadership to foreign and defence policy. There may indeed be a paradox here in the sense that it was the non-Thatcherite ministers who presided over the period of confrontation and cold war with the Soviet Union, while the more Thatcherite ministers have helped cultivate the remarkable improvement of relations with Gorbachev's Soviet Union.

This book, then, is an attempt to explore the foreign policies of the Thatcher governments and to complement studies of domestic politics in the Thatcher era.

References and Further Reading

Drucker, H. (1986) *Developments in British Politics*, Macmillan.
Kavanagh, D. (1987) *Thatcherism and British Politics, the End of Consensus?*, Clarendon Press.
Pym, F. (1984) *The Politics of Consent*, Hamish Hamilton.
Riddell, P. (1985) *The Thatcher Government*, Blackwell.
Young, H. and Sloman, A. (1986) *The Thatcher Phenomenon*, BBC Publications.
Smith, M., Smith, S. and White, B. (eds) (1988) *British Foreign Policy: Tradition, Change and Transformation*, Unwin Hyman. This is the most recent analysis of foreign policy in the analytical or thematic style referred to above.

CHAPTER 1

Britain and the United States: Beyond the 'Special Relationship'?

MICHAEL SMITH

More than any other bilateral relationship, that between Britain and the USA permeates all areas of British foreign policy. Historically, it has been both more salient and more significant to British foreign-policy makers than relations with the countries of Western Europe or the Third World. Often it has been presented as a 'special relationship', implying an intimacy and mutual responsiveness on the part of those involved in it which transcends the more normal pursuit of national interests or the conclusion of formal alliances. As a result, it can be argued that the link with Washington has constituted an intangible, yet exceptionally powerful, constraint on the direction of British foreign policies, especially during the twenty years immediately following the Second World War. As Coral Bell notes, the 'special relationship' is strong and resilient because 'it is not a construction but a capacity — a capacity to see the elements of common interest in whatever international storms the time may bring' (1973, p.119).

Not surprisingly, given this essentially informal yet apparently powerful influence, the precise nature and effects of the 'American connection' in British foreign policy has been a constant source of debate and controversy. For some, the association with the USA has been a means whereby the decline of British foreign policy has been moderated, and through which the beneficial effects of British diplomatic skills have been felt in Washington. For others, the impact has been illusory and pernicious, giving policy makers in Whitehall ideas above their station and preventing them from seeing the logic of Britain's changed international position. (For examples of both views, see Louis and Bull 1986; Reynolds 1985–6.) In particular, it has been argued that the reorientation of British policy towards Western Europe was hindered, not so much by any concrete actions on the part of American administrations as by the psychological 'blinkers' worn by successive generations of the British foreign-policy-making élite (Bell 1973; Manderson-Jones 1972). Essentially complicated and ambiguous, British–American relations have taxed the ingenuity and imagination of successive analysts and commentators as much as they have the skills of the policy makers. The 'special relationship' has been described also as 'natural, uneasy, ambiguous, ambivalent [and] sweet and sour' (Edmonds 1986, p.6). Community appears to coexist with contention, interests with intimacy, and affection with recriminations.

The place of the USA in the foreign policy of any British government is thus central but contested. In no case is this more true than that of the Thatcher governments since 1979. Before the Conservative victory of that year, it appeared that the 'special relationship' had largely disappeared, to be replaced by a more generalised condition of 'complex interdependence' such as that which can be said to exist between many of the advanced industrial societies (Smith 1981). Thatcherism in many respects challenged and attempted to reverse this trend, especially when, in 1981, the Reagan administration took power in the USA. Not only was the 'special relationship' reinstated as the centrepiece of British foreign policy, but it also seemed to become part of an intense ideological and personal alliance centred around the two leaders themselves, bolstered by the influence of the 'New Right' in general. As the Prime Minister herself proclaimed during one of her visits to Washington, 'We see so many things in the same way and you can speak of a real meeting of minds. I feel no inhibitions about describing the relationship as very, very special' (*Financial Times*, 23 March 1985). Such manifestations of renewed intimacy can be interpreted in many ways – as the natural convergence of two imperial powers in decline, perhaps (Krieger 1986), or as the triumph of nostalgia and sentiment over reality (Hill 1986) – but they undoubtedly pose an intriguing problem in the analysis of Thatcherite foreign policy. Part of the intrigue arises from the fact that the apparent intimacy has been unable to gloss over the evidence of continuing and substantial clashes of interest, and the tension between an 'Atlantic' and a 'European' thrust for British foreign policy in general. Significantly, these tensions can also be observed within the structure of British governments, throwing into question the assumption of a dominant or monolithic Thatcherite orthodoxy.

Problems such as these are by no means confined to British–American relations. Any assessment of foreign policy and of international relationships must distinguish between broad, far-reaching forces and specific factors. While broad forces (of values, institutions and international structure) establish the overall direction of policy and set the limits of manoeuvre for the policy makers, specific factors (such as personalities, political fluctuations and the pressure of events) will inevitably operate to shape policy responses in particular situations or on particular issues. Part at least of the skill of the foreign-policy maker lies in recognising the limits to manoeuvre whilst maximising the ability to cope with or profit from specific events or trends. The discussion in this chapter suggests that this tension between forces and factors is especially important in an assessment of British–American relations during the Thatcher years. Has the Prime Minister's 'very, very special' relationship with the USA, and specifically the Reagan administrations, really changed the underlying realities of British foreign policy? What has happened when the force of sentiment and nostalgia has come up against clashes of material interest? Are changes in the international system producing structural shifts which will make British foreign policy less 'Atlantic' and more 'European', or which will produce internal conflicts within the British government as different preferences and priorities make themselves felt? These general questions will be addressed by the remainder of this chapter in two ways: first, through a discussion of the affinities and tensions between Thatcherism and successive American administrations; second, through analysis of four policy areas – East–West relations, regional conflicts, the management of the world economy and the handling of 'intermestic' affairs.

Thatcherism, Carterism and Reaganism: the Policy Context

Relations between the Thatcher governments and the United States are often presented – both by outsiders and by those personally involved – as a kind of love-affair, in which the main protagonists are Mrs Thatcher and President Reagan. On the basis of the discussion so far in this chapter, it is important to retain a sense of perspective about such caricatures, but it is nonetheless important to note the assumed intimacy underlying the stereotypes. This intimacy was based from the start on three central foundations: personalities, domestic policies and perceptions of the international system. Mrs Thatcher's style of prime ministerial government reflects not only certain tendencies in the British political system but also a personal conception of leadership and of the relationship between ideas and action. From the outset, this style was projected into foreign policy, in terms both of the appropriate role for Britain and of expectations of the role to be played by the USA. The Prime Minister stood ready to present herself as Washington's best friend in the international arena and eager to respond to kindred spirits in the White House. Part of this eagerness was a reflection of Thatcherism in its domestic context: the unleashing of national energies and the liberation of market forces was seen as closely connected to – and perhaps unattainable without – similar priorities in the United States. 'Thatcherism in one country' was not the aim of the British government, least of all of its leader, and would depend on the evolution of US policy above all. This perception was allied closely to a particular view of the international system, which emphasised the threat to freedom from Soviet expansionism and argued that the economic and social energies of Western capitalism could only be maximised if security was first ensured. It was almost axiomatic in Mrs Thatcher's foreign-policy stance that security for the West could not be ensured without strong leadership from the United States, centred around the refurbishment of American military might.

National needs and Mrs Thatcher's personal inclinations seemed happily to coincide, and to point directly to a renewal of a 'special relationship'. It is important, though, to note some of the other, and often contradictory, implications of Thatcherism's world-view. In the first place, the predilection for strong leadership and a positive, assertive style meant that there was a distinct possibility of friction no matter who occupied the White House: on the one hand, the Prime Minister was not one to suffer fools or the mistaken gladly, and on the other, her expectations of American leadership meant that any shortcomings in Washington's performance might be severely punished. Secondly, the Thatcherite preoccupation with national regeneration in Britain implied the need not only to 'convert' the USA but also to focus very firmly on British interests. As Hugo Young was to note, Thatcherism in its international manifestation 'sees Britain's only important role as looking after its own business' (*The Guardian*, 26 March 1987). David Allen points out in Chapter 2 that this was central to Thatcherite policies in Western Europe; similarly, in the context of British–American relations, it could not be taken for granted that 'Britain's business' would always coincide neatly with the American connection, or that all parts of the British government would share this priority. Finally, it should be noted that, while many of the Prime Minister's aspirations lay in the global arena, and thus with the USA, many of her pressing policy needs – and the developing lines of policy pursued by important departments of state – lay in the area of the European Community or the pursuit of European security through Nato. In the terms used earlier in this chapter, neither broad forces nor specific factors pointed unequivocally in the direction of Washington, and the extent to which Thatcherism could or should redirect them was open to question.

These initial tensions were compounded by the course of American foreign policy between 1979 and 1987, which meant that the assumptions and expectations of Thatcherite foreign policy were thrown into continual doubt and occasional confusion. In this context, it is important to remember that the first two years of the Thatcher era were the last two years of the Carter Presidency in the United States. 'Carterism' was if anything distinguished by the absence of the qualities which the Prime Minister demanded of the Americans. It was uncertain, often indecisive, and given to internal disputes and ineffectiveness in operation – a set of qualities perhaps best demonstrated in the fiasco of its attempts to rescue the

American hostages in Iran in April 1980. Nonetheless, by the end of 1980 the retiring administration had set in place at least some of the features that were to formalise the 'new cold war'. The Soviet invasion of Afghanistan, coupled with the impact of the Iranian crisis, had led to the beginnings of a major defence build-up, to the demise of US–Soviet détente and to the proclamation of American responsibility for order in areas such as the Persian Gulf. The American economy was still in disarray, and the dollar a source of international instability, but the omens indicated a reassertion of American leadership and its convergence with the international posture of Thatcherism.

The election of Ronald Reagan in November 1980 did more than simply consolidate this set of trends. From the point of view of British foreign policy under Thatcher, it consummated many of the desires which were central to its general direction. At one and the same time it promised a new reliability and consistency in policy making, a rejuvenation of American strength in both the economic and the military fields, and a reassertion of Washington's leadership in the struggle against Soviet expansion. The Reaganite programme appeared to dovetail neatly with the aspirations of the Prime Minister and with the practical need for a more effective performance of the USA's international role. Not only this, but the Prime Minister and the President rapidly developed a cordial, not to say gushing, personal rapport – the basis for the 'love-affair' noted earlier. As might be suspected, though, the development of Reaganism in practice did not fit the rather simplistic notions embodied in some of the President's rhetoric. Where the President was wont to talk of 'a shining city on a hill', it turned out that Washington remained a rather intractable and chaotic place. Constant internecine warfare was carried on by the President's advisers, who came and went at times with bewildering frequency and uncertain impact. The ultimate expression of this policy confusion came with the 'Irangate' revelations of 1986 and 1987, which threatened to call into question the credentials of US foreign policy as a whole. Meanwhile, the defence build-up continued and even accelerated, but its ultimate objectives remained unclear. A policy of muscular insularity, with few concessions either to allies or adversaries, seemed to lie at the heart of Reaganism; whilst this was dramatically illustrated by the defence 'binge', it was no less tellingly demonstrated by the implementation of 'Reaganomics', which threatened friend and foe alike with high interest rates and retaliation against unfair competition. The gradual retreat from confrontation, both in the defence and the economic spheres, did little to reassure the outside world, given the internal confusion of American policy and a continued inability to transcend the influence of domestic pressures.

From the point of view of British–American relations, the contradictions and fluctuations of 'practical Reaganism' are at least as important as the ideological postures and long-range goals espoused in Washington. As noted earlier, it should by no means be taken for granted that Thatcherite foreign policy would dictate passive subordination to Washington in all circumstances, or that the Prime Minister's preferences would be shared by her colleagues. Given the mercurial nature of policy as it developed under President Reagan between 1981 and 1987, it is far from clear that the context for special intimacy or mutual influence between Britain and the USA was any more promising then than under the Carter administration. Once again, the argument returns to the relative impact of broad historical forces and more specific factors: were the prospects for Thatcher and Reagan, despite their personal intimacy and shared aspirations, really no better than would have been those of any other British and American leaders in the 1980s? To explore this issue further, it is necessary to turn to the substance of policy itself and to consider the four areas to which we referred earlier.

The Substance of Policy

East–West Relations

It has already been noted that, for each and every British government since 1945, a major task has been the definition of a position in relation to East–West relations. In pursuit of this objective, British–American relations are of special significance: the definition of a British role in cold war or détente necessarily entails the definition of a position *vis-à-vis* the United States. By implication, it also entails defining a position in 'West–West' relations – the links between the USA and its major allies in Western Europe. Historically, British policy makers have often found themselves in an ambivalent position in the East–West conflict: whilst wishing to be seen as America's closest ally, they have also nurtured hopes of being able to exert some autonomous influence on the course of events. Their difficulties have been compounded by the steady decline in Britain's military and economic muscle – at least in relation to the superpowers – which has forced them into a delicate balancing act. Neither partner nor puppet, the British have been peculiarly subject to changes in the climate of relations between the 'Big Two', and the defence or pursuit of specifically British interests has been frequently threatened by the *force majeure* of superpower politics.

The onset of the 'new cold war' in 1979 and 1980 underlined this central tension in British policy. Ideologically, the Thatcher government had much sympathy with the Americans' new determination to stand up to Soviet expansionism and to contain instabilities in the Third World. Mrs Thatcher was among the first and most enthusiastic supporters of President Carter's firm stand against the Soviet invasion of Afghanistan, and shared Washington's opposition to terrorism and hostage taking of the kind that occurred in Iran. This was one of those occasions, though, when declaratory and operational policies followed rather different paths. The concrete demands posed by American policies, particularly in respect of economic and diplomatic sanctions against the USSR in the wake of the Afghanistan crisis, met with a distinctly muted British response, despite the Prime Minister's public support in general terms. In this, London was far closer to the line pursued by other European Community members, and the FCO in particular was not averse either to the pursuit of a self-consciously 'European' line or to the use of the need for European agreement as a cover for inactivity.

A similar pattern of behaviour was brought out, in much sharper relief, by the American demand for sanctions against the Soviets after the imposition of martial law in Poland (December 1981). Despite successive declarations of support for the Americans' position, the British government hedged noticeably in the face of increasingly peremptory demands for action to obstruct the progress of the Siberian gas pipeline project. As before, the British response had much in common with those of its major West European partners: when in the summer of 1982 the White House suddenly escalated its demands, the response from Whitehall was positively frosty. Confronted by the possibility that punishments would be inflicted upon British firms without their consent, the Thatcher government moved swiftly to invoke the Protection of Trading Interests Act, a step which would have put it in the position of ordering British firms to defy American policy. The Americans retreated from the final confrontation, and the issue was defused; but the episode had demonstrated two vital features of Thatcherite policy. First, the British government after 1979 consistently opposed the use of economic measures by themselves as a means of punishing the Soviets or other transgressors (the Falklands crisis was no exception to this – see below). Second, when the fighting of the 'new cold war' or other conflicts threatened concrete British interests, the government was prepared, despite the Prime Minister's instinctive pro-Americanism, to fight tooth and nail to prevent them being damaged.

A similar picture can be painted in respect of one of the central themes of US foreign policy throughout the Thatcher years: the arms build-up and its implications for arms control. One of the victims of the post-Afghanistan superpower 'freeze' was the arms control process, killed by the failure of the United States to ratify SALT II and by the widespread perception in the USA that the USSR had profited both from the negotiations and from the shifting nuclear balance in the 1970s as a whole. The British government, in common with others in Western Europe, was faced with a dilemma: on the one hand, they wished to reinforce the American commitment to Europe and to meet the threat of new Soviet weapons such as the SS-20, but on the other hand, they did not want a new and unrestrained arms race which would undermine strategic stability. For the British, there was the added complication that they were about to make key decisions on the future of their own nuclear deterrent – decisions that were in all respects dependent on the developing American strategic posture. No wonder, then, that the unfolding of the nuclear issue prompted wary, and in some cases profoundly worried, British responses.

From 1981 to 1983, the British position on nuclear weapons took two major forms. First, the government was concerned to demonstrate its commitment to Nato policy – and thus to the American position – by achieving the deployment of cruise missiles. By firmly adhering to this line, the Thatcher government established itself as a loyal lieutenant for the Americans in Western Europe, but it also incurred significant domestic costs in the form of political opposition within and outside Parliament. Less obvious, but equally persistent, was the other side of British policy: continuous polite but insistent pressure on Washington to implement the other half of the 'twin-track' policy and to begin negotiations with the Soviets. The repeated rejection of Soviet offers by the White House during 1982 brought forth open expressions of British concern, and the start of talks during 1983 was equally hailed by Downing Street as a justification for all their efforts over the preceding two years.

As the talks proceeded, however, the British were not altogether reassured. In particular, they took considerable efforts to ensure that the Americans came to no deals involving British – and French – nuclear forces. Thus when Mrs Thatcher visited the USA in September 1983, she found herself having simultaneously to reaffirm her commitment to cruise missiles, stress the need for substantive US–Soviet negotiations and defend the British nuclear force. There is every indication that the British achieved their objectives, at least in the short term: the British nuclear force never became a central issue in the talks, and the Americans were reinforced in their growing inclination to look for a genuine deal with the USSR. As the prospect of an agreement became more definite, the British again showed the ambivalence of their position in relation to the USA. On the one hand, they were concerned to remove obstacles to an agreement – the most obvious being President Reagan's dogged commitment to the Strategic Defense Initiative (SDI), which the Soviets insisted on including in any strategic weapons agreement. On the other, they were concerned to prevent the 'decoupling' of Western Europe from the USA – a threat which was inherent in any proposal that all intermediate-range nuclear forces should be removed from Europe. After the Reykjavik summit of October 1986, which appeared to raise the spectre of such a deal, Mrs Thatcher's instant response was to fly to the USA and obtain reassurance from the President – a reassurance which was then pursued in Nato and other settings during 1987. Clearly the British–American consultation at this stage was effective, or at least convincing to Mrs Thatcher, since her support for the later Soviet–American agreement on a 'double-zero' arms control plan was readily forthcoming.

Although it appears that British–American relations functioned effectively on intermediate nuclear forces, the same cannot be said of the British attempts to influence the SDI. This visionary plan, announced by President Reagan in March 1983 (with no warning to America's allies or even to larger parts of the US administration), posed a double threat to British interests. First, as already noted, it seemed to reduce the chances of arms-control agreements, since the President saw it as essentially non-negotiable. Second, the SDI promised to make all offensive nuclear forces obsolete, or at least to increase greatly the costs of making them effective: the implications for Britain's comparatively limited force did not need to be underlined. There was, however, a third dimension to the British dilemma, arising from the assumed technological and economic benefits for those involved in the project. Could the British sign up for the research and development, and at the same time continue to express their reservations about the strategic implications of the SDI? At least until 1987, it appeared that they could, since the signing of a 'framework agreement' for SDI research in December 1985 did not prevent the British government from criticising the American stance on observance of two key arms control agreements, the Anti-Ballistic Missile Treaty and the unratified (but generally observed) SALT II agreement (Taylor 1986). What this process did reveal, though, was a series of often sharp disagreements within the British government itself. Most obviously, the Prime Minister's sympathetic attitude towards the Americans' policy was not reflected in the stance adopted by the Foreign Secretary, Sir Geoffrey Howe. In March 1985, he made a speech to the Royal United Services Institution in London, in which he accused United States policies of reflecting a 'Maginot mentality' and called for the inclusion of SDI in negotiations. American reactions were sharp, and it was apparent that both in making the speech and in more generally supporting the growth of a 'European voice' in defence matters the Foreign Secretary was pursuing a rather different line from that advocated elsewhere in Downing Street.

It appears from this evidence that the Thatcher governments had measurable, if limited, success in resolving the dilemmas emerging from the development of East–West relations up to 1987, and in ensuring that British interests were considered in Washington. Where it appeared that those interests might be ignored or damaged by American policy makers, the British government could adopt either or both of two tactics. The first was essentially a national or bilateral response: asserting the British position, and being prepared to defend it either by unilateral action or by direct contact with the American administration (Washington was certainly Mrs Thatcher's favourite destination). The second, and perhaps in the long term the more important, could be described as a 'European' response, through which Mrs Thatcher – willingly or unwillingly – came under the influence of those departments or other governments which stressed the growing salience of West European interests either in the context of Nato or through other channels. On SDI and on arms control, the Prime Minister flew to the President's side, but only after consulting with her major European partners; equally, when she visited Moscow in 1987, she allowed it to be known that she was 'speaking for Europe'. In formal terms, the revival of the Western European Union as a defence forum for Western Europe was greeted with qualified approval by the British, not least because it might provide another channel of influence with the Americans; this adds to the overall impression that British policies by no means embodied a slavish adherence to American positions, whatever the Thatcherite rhetoric might have implied.

Regional Conflicts and World Order

Conflicts outside the central theatre of the cold war and détente have always occupied an important place in British–American relations. The Middle East and south-east Asia, to name only two regions, have witnessed some of the more turbulent episodes in the 'special relationship'. As time has passed, though, the nature of the British–American link has changed. Whereas at one time it was conceivable either that the two countries could operate in quasi-partnership to maintain order in far-flung parts of the world, or that each could independently intervene in pursuit of its own interests, it has become ever more obvious that the USA alone is capable of pursuing a truly global approach to regional problems. This means that the problem has changed for British foreign-policy makers: in the 1980s, their calculations are concerned not so much with British entanglement in regional conflicts as with evaluating, and if necessary moderating, the consequences of American intervention. If the British are to have more than a marginal influence in these cases, they will do so not by the exertion of military or economic muscle but by the use of diplomacy or multilateral collaboration; not by the exertion of power but by the establishment and maintenance of principles. Given the 'policy of strength' espoused by the Reagan administration, it might thus have been expected that British policy would face some sharp challenges.

Perhaps the longest-standing area of mutual involvement for the British and the Americans outside Europe – and the scene of some key crises in postwar British–American relations – is the Middle East. By the end of the 1970s, though, it could be argued that Britain's historic role in the area had almost disappeared. It had been replaced by two types of outside involvement which continued to entangle both the USA and the countries of the European Communities. The Americans had increasingly become drawn actively into the safeguarding of international order in the Middle East, and into the search for a settlement of the Arab-Israeli dispute, a search which had led in 1978 to the Camp David Accords between Israel and Egypt, with the United States as active sponsor. Meanwhile, the Middle East, and particularly the Arab world, had seen the growth of a common policy stance on the part of the European Community, which was expressed in economic terms through the 'Euro-Arab dialogue' and in diplomatic or foreign-policy terms by the Venice Declaration of 1980. The British found themselves in the middle of the forces set up by these coexisting initiatives: on the one hand, they contributed part of the force which observed Israeli withdrawal from the Sinai desert under the terms of the Camp David Accords, whilst on the other they found themselves engaged in, and at times leading, the European initiative. Both the Carter and the Reagan administrations were hostile to the Venice Declaration, especially insofar as it called for the recognition of the Palestinians as parties to the peace process, and this was to form a continuing undercurrent of tension in the British–American dimension of the issue. As in other areas of policy, it was also apparent on more than one occasion that sympathies with American positions were by no means uniform across the British government.

A more tangible – and more perilous – area of British–American interaction was the conflict in the Lebanon. After the Israeli invasion of 1982, the Americans became embroiled through their participation in a Multi National Force (MNF) stationed in Beirut, and the British, along with several other European countries, also established a presence. In Britain's case, the contribution amounted only to a hundred men, but this largely symbolic effort began to appear distinctly dangerous as the situation deteriorated in 1983. Most tellingly, it appeared that British participation did not entitle them to any consultation with the Americans, who were taking an ever more active role in the conflict. The crisis came in late 1983, with suicide attacks on the American forces and increasing pressure for their withdrawal. The British – or, at least, the FCO – seemed to toy with the idea of establishing a United Nations presence in Beirut, but this had little impact on an American policy which was responding at least as much to domestic pressures as to events in the Lebanon. Meanwhile, Washington continued to attack any hint of a diplomatic solution that gave a role to the Palestinians. From the American withdrawal in 1985 on, a new phase seemed to emerge, and one that was again to entangle the British with the Americans. Increasing terrorist activity, aimed either at American aircraft and ships or at individuals in Beirut itself, created an atmosphere of near-hysteria in the USA especially, and after attacks on Rome and Athens airports at Christmas 1985 Washington's hostility turned more and more towards Libya. As in other cases, the British and their European partners were reluctant to impose economic sanctions on the Qaddafi regime, believing that they simply would not work. The Americans, dissatisfied with the European response and more than ever convinced that Libya was the fount of all terrorist activity, demanded more positive commitment from their allies, if necessary including the use of force. This led in April 1986 to the bombing of Tripoli by F1-11 aircraft based in Britain, with the agreement of the British government.

On the face of it, the Tripoli raid confirmed the existence of something that might be called a 'special relationship'. Of all European countries, only the British responded to the American call; others even refused overflying rights to the F1-11s. Two things stand out in the aftermath of the raid, though: first, the Thatcher government was at pains to emphasise its reluctant acquiescence in the scheme, and to stress that it was very unlikely to happen again; second, it was clear from public reaction to the events that the government did not reflect the British national mood, which was profoundly suspicious of American policy. There is no doubt that the cost for Britain was high, with some hostages being killed and more being taken in the Lebanon, and with an eventual rupture with Syria as an indirect consequence of Britain's association with American actions. Arguably, Britain's diplomatic credibility in the Middle East was severely dented, and the association with the USA carried on into later entanglement with the Gulf War during 1986 and 1987. Despite the official line in the latter case – that British action was aimed at preserving the freedom of the seas, and that a solution under the auspices of the United Nations would be the best way out of the impasse – the suspicion lurked in some minds that the Americans had once again put to the British a request they could not refuse.

Part of the reason for the Americans' ability to persuade the British to their way of thinking about the Middle East lay in events in a very different part of the world. Whereas the Middle East is a long-established theatre of British–American competition and collaboration, there is no doubt that the most dramatic instances of regional conflict under the Thatcher governments occurred in the Western Hemisphere. The Falklands War of 1982 is covered in detail elsewhere in this volume, but it is important to note that the United States played a vital part in shaping its course and determining its conclusion. This is not to imply, though, that the 'special relationship' operated to ensure American support and single-minded commitment to the British cause. Indeed, it was the very ambivalence of the American position that made it such a central focus of British attention; to achieve influence, the British had to penetrate the Reagan administration, to understand its internal workings and to exert pressure on the strategic points in the American foreign-policy process. As one commentator later recorded, 'During the Falklands crisis, the British Ambassador in Washington saw the National Security Adviser, went daily to Capitol Hill, lobbied the individual members of the Senate Foreign Relations Committee, and appeared on television seventy-three times. It was a masterly example of diplomatic skill' (Steiner 1987, p. 15). Matters were complicated by the fact that several members of the President's entourage were decidely unsympathetic to the British cause, even though American public opinion was strongly supportive. Crucially, it appears, the Secretary of Defense, Caspar Weinberger, both favoured the British and was in a position to authorise material assistance with military supplies and intelligence. The part played by the United States in the episode stands in considerable contrast to the role of the European Community: here Britain was able to gain initial support for sanctions, but the EC simply could not give the kind of concrete support in the field that was forthcoming, despite all the uncertainties, from Washington

(Edwards 1984). No wonder, it might be suggested, that when the call for help in Libya and the Gulf was heard, the British were not well placed to deny it.

The Falklands, undoubtedly the most dramatic episode in British foreign policy under Thatcher, was not the only instance in which British and American policies came together in relation to Latin America. Although they were less sensational, events in Grenada and Central America carried considerable significance as indicators of rather different dimensions in the British–American relationship. When the Americans invaded Grenada in October 1983, they established a military occupation of a Commonwealth country, and they did so without consulting the British government. One theory had it that the State Department itself did not know what was going on, and thus was in no position to keep the British informed even if it had wanted to (Steiner 1987, p.9). Predictably, the British – specifically, the Prime Minister's – reaction was one of outrage, and President Reagan experienced one of the less pleasant telephone conversations of his political life in consequence. Little that the British government could do would have had any effect on the American position; although Sir Geoffrey Howe, the Foreign Secretary, called at one stage for a united West European stand against American high-handedness, this was set against an overall desire not to rock the boat in the run-up to deployment of cruise missiles. Significantly, opinion polls indicated a distinct suspicion of American policies in general among the British public, a trend that was to recur in 1986 after the Libyan raids. But the fact remained that there was very little the British could do, just as there was in December 1983 when the United States lifted its ban on arms sales to Argentina. Much the same was true, in a different context, of the crisis in Central America. The British have a token presence in Central America, in Belize, but could exercise no influence over the course of American policy. Indeed, the most significant British involvement in the conflict was through European Political Co-operation, the 'foreign policy' of EC members, which supported the peace efforts made by the local states, in indirect opposition to the Americans' policy. On at least one occasion, the Foreign Secretary was led openly to distance these efforts from those enshrined in the 'Reagan Doctrine' and implicitly supported by the Prime Minister (Allen and Smith 1988).

The one remaining area of British–American interaction in

relation to regional conflict is South Africa. As noted by James
Barber in Chapter 5 of this volume, the British attitude to economic
sanctions against the Botha government was decidedly unsympathetic throughout the Thatcher years. For many of those years, they had
the support of the Reagan administration, whose policy of
'constructive engagement' coincided neatly with the preferences of
the government in London. During 1985 and 1986, though, the
pressure from Congress and other groups in the USA for the
application of sanctions began to tell on the administration. As a
result, selective sanctions were first applied and then extended, over
the President's veto. This reversal, in addition to revealing much
about the policy process in Washington, had the effect of
undermining the British diplomatic effort and increasing the
pressure on the Thatcher government to impose sanctions itself.

   This brief review of regional conflicts in terms of British–
American relations presents much that is seemingly contradictory.
The Thatcher government between 1979 and 1987 stood in almost
all cases for diplomatic solutions and the maintenance of international order, yet in many cases it was entangled in or went along
with the use of coercion or force. It made persistent efforts to
influence American policies on a variety of issues, yet it was
consistently rebuffed or ignored; even on the Falklands it can be
argued that it was touch and go before the final American
commitment was obtained. Consultation, affected by the internal
turmoil of policy making in Washington, was often fragmentary
and sometimes non-existent. Although on some issues the European
dimension provided a cover or an alternative channel for British
efforts, it seems that the brute facts of American globalism and
British regionalism, American capability and British lack of it, were
never far from the surface.

Managing the World Economy

It was noted earlier that one of Thatcherism's central priorities from
the outset was the generation of national economic recovery. Indeed,
the word 'recovery' could be seen as an understatement, since the
Prime Minister and her supporters were intent on an economic and
social transformation which would incidentally restore the vitality of
the economy. As argued earlier, though, it was impossible for any
such policy to be carried out in isolation, either from the

BRITAIN AND THE UNITED STATES   25

international system and the world economy in general or from the
United States in particular. Britain has always been heavily
dependent on international exchange and collaboration for the
furtherance of its domestic and international objectives, and since
1945 the relationship with the USA has been one of the central
pillars of Britain's role in the world political economy. It is clear –
and it was clear as early as the 1940s – that although Britain is
intensely concerned and involved with the world political economy,
and with the USA as the dominant Western capitalist country, its
position is one of considerable vulnerability. The 'multilateral era' of
trade liberalisation and currency convertibility which was established in principle after 1945 owed a good deal to British ideas, but
a lot more to American economic power, and Britain's position as
the 'sick man' of the industrialised nations seemed to be confirmed
by poor economic performance during the 1960s and 1970s (Smith
1988). At the same time, especially in the 1970s, American
economic power became a more erratic and destabilising influence in
the world economy, with burgeoning trade deficits and an unsteady
dollar.

   This meant that the place of Thatcherism in the world political
economy was bound to be a major preoccupation for the government
after the 1979 general election, and that the position and policies of
the USA would themselves be central to the prospects of success.
True, the Americans were not the only manifestation of international interdependence with which the government had to deal; the
European Community was an unavoidable and often compelling
feature of the economic landscape, as can be seen in Chapter 2.
Under both Carter and Reagan, though, it was American policy that
shaped much of the international economic agenda. Not only that,
but it was in Reagan's domestic economic programme – the
phenomenon of 'Reaganomics' – that Thatcherism found at least in
some respects an international echo. Finally, the United States,
directly or indirectly, had by the late 1970s a strong and growing
presence within British society and the British economy. For any
government in the industrial world of the 1980s, the management
of 'intermestic' affairs – those that are simultaneously domestic and
international – is a major task. For Britain, given its dependence on
international transactions, this is especially true; and in the
'intermestic' affairs of Britain, the USA would inevitably loom
large.

Despite the ideological similarity between Thatcherism and 'Reaganomics', the development of economic policy in Reagan's America came to constitute one of the most worrying and least tractable of the problems facing the British economy. Although the Carter administration had been criticised for failing to establish consistency in its monetary and exchange-rate policies, the failings of the late 1970s paled in comparison to those of the 1980s. Tax cuts, combined with massive increases in military expenditure and declining industrial competitiveness, created the need for high US interest rates which threatened to choke off any recovery in British (and West European) growth. The American recession of 1981–2 was then followed by an equally intense boom, fuelled by massive and growing deficits both in the US Federal budget and in American external trade. In all of this the pound, and the British economy, were buffeted remorselessly. First the pound reached new heights, buoyed up by its 'petrocurrency' status; then, in 1984 and 1985, it reached new depths against the 'almighty dollar'. The British problem was not unique, but it was severe, and the irony was only increased by the supposed affinity between Thatcher's and Reagan's economic programmes.

In this situation, the British had recourse to a variety of strategies. The first could be described as persistent and often strident hectoring. Mrs Thatcher missed no opportunity, either in personal meetings with the President or at the annual Western Economic Summits, to lecture him on the need for financial rectitude and on the irresponsibility of his deficit financing. Such advice was on the whole politely ignored: indeed the President's response to criticism from many of the allies was that they should expand their own economies in the same way as the Americans were attempting to expand theirs. During the golden days of dollar strength in 1984 and 1985, Mrs Thatcher's homilies had if anything even less effect. At almost the same time as the Prime Minister was describing the British–American relationship as 'very, very special' (March 1985), the President was talking the dollar up to ever greater heights in defiance of his visitor's advice. Another strategy adopted, with qualifications, by the British, was to co-ordinate their policies with the Europeans. Although this provided some shelter for the pound, its usefulness was limited for a long time by the Prime Minister's aversion to membership of the European Monetary System (EMS). By 1986 and 1987, though, a viable strategy appeared to be emerging: first, the pound was operating as an 'informal member' of the EMS, and second, the British were active in promoting co-operation on exchange rates between members of the so-called 'Group of Five', and of its successor the 'Group of Seven', industrial countries. It must be noted that this improvement, while coinciding with British preferences, owed as much to changes in the American position and those of West Germany and Japan as to any triumph for British economic muscle. As in other areas of policy, though, it is important here to distinguish between the positions adopted by different members of the government. The Prime Minister, as noted above, was consistent in her opposition to collaborative management through active intervention, and particularly through the EMS. On the other hand, as became increasingly apparent during 1987 and 1988, the Chancellor of the Exchequer, Mr Nigel Lawson, was strongly in favour both of a fully co-ordinated approach to monetary management and of Britain's full membership of the EMS (a view in which he was supported by Sir Geoffrey Howe).

Another issue of particular importance to British involvement in the world political economy is that of trade, aid and development. As in the case of economic and financial strategy, there was a good deal of similarity between the trade and aid programmes of the Reagan and Thatcher governments. Both were unequivocally for the maximum possible freedom of trade, and for the liberation of market forces on a world scale so that poor countries could help themselves to achieve Western-style development. In both Britain and the United States, though, there were forces working to dilute this ideological alignment. For Britain, membership in the European Communities meant that much of its trade policy was decided in Brussels rather than in London, and that the dictates of the Common Agricultural Policy and other EC mechanisms limited any possibilities of national action. In the United States, the surge of imports resulting from economic expansion and loss of competitiveness meant that the Reagan administration faced growing protectionist pressures, and that it was largely on the defensive. Nonetheless, there is evidence that, in the preparation of a new round of global trade negotiations under the auspices of the General Agreement on Tariffs and Trade (GATT) during 1985 and 1986, the British and the Americans found themselves in close alliance. Broad philosophical agreement there might have been, but as noted earlier there were sharp disagreements between the British and the Americans over East–West trade; and other specific contentious issues concerned trade in steel and high-technology products.

On developed world trade, therefore, it appears that the material stakes and organisational commitments of Britain and the USA operated to dilute the ideological affinity in their governments' programmes. Perhaps because the stakes were less high and the commitments less constraining, there was greater convergence in matters of aid and development. Both the Reagan and the Thatcher philosophies emphasised national priorities in the allocation of aid, and, with the encouragement of 'New Right' lobbyists and pressure groups, they instinctively reacted against the 'softness' or ideological unreliability of many international agencies. As a result, both governments set out to release themselves from some of the more irksome obligations to which they were subject and to distance themselves from the prevailing orthodoxy of development strategies. There was more than a hint of co-ordination and of the effects of 'New Right' lobbying in the American and British withdrawals from UNESCO, their reactions to the Brandt Report and its accompanying international conferences, and their hostility to the UN Conference on Disarmament and Development in 1987. Both in Washington and in London, there was reluctance to increase the resources allocated to multilateral agencies, and a corresponding willingness to reward the faithful poor (as well as domestic manufacturers through contracts and 'tied aid'). On a more positive note, both the USA and Britain responded to the growing pressures during 1986 and 1987 for rescheduling and otherwise alleviating the burden of Third World debt, although this represented in some ways an acceptance of the inevitable.

Handling 'Intermestic' Affairs

For advanced industrial countries such as Britain and the United States, many of the symptoms of interdependence do not manifest themselves 'out there', beyond national boundaries in the world economy or the international political system. The growth of transactions between societies and the spread of interpenetration between industries and other institutions mean that the line between 'domestic' and 'international' is often meaningless (Wallace 1986). Because of the complexity of many 'intermestic' issues, and their importance for national economic and social well-being, they have proved to be some of the most taxing and fraught problems facing national governments. Even where two governments are agreed on economic strategy, they may either be unable to control the handling of these problems or incapable of preventing costly conflicts and misunderstandings. Given the high level of interpenetration between the British and American economies, and their interests in many shared activities, it is easy to predict that the management of 'intermestic' issues will be a problem for all governments in London and Washington. During the 1980s, the problem has been particularly (but not solely) apparent in two areas: first, the field of national security, and second, the sphere of industry and investment.

It is clear from the discussion so far that the United States and Britain have developed and maintained a high level of shared activities in the field of national security. There is considerable interpenetration between the military and intelligence establishments of the two countries; there is collaboration on particular projects and activities; and there is in Britain a considerable American military presence. All British governments – the Thatcher government in particular – have been at pains to cultivate and to maintain this network of contacts, and it has been seen as central to the 'special relationship'. During the 1980s, however, it has increasingly become a matter of disagreement and contention within Britain, and thus a source of pressures to which the government has had to respond.

Three examples will give an indication of the ways in which 'foreign policy' has penetrated the domestic context of national security. First, and most continuously, the Thatcher government experienced the forces generated by the deployment of cruise missiles during 1983. At one and the same time, the government had to pursue its objective of reassuring the Americans that it was the most loyal of allies and countering the presence of the peace movement at national and even local levels. The problem did not disappear with the deployment of the missiles, and remained to play a part in the progress towards a disarmament agreement during 1986 and 1987. A connected problem was that of intelligence collaboration – one of the least public but most persistent aspects of the 'special relationship'. In the international domain, this relationship played a crucial part in the Falklands War, when the Americans repositioned one of their satellites to provide British forces with vital information on Argentine movements. At the national level, the supply of information to the USA from the Government Communications Headquarters (GCHQ) at Cheltenham became controversial in the light of the Thatcher government's attempts to eliminate trade unions there – an attempt which some claimed to have been prompted by American security concerns. Finally, as noted earlier, the launching of the April 1986 raids on Libya from British bases caused widespread concern about the ability of the government in London to assert itself in the light of determined US pressure.

Although it is convenient to draw a line between 'intermestic' problems in the national security and the economic spheres, it can be misleading. For instance, the Thatcher government found itself in a difficult position when faced with American demands for controls on the export of so-called 'sensitive technology' to Eastern bloc countries. Since this description could apparently be applied to home computers or video games, the government had to spend much diplomatic energy in attempts both to find out what the Americans really meant and to prevent the blanket imposition of controls on an extra-territorial basis. More dramatic was a series of tensions arising from the shifting control of British industries, some of them with a national security significance and all of them raising the spectre of anti-Americanism. The battle for control of Westland Helicopters in early 1986 brought forth explicit conflicts between a 'European' and an American affiliation, and split the Cabinet. At the same time, suggestions that parts of British Leyland, the motor manufacturer, might be sold off to Ford or General Motors aroused a strong nationalistic reaction. The anti-American card was also played, with little success, in the dispute over the future of the Nimrod airborne surveillance aircraft during 1986 and 1987.

The problems raised by American penetration of British economic life will not go away, given the global scale and weight of the USA's financial resources and the fact that Britain simply cannot sustain single-handedly its presence in many advanced sectors. This was not the whole of the story during the 1980s, though, and two additional features should be pointed out. First, the American presence might have been the most intrusive and sensitive, but it was not the only one: Britain during the 1980s continued to be an attractive home for investments from both Japanese and European companies. Second, the trend was not all in one direction, and the liberalisation of exchange controls by the Thatcher government led to massive British investment in the USA. By 1987, even those ultimate bastions of Americanism, the Hilton and the Holiday Inn, had fallen at least partly into the hands of British investors.

It was suggested earlier in this chapter that the growth of interdependence and interpenetration between Britain and the USA meant that British governments faced considerable problems of management. Given the ostentatious commitment of Thatcherism both to national economic and social regeneration and to the maintenance of an open world economy, it was predictable that conflicts would arise with American policy either at the level of international co-ordination or at the level of domestic political and economic life. The 'intermestic' arena raises the possibility of such conflicts — and of policy convergence — in a particularly challenging way, confronting governments with the need for management in several dimensions and several contexts at once, and often bringing a wide variety of non-governmental players into the game. In addition to the examples given above, it would have been possible to cite the affairs of Northern Ireland, which led to intensive British attempts to influence the US Congress as well as the White House; or the attempts by some American states to extend so-called 'unitary taxation' to American firms operating in Britain; or the tangled relations between British government nuclear policy, the Labour party's programme and the position of the Reagan administration, which aroused fears of US intervention in the 1987 general election campaign. There is much about these relationships that is intimate, but their management is not necessarily ensured by mystical notions of a 'special relationship'. Rather, it entails hard and detailed work to ensure that things do not get out of hand, that the relevant interests both within and outside government are taken into account and that the domestic consequences of international actions are thoroughly considered.

Conclusion

At the beginning of this chapter, it was argued that despite the perceived existence of a 'special relationship' between Britain and the United States — a relationship given both high priority and a high profile by the Thatcher governments after 1979 — a number of important elements could intervene to modify or divert British–American relations. These elements were described as 'broad forces' and 'specific factors', the former setting the general context of foreign policy and the latter conditioning actions in particular situations or on specific issues. It was also noted that the convergence of Thatcherism and Reaganism at the level of rhetoric and ideology was accompanied by a far less harmonious picture at the level of policy development in the real world of the 1980s. Personal and doctrinal harmony was accompanied by practical tension, ambivalence and constraint.

These initial impressions are confirmed by a more detailed analysis of the issues around which British–American relations have centred during the 1980s. In a number of areas the assumption of harmony was challenged by real-world tensions, and by a British determination not only to support the United States but also to defend Britain's own interests and obligations. On arms control and economic warfare, on regional conflicts and the politics of the world economy, the Thatcher governments combined an instinctive desire – especially on the part of the Prime Minister – to conform to American leadership with an equal readiness to criticise or to recommend alternatives. The extent to which such British pressures succeeded in influencing American policies was distinctly variable, and appeared to depend on at least three elements: the degree of commitment and coherence in both British and American policies, the ability to penetrate the policy process in Washington, and the capacity to align British actions with those of other West European countries. Favourable scores on all three counts could bring success, whereas failings in any one or more of them could make British–American relations very hard work.

What does this imply for the operation of broad factors and specific forces, in the recent past and the foreseeable future, in British–American relations? First, it demonstrates that specific factors are important, but that their significance varies according to situations and issues. The notion of a blanket relationship, 'special' or not, flies in the face of the facts, and ignores the manifest tensions and conflicts noted in this chapter, many of which have penetrated deep into British policy making. Arguably, this has always been the case in British–American relations: a study in the 1960s was aptly entitled *Community and Contention* (Russett 1963), and there have been many instances of disagreement within Whitehall. During the

1980s, though, it can be argued that the habitual ambivalence of the relationship has been played out against a backcloth that is shifting inexorably. As a result, British policies have become more 'regional' and 'European' (but not completely so), whilst American orientations have become a strange hybrid of globalism and insularity. Personalities, issues and actions can delay or divert this process, but they cannot halt or reverse it.

For British policy makers in the late 1980s, the context presents limited but important choices in the conduct of relations with the United States. On the one hand, they might accept the logic of 'Europeanisation', recognise that British interests are marginal and often opposed to those of the USA, and present themselves as partisans of a growing 'third force' based on the European Communities. On the other, they might see themselves as operating within Europe to represent a broader transatlantic and even global set of priorities and to prevent the growth of a narrow regional caucus. Reality is likely to be a shifting and uneasy combination of these two positions. As William Wallace noted in the early days of Thatcherite foreign policy (*The Guardian*, 15 May 1980):

> The problem for Britain . . . is where to place the main emphasis – in our foreign and defence policy and in our economic and financial diplomacy – between an America which has lost the capacity to respond sensitively and sympathetically to its transatlantic partners, and a Europe which neither fully shares British conceptions of international order nor offers us a comfortable basis for economic co-operation.

References and Further Reading

Allen, D. and Smith, M. (1988) 'Western Europe in the Atlantic system of the 1980s: towards a new identity?' in Gill, S. (ed.) *Atlantic Relations in the Reagan Era and Beyond*, Wheatsheaf.

Bell, C. (1973) 'The special relationship' in Leifer, M. (ed.) *Constraints and Adjustments in British Foreign Policy*, George Allen & Unwin, pp. 103–19.

Edmonds, R. (1986) *Setting the Mould: the United States and Britain, 1945–50*, Clarendon Press.

Edwards, G. (1984) 'Europe and the Falkland Islands crisis, 1982', *Journal of Common Market Studies*, vol. XXII, no. 4, pp. 295–313.

Hill, C. (1986) 'Reagan and Thatcher: the sentimental alliance', *World Outlook*, vol. 1, no. 2. pp. 2–18.

Krieger, J. (1986) *Reagan, Thatcher and the Politics of Decline*, Polity Press.

Louis, W.R. and Bull, H. (eds) (1986) *The Special Relationship: Anglo-American Relations since 1945*, Clarendon Press.

Manderson-Jones, R.B. (1972) *The Special Relationship: Anglo-American Relations and Western European Unity, 1947–56*, Weidenfeld & Nicolson.

Reynolds, D. (1985–6), 'A "special relationship"? America, Britain and the international order since the Second World War', *International Affairs*, vol. 62, no. 1, pp. 1–20.

Russett, B. (1963) *Community and Contention: Britain and America in the Twentieth Century*, MIT Press, Cambridge, Mass.

Smith, M. (1981) 'Britain and the United States in the eighties', *Yearbook of World Affairs*, pp. 165–80.

Smith, M. (1988) 'Britain and the advanced industrial countries' in Smith, M., Smith, S. and White, B. (eds) *British Foreign Policy: Tradition, Change and Transformation*, Unwin Hyman.

Steiner, Z. (1987) 'Decision making in American and British foreign policy: an open and shut case', *Review of International Studies*, vol. 13, no. 1, pp. 1–18.

Taylor, T. (1986) 'Britain's response to the Strategic Defense Initiative', *International Affairs*, vol. 62, no. 2, pp. 217–30.

Wallace, W. (1986) 'What price independence? Sovereignty and interdependence in British politics', *International Affairs*, vol. 62, no. 3, pp. 367–90.

CHAPTER 2

British Foreign Policy and West European Co-operation

DAVID ALLEN

This chapter seeks to examine the policies of the Conservative government since 1979 towards the process of West European co-operation, in which the states of Western Europe seek to manage their political, economic and security interdependence via a variety of formal and *ad hoc* arrangements. The central focus will inevitably be the European Community, which has enlarged both its geographical scope and its agenda in the 1980s. As well as playing a significant part in the Community's development, the Thatcher government has also consistently argued against a rigid insistence that all aspects of West European co-operation must somehow be made a part of the formal Community process. Thus Britain has continued to support the European Monetary System (EMS) whilst still not joining its exchange-rate mechanism, has encouraged discussion of security matters within European Political Co-operation but also supported the revival of Western European Union, and has sought to extend EC agreements on coping with terrorism to the wider group of states in the Council of Europe. In her general approach to Western Europe Mrs Thatcher has been anxious to downgrade the theology of

European integration and emphasise what she regards as the
'practicalities' of intergovernmental co-operation. In the political
climate of the 1980s, however, such an approach has gradually come
to be seen by many of Britain's partners as contributing to, rather
than undermining, their own aspirations for the future development
of Western Europe.

There is no doubt that during the nine years that Mrs Thatcher
has been in power the nature of the European Community and of
Britain's relationship with it has changed fundamentally. In 1979
the European Community consisted of nine member states, with
Britain one of three that had joined in 1973 and were just coming
towards the end of their transitional periods. Britain was essentially
isolated as an 'awkward' member, at odds with the others over the
inequities of the budget arrangements and with no apparent
enthusiasm for the Community's major policy achievement, the
Common Agricultural Policy. Moreover, whilst there was a clear
British enthusiasm for the development of the Community's role in
the international system, via both external economic policies and
political co-operation, this tended to be countered by the absolute
refusal to consider, in other than the most negative of lights, the
future development of the Community towards some sort of
European Union, however loosely defined. Furthermore, in the first
six years of membership successive British governments had made
little or no effort to try and explain to the British people either the
costs or the benefits of membership. As a result, the British and
their fellow Europeans regarded each other with mutual suspicion
and hostility at both the governmental and general-public levels and
it was commonly held within Britain that a number of economic
problems, along with a loss of political sovereignty, were the direct
result of our membership of the European Community.

It will be argued below that Britain has moved, between 1979
and the present, from an uncomfortable outsider to an established
and important member of the European Community, now occupying
what was described at the time of the last London meeting of the
European Council as 'the middle ground of European affairs'
(*Financial Times*, 4 December 1986). The transition has not,
however, been a smooth one, involving as it did five years of intense
and often acrimonious negotiations over the question of the size and
equity of Britain's net contributions to the Community budget, and
it may not be permanent. Although, as we shall see, the present

government has been able to play a much more positive role since the apparent resolution of the British budgetary problem at the Stuttgart (1983) and Fontainebleau (1984) European Council meetings, the agreements themselves are now due for review and public opinion in Britain remains in such an ill-informed and unprepared state that it could easily still prove more responsive to political leaders who present an image of standing up to, rather than working with, Europe.

However there is also a sense in which changes in the nature of the Community itself since 1979 have made Britain's position more comfortable. Enlargement to include the three southern countries of Greece, Spain and Portugal, which was enthusiastically supported by Britain, has meant that the Community is now a much more diverse and less cohesive body than it was when Britain first joined or when Mrs Thatcher was first elected. The distinct profile of the original six has become diminished, as has the domination of Community proceedings and developments by the Franco-German relationship. Here too, however, as recent developments in the security field suggest, there is some way to go before a triangular relationship, in which each bilateral link is of equal significance, develops between the three most important states. Although no longer predominant, the Franco-German link remains closer in relation to European co-operation across a broad spectrum of issues than that between Britain and either France or West Germany.

Similarly there have been significant changes in the priorities of issues on the Community agenda in the 1980s which have tended to diminish Britain's isolation from the other member states. First of all, thinking about the budget and the Common Agricultural Policy has evolved towards the British position and it is now generally accepted that the CAP must be reformed and a new and fairer basis for raising and dispensing revenues developed. Second, in the medium term, attention has moved away from the target of economic and monetary union, with which the Conservatives have problems, towards that of completing the internal market which they by and large endorse, as they also do the various proposals to enhance high-technology (though not in space!) and research co-operation. Where there are proposals to spend considerably more on intervention in the areas of social and regional policy, the Thatcher government has not felt quite the same need to lead the opposition because there are other member states with similar reservations about such policies.

Finally, in initially advocating and then playing a leading role in advancing the closer integration of Community activity with both foreign policy and security co-operation, the British government has found an area of European activity in which its general credentials can be enhanced rather than diminished. In similar fashion, and despite its continued hostility to ideas that can be seen as federalist or supranationalist, the Thatcher government has become increasingly interested in making European institutions more 'efficient' and to that end has come forward with a number of well-received and useful proposals for their adaptation or reform.

In the following sections we shall first of all examine the question of the Community budget, which is absolutely central to an understanding of the British approach to the internal development of the Community as a whole – which we will then proceed to consider in the second section. The third section will cover the Conservative government's approach to the development of foreign and security policies at the West European level, and the survey will conclude with a brief examination of the government's role in the development of European institutions.

The Central Role of the Budget Problem

The budget of the European Community has dominated Mrs Thatcher's approach to internal policies for her entire period in office. She came to power just as the extent of Britain's net contribution, once the transitional period was ended, was beginning to cause real concern. The solution that Harold Wilson had accepted at Dublin, which was successfully designed by the German Finance Ministry never to be triggered, had to be replaced but there seemed little prospect that a new and inexperienced British Prime Minister would have much chance of extracting concessions from the well-established 'gang of two', President Giscard d'Estaing of France and Chancellor Schmidt of West Germany. This was indeed the case at Mrs Thatcher's first European Council meeting at Strasbourg in June 1979. In response to her claims that Britain's likely net contribution of over 1,000 million ECUs in 1979 was unfair and that a permanent corrective measure should be developed to alleviate the problem in the future, the French Presidency, supported by the rest of the EC was prepared to offer only a small 'one-off' lump-sum repayment, along with the suggestion that Britain support the development of new Community policies from which it might be better able to profit than from the CAP.

At the next European Council meeting in Dublin, Mrs Thatcher was to make her famous declaration that she intended to 'get our money back' (Butler 1986, p. 95) and it was following the lack of progress there that Britain decided to link the resolution of its budget demands to the 1980 CAP price-fixing, threatening to veto any farm deal if there were no concessions on the budget. This strategy eventually succeeded and Lord Carrington was able to negotiate a three-year deal, which he then had to sell to Mrs Thatcher, possibly the more formidable of his tasks. The agreement was that Britain would get back roughly two-thirds of the Commission's estimate of her net contribution for 1980 and 1981 and that the Commission would also be given a mandate to produce a report on all the Community's policies, on suggested changes to the CAP and on the problem of budgetary imbalances. These were all issues that the Community should have resolved before considering the accession of Greece, and the British position, although motivated by an obvious national interest, could be argued to have been in the long-term interest of the Community as a whole. It is certainly the case that most of the issues that Britain sought to link to her particular budget problem back in 1980 were regarded by most member states as being in need of urgent attention by the time of the Copenhagen European Council meeting in December 1987.

Despite the impetus of the mandate, little progress was made during what turned out to be a lacklustre British Presidency in the second half of 1981. Helen Wallace has argued (1986, p. 584) that during this Presidency Britain had difficulty in persuading the other members states that its arguments about finance and agriculture were relevant to the Community as a whole and not just to British interests. In other words, there was little confidence in British impartiality despite the evident efforts that were made to create that confidence. Wallace also refers to the problems that the British Presidency had in mediating in Community negotiations, and attributes this partly to inexperience and partly to the fact that 'the British political style (and particularly that of Mrs Thatcher?) was ill-suited to the role of coalition-building' so necessary in a Council of twelve states (1986, p. 585).

Of course 1982 was the year of the Falklands War and it was also to see the collapse of the budget-negotiating tactic that Britain had used successfully the year before. After the Argentinian invasion of the Falklands in April, the Community managed an impeccable response, agreeing to a trade and arms embargo within a few days. If anything the response was too good, for a number of EC stages were later to complain that Britain had taken the Community far too much for granted and had devoted most of her diplomatic effort to winning US and UN support. It was argued that, whilst the British got exactly what they wanted, they showed little understanding of the genuine problems faced by several EC states in supporting British policy. Some of the flavour of this dissatisfaction, along with a concern that Britain was not making any serious effort to solve the Falklands problem by diplomatic means, obviously spilt over into the CAP price-fixing/British rebate negotiations. The outcome was that a British attempt to invoke the Luxembourg compromise on the farm-price deal was rejected by other members, who proceeded to take and win a majority vote. Although this represented a major setback for the British budget strategy, it was inevitably overshadowed by events elsewhere and by the fact that Francis Pym was able eventually to secure an 850 million ECU rebate for 1982.

However, two attempts to get a long-term solution to the British budget problem had now failed and the issue was clearly damaging all other aspects of Britain's relationship with the European Community. The problem itself had now become more pressing for the Community as a whole since the total budget was rapidly approaching the 1 per cent VAT ceiling that marked the limit of available resources. Just before what was to prove to be the critical Stuttgart European Council meeting in 1983, Mrs Thatcher accepted a Foreign Office proposal that she should go for a new set of negotiations linking any increase in the VAT ceiling (which some states wanted, but which would require unanimous agreement and ratification) to the reform of the CAP, budgetary discipline and a permanent formula for resolving the problem of budget imbalances – the British problem in other words. This line was eventually accepted at Stuttgart and formed the basis of the settlement made at Fontainebleau the next year. Once it became clear that the budget problem was going to be cleared up, claim supporters of the argument that the Thatcher government is more pro-European than its record over the first five years might suggest, the government was able for the first time properly to set out its European stall.

Between Stuttgart and Fontainebleau, and after the Conservatives had been convincingly re-elected, Sir Geoffrey Howe gave a carefully prepared lecture at Chatham House in which he repeated Britain's conditions for accepting an increase in EC resources but also suggested ways in which the Community might move on from the budget negotiations (Howe 1984). Much of what he had to say was to be repeated by Mrs Thatcher at Fontainebleau when she presented a paper entitled 'Europe – The Future' as a 'contribution' to the next stage of Community development (JCMS 1984). In both documents the British surprised their fellow members, who had perhaps come to believe that Mrs Thatcher had no other objectives beyond getting her money back, with the depth of their vision for the future. In particular, both Howe and Thatcher called for the completion of the internal market, with Howe claiming that non-tariff barriers within the supposed 'common market' were costing some £6,750 million. In calling for the completion of a truly free market, the British in 1984 made their first major contribution to setting the Community's agenda – reaching that objective by 1992 has now become the EC's major priority.

The British were less enthusiastic about advocating major new spending programmes for the EC, although lip-service was paid to the need for industrial co-operation (particularly in research and development) and to the need for an energy strategy and for measures designed to protect the environment. Improvements in the internal workings of the Community were to provide the base for expanding the international competence of the EC, but we shall examine these matters in a later section. Suffice it at present to say that the Fontainebleau agreement on the future financing of the budget and the acceptance of a formula whereby Britain receives an annual rebate amounting to 66 per cent of the gap between its total VAT contribution and Community expenditure in Britain (Denton 1984) represented a watershed in the Conservative government's relations with its Community partners.

The question of the budget has not of course been finally resolved. Since 1985 the Community has sunk deeper and deeper into near bankruptcy as the costs of the CAP have soared through overproduction and through the rising cost (as the dollar declines) of export subsidies and as the Fontainebleau 'own resources' VAT limit of 1.4

per cent (with a possible extension to 1.6 per cent, which would require unanimous agreement) proves inadequate. The difference in the budgetary debates from 1984 onwards was that Britain was no longer isolated in the role of demander but merely one of a number of states which recognised there was a problem but could not find a solution. In relation to CAP reform the British, whilst still protecting their own farmers' interests, have found it easier to go along with Commission proposals for 'stabilisers' and set-aside schemes than either the French or the Germans, and as both these countries are now net contributors to the EC budget Britain is no longer alone in expressing reservations about the large increases in spending on the Social and Regional funds advocated by the southern countries and the Delors Commission. However the possibility of future isolation still remains, particularly now that the Prime Minister has reason to believe that resolutely sticking to the British position of no budgetary increases without CAP reform and real indications of budget discipline is a line that must eventually prevail. There is always a danger that the whole Fontainebleau deal could once again be questioned and, although Mrs Thatcher's behaviour at the disastrous Copenhagen European Council was exemplary (mainly because of her concern to preserve European solidarity in the face of US–Soviet developments at their own summit in Washington), there have been signs since that the rest of the EC might seek a less 'disciplined' way out of their agri-budgetary crisis than the British government envisages.

We shall return to the problem of the British domestic consensus in the conclusions, for it is quite clear that the manner of her eventual budget victory was such that Mrs Thatcher would have great problems in settling for anything less in the future, even if other possible benefits, such as progress on the internal market or Community solidarity towards the outside world, could be seen to outweigh the costs. Nevertheless, in conclusion, the British budget campaign has to be judged as a diplomatic success in the short to medium term. Not only did Britain win financial compensation, but subsequent developments have also confirmed the logic of Mrs Thatcher's arguments. Once the issue was settled the British government was able to demonstrate a much more positive approach to the development of the European Community and, as we shall see in the last section, this was well demonstrated by the process that culminated in the Single European Act coming into force. In the next section, however, we shall briefly examine the Thatcher government's line on other aspects of the Community's internal development.

Internal Policy Developments

By and large the Thatcher government has sought to relate its responses to various proposals for action at the European level to its monetarist and free-market principles. This has not prevented it from accepting high agricultural prices for British farmers or from seeking to preserve their interests via manipulation of the green exchange rates. Under Mrs Thatcher Britain has become increasingly self-sufficient in food and has in particular become a significant contributor to the grain and beef surpluses. However the government has probably gone further than its major partners in preparing its farmers for the time when the CAP is reformed and at present Britain, unlike West Germany, would probably be able to implement any CAP changes that called either for production cuts or price reductions. Mrs Thatcher was confident enough about her control of British agriculture and of her domestic budgetary flexibility, to suggest at Copenhagen in 1987 that each country could resolve the budget and agricultural surplus problem by agreeing to write off the costs of all surpluses against their national, rather than the Community, budget. This line of argument suggests that, if it came to it, the current British government would not object to the 'renationalisation' of the CAP. In the past such suggestions were interpreted as indicative of a British desire to undermine the very basis of the European Community. These days it is the CAP in its present form rather than proposals for its improvement that is seen as threatening the continued existence of the Community. Finally, with regard to agriculture the Thatcher government conducted a long and ultimately successful negotiation to agree a Common Fisheries Policy, primarily because it was more prepared than its predecessors (with the exception of Mr Crosland, who died just as he was getting to grips with the portfolio) to face up to the domestic political consequences of sharing access to and introducing conservation measures in what had been British but now became Community waters.

It was the monetarist stance of her incoming government which

ensured that Mrs Thatcher followed Mr Callaghan's line of
participating in the European Monetary System but not in its
exchange-rate mechanism. Whilst the more doctrinaire monetarists
argued that there was no need for any sort of exchange rate policy
and that to have one would be to lose control over the money supply,
the Treasury stuck to its unwillingness to give up the flexibility
implicit in freely-floating rates. Once the decision not to join had
been taken in 1979, there was always going to be an extended
argument not just about the principle itself but over when would be
the right time to join. Whilst both Sir Geoffrey Howe, as Foreign
Secretary and an ex-Chancellor, and Nigel Lawson the present
Chancellor of the Exchequer now advocate membership, and despite
the fact that for the past couple of years Britain has been quite
obviously following an exchange rate policy of trying to keep the
pound between upper and lower limits *vis-à-vis* the Deutschmark,
Mrs Thatcher herself has held out resolutely against such a move.
Britain's Community partners continue to cite this reluctance as
indicative of Britain's different approach to European co-operation
and to regret the fact that the pound's absence diminishes the role
that Europe can play in global economic management.

    As far as industrial policy is concerned, the Conservatives have
gone along with various crisis measures in the steel sector but have
shown no great enthusiasm for extending the Community's
interventionist scope. During the third British Presidency in 1986
the government, fearing calls for some form of Community-wide
infrastructure project to reduce unemployment, came up with a plan
which placed a great deal of emphasis on deregulation, promoting
small business and training schemes, all of which were designed not
so much to alleviate unemployment as to fill up the agenda of the
Employment Council with non-controversial material. The British
government has been accused of following its pro-American rather
than European tendencies over the Westland affair and over its
support for British Airways' purchase of Boeing rather than Airbus
planes. On the Airbus itself, the government has been prepared to
assist British Aerospace with the R & D costs of participation in the
A320 and A330/340 programmes but has in both cases given
significantly less than requested whilst insisting on the repayment of
earlier loans for the A300/A310 programme. The British government was instrumental in encouraging Airbus Industries to seek to
collaborate with McDonnell Douglas to build a plane to compete

with the Boeing 747 rather than sticking to a purely European alternative, and it will probably continue to pursue this line of thinking in the future even though initial talks got nowhere.

In the area of co-operation in research and high technology, the Conservative government has cautiously supported programmes like ESPRIT and RACE within the Community framework (although it withheld agreement to the necessary funding for some time in 1987) and has also come round to support the French-inspired EUREKA programme, which includes eighteen European countries and was initially designed as a civilian response to the US Star Wars (SDI) research programme. There are significant differences between the major European governments on how and with whom high-technology projects should be funded. The British approach has been characterised by a desire not to exclude co-operation with the US – only the British responded enthusiastically to US promises of SDI contracts, but it is notable that this enthusiasm has not to date been turned into research work of any significant value – and by a preference for financing projects from private markets (Sharp and Shearman 1987, p.79) and existing support schemes rather than from new government money. Over both SDI and the source of funding, the Thatcher government has been at odds with the French and the Germans in particular. More generally, the British government has been criticised for its rigid insistence that any money diverted to European programmes of whatever kind should be deducted from the existing grants of government departments. Finally in the area of high technology, the British government has been strongly criticised recently for its lack of enthusiasm and support for the ambitious plans of the European Space Agency (Marsh 1987).

As we stated above, it is in its support for the concept of the internal market that Britain has been able to appear most *communitaire* in recent years, although even here there are major reservations about the desirability of harmonising tax rates, especially those of income tax and VAT. The British government has tended to argue the validity of the US example – not necessarily designed to endear it to all its EC partners! – in both advocating a freer market in financial services or in, say, air transport and continuing to defend the preservation of individual tax regimes. Despite the enthusiasm for the general principle of the internal market the Thatcher government has continued to resist what it sees as harmonisation for its own sake and to support constant scrutiny of Commission proposals to ensure that the advantages to be gained from legislation are greater than its administrative costs or any burden it may place on free enterprise.

In its approach to policies at the European level, Britain under Mrs Thatcher has therefore placed considerable emphasis on the advantages of negative integration (removing barriers to trade) and the disadvantages of positive integration (extending interventionist policies). Her government has also advocated, and seeks to gain from, a relaxation of the view that everything must be done within the Community framework, and that everything that is done within the Community framework must be done at the same time and at the same pace by all the member states. Whilst this policy of Europe 'à la carte' enables Britain to pick and choose the areas in which it is prepared to co-operate at the European level, it can also have its own disadvantages. There are a number of issues to do with the internal market where the smaller and poorer members states stand to gain little and in some cases clearly lose out to the larger states. As Hellen Wallace has pointed out (1985, p.88) the British still have to recognise that their own expectations of differential treatment – over the budget, EMS or, indeed, harmonisation of tax rates – must be reconciled with their partners' needs for similar consideration, needs which if met could undermine the achievement of the internal market. In other words, it remains to be seen whether the Community that the British Conservative government has played a recently significant part in creating will be capable of meeting that government's expectations in the long term.

Foreign and Security Policy in Western Europe

Whatever their feelings about the internal policies of the European Community, every British government since 1973 has enthusiastically participated in and sought to develop the process of European Political Co-operation (EPC). Even though Mrs Thatcher herself is perhaps best known for the closeness of her relationship with President Reagan and her endorsement of many of his foreign policy stances, the main lines of British foreign policy in the last decade have come closely to resemble those pursued by the West Europeans collectively. This fact reflects as much the influence of EPC on

British thinking as it does the reverse, although on a number of issues, in particular policy towards the Middle East conflict and East–West relations, Britain has played a key role in determining European policy. In the period before Mrs Thatcher came to power, EPC had reached a kind of plateau after its rapid early development. The Soviet invasion of Afghanistan, which heralded the start of a renewed period of East–West tension, and the need to fill the void in Western policy created by the transition from the crippled Carter administration to the initially inexperienced Reagan administration, gave the process of European foreign policy co-operation a much needed stimulus. It was during the British Presidency of 1981 that the London Report was published, which codified Lord Carrington's call for EPC to be extended to include discussion of security matters and established a more effective crisis mechanism in an attempt to improve on the six weeks it had taken the EC countries formally to react to events in Afghanistan. Also during this early period, the British government played a key role in both the development of and the follow up to the Community's Venice Declaration on the Middle East, which was made in 1980. This declaration played a significant role in broadening the scope of the Camp David peace process to include other interested parties, and in particular to recognise the rights of the Palestinians as well as those of Israel.

The Venice Declaration was not well received in the United States for it appeared to challenge the broad lines of US policy. It was, however, to be the first of a number of such challenges from the Europeans in the 1980s. What is notable is that the Thatcher government has not just gone along with but in many cases has initiated lines of policy in EPC that differ from those being pursued or advocated by the US. On occasion the British have been pleased to seek European solidarity in the face of events such as the American invasion of Grenada or American attempts to extend the application of its domestic laws to British firms participating in the sale of technology to the Soviet Union. In some instances there has been a suspicion that the Foreign Secretary and the Foreign Office have used the need for agreement within EPC to persuade the Prime Minister to soften her own natural inclination to line up with the United States. There have also been instances where Britain has chosen to act alone and where the Community has been called upon to endorse that action. Thus, as we have seen already, the EC member states came up with the goods at the time of the

Falklands – the United States noted at that time that the Community was a lot quicker to act against Argentina than it had been against Iran at the time of the American hostage crisis. Also, after some hesitation, the British government received EC support at the time of the British break with Syria over that country's support of terrorism. Although Mrs Thatcher stood out from all other members of the Community in her willingness to endorse the American bombing raid on Libya, public reaction in Britain to that event suggests that she would not be anxious to respond in similar fashion again.

European foreign policy co-operation has, then, developed quite distinctly in the 1980s with Mrs Thatcher's Britain at the forefront of its institutional and substantive development, its progressive integration with the external relations of the Community itself culminating in its acquisition of a Treaty base as part of the Single European Act and the extension of its scope within that Treaty to include the economic and political aspects of security. The transformation of the British foreign policy process was such that Lord Carrington, when Foreign Secretary, stated that 'British foreign policy must now be conducted essentially in an European framework'. More specifically, his deputy Douglas Hurd, who had previously been a diplomat, claimed that since the 1950s 'the biggest single change of diplomatic method stems from European Political Co-operation. Then it was broadly speaking with the Americans only that we shared information and assessments: policy making was a national preserve. Now in some areas of diplomacy our policy is formed wholly within a European context; and in no area is the European influence completely absent' (Hurd 1981).

Much the same sorts of argument could be made about the context within which most of Britain's external economic policy is now formulated. Although acting on a mandate given to it by the Council of Ministers, it is the Commission which is now the major trade negotiator on behalf of the member states. Whilst the Thatcher administration has been anxious to prevent calls for protectionism, particularly in response to actions by the United States, it has, in the main, been glad to seek shelter from the international economic storm within the defensive walls of a common Community stance. In areas where there is no Community policy, Mrs Thatcher's Britain has tended to align with West Germany and France in calling for corrective action from the United

States and Japan. In most aspects of international economic management, and despite the frequently proclaimed strength of the British economy under the Conservatives, there has been little pretence that Britain can do anything other than co-operate with its Community partners.

The development of British foreign policy within a West European framework reflects a fundamental transformation of European politics, with all West European states increasingly recognising their interdependence and their individual inability to exert influence in an international system dominated by the two superpowers. Although the Thatcher government has willingly gone along with the 'Europeanisation', it has been anxious at every available opportunity to make clear that it sees such a development as a contribution to the continued solidarity of the Western Alliance as a whole rather than, as some other European states see it, an alternative to the Alliance. Mrs Thatcher has been a firm exponent of the old Kennedy notion of Western Europe and the United States being the twin pillars of the Atlantic Alliance. This attitude has been tested on a number of occasions but no more so that at the time of the US–Soviet Summit in Reykjavik when President Reagan came close to agreeing a far-reaching arms-control agreement that Mrs Thatcher for one would have had great difficulty living with. There is, then, an inherent conflict implicit in West European progress towards a common foreign and security policy stance. As the West Europeans begin collectively to define their own identity and to pursue their own joint interests they will inevitably come into conflict with the United States, and when such conflicts break out it is the British government that feels most exposed.

This is much what has happened in the security sphere. In the early 1980s the Thatcher government argued against the protests of the Irish, the Greeks and the Danes that EPC should extend its scope to consider security matters. This call was soon taken up and furthered in the rhetoric that surrounded the Genscher–Columbo proposals for progress towards European Union. Britain was already involved in attempts, via the Eurogroup of Nato which it had founded in the late 1960s and the Independent European Programme Group, to rationalise arms production and to reassure the United States that Western Europe was prepared to share the burden of its collective defence. In the 1980s the Conservative government was initially enthusiastic about the revival of West European Union

although it was soon apparent that at least part of the enthusiasm
had to do with a concern to keep an eye on exactly what the French
and the Germans were up to. More recently British support for some
sort of West European defence identity has been more muted, with a
degree of concern being shown about the latest Franco-German
developments. The celebrations that accompanied the 25th anniver-
sary of the Franco-German Treaty of friendship and the decision to
establish a joint brigade and to share targetting information was met
quite swiftly by warnings from London about the possible dangers
involved in splitting the Alliance. Thus, whilst the Thatcher
government has been prepared to play its part in European defence
co-operation and to take a lead in establishing a link between EPC
and security considerations (particularly outside the Nato area), it is
not interested in participating in any fundamental changes in the
European security system. Unlike many of its Community partners,
the British government has its doubts about continued superpower
arms reductions in Europe because, perhaps more than any other
West European state, it fears the consequences of any American
decision to scale down its commitment to Europe. For Mrs
Thatcher, the value of any European defence collaboration is
measured in terms of a continued American commitment; some of
her European colleagues are beginning to think of it as an
alternative.

Institutional Developments

Despite a number of reservations about the symbolic significance of
European institutions, the record of the Thatcher government is a
surprisingly good one when it comes to considering its willingness
to either propose or go along with institutional reform. As long as it
could not be accused at home of favouring the development of a
federal Europe, the British government has adopted a practical and
usually positive approach towards institutional change. Perhaps the
biggest turnaround came over the Single European Act. At the
European Council in Milan, Mrs Thatcher, in the uncomfortable
company of Greece, stood out against proposals of the Dooge
Committee (established at Fontainebleau) for the reform of the
Treaty of Rome in order to speed up the Community decision-
making process by limiting the power of individual states to block

legislation. However, once she had been outvoted in Milan, the Prime Minister took the work of the Intergovernmental Committee extremely seriously and in the event probably contributed far more to its eventual success than many of the countries that had most enthusiastically argued for it in principle. Indeed the Single European Act itself, with its provisions for majority voting in the Council on proposals to perfect the internal market and its Treaty on Political Co-operation that provides both for a secretariat and for the economic and political aspects of security to be considered, has caused far more of a stir in Germany, France, Eire and Denmark than in Britain. Much of the detailed drafting was done by British officials in what has to be seen as a victory for pragmatism over idealism with regard to the development of West European co-operation.

In the European Council Mrs Thatcher has emerged as the senior European Head of Government and has recently succeeded in persuading her colleagues that just two well-prepared meetings a year were necessary instead of three. British proposals to reduce the size of the Commission by allocating just one Commisioner per country have not yet been taken up and there are still bad memories of Mrs Thatcher's interference with the independence of the Commission in 1981 in order to secure Christopher Tugendhat the Budget portfolio. Inside the Commission there are those who have enjoyed a wry smile at the irritation that Internal Market Commissioner Lord Cockfield has caused some of his former UK Cabinet colleagues with some of his proposals and there was genuine surprise recently when Mr David Williamson, who had previously worked in the Cabinet Office for Mrs Thatcher and who had just succeeded Emile Noel as the Secretary-General of the Commission, gave an extremely upbeat speech about the Community's chances of solving its agri-budget crisis in the near future – not, many thought, a speech of which Mrs Thatcher would have approved.

Britain has run two Presidencies during Mrs Thatcher's term of office, neither with startling results but both sufficiently uncontroversial to suggest that Britain is learning to play the European game to greater effect than before. Many saw the recent London European Council as a masterful example of how to stage an event that avoids all the really difficult issues. More positively, Britain was responsible in 1980 for developing the troika system of linking three successive Presidencies together to achieve continuity in EPC, and in 1986 introduced the same idea, this time known as the 'rolling action programme', to co-ordinate better the work of succeeding Presidencies on the internal market.

Conclusion

Much of what has been written above has suggested a rather more positive view of Britain's relationship with its West European partners than one might have expected from the tone of Mrs Thatcher's budget campaign. During her period of office, Britain has certainly moved from the periphery of the Community towards the middle ground. Most aspects of Britain's relationship with the Community and with other member states reflect an acceptance of interdependence and a constructive attempt to manage it so as best to advance Britain's interests as interpreted by the government. The one thing that is missing, however, is any attempt by the Conservative government to build a domestic consensus for its European policies. Although Sir Geoffrey Howe recognised this problem in his 1983 Chatham House speech, when he spoke of the government's duty 'to provide information and explanation' so as to overcome the public's 'insular reflex' (Howe 1984, p. 187), neither he nor any other member of the political establishment in Mrs Thatcher's Britain have made any attempt to educate the British public in the realities of European interdependence or the ways that its government is seeking to cope with it. Mrs Thatcher has gone out of her way to cultivate the impression of her constant struggle with our European partners to safeguard British interests. The danger is that this distorted picture could one day backfire on her and prevent Britain from fully benefiting from the constructive work that has been put into changing the nature of our relations with Western Europe.

References and Further Reading

Butler, M. (1986) *Europe: More than a Continent*, Heinemann.
Denton, G. (1984) 'Re-structuring the EC Budget: implications of the Fontainbleau Agreement', *Journal of Common Market Studies*, vol. XXIII, no. 2.
Howe, G. (1984) 'The future of the European Community: Britain's approach to the negotiations', *International Affairs*, vol. 60, no. 2.

Hurd, D. (1981) 'European Political Co-operation', *International Affairs*, vol. 57, no. 3.

JCMS (1984) 'Europe – the future', *Journal of Common Market Studies*, vol. XXIII, no. 1.

Marsh, P. (1987) 'Britain's Space Programme', *Financial Times*, 18 September 1987.

Sharp, M. and Shearman, C. (1987) *European Technological Collaboration*, Routledge & Kegan Paul.

Wallace, H. (1985) *Europe: The Challenge of Diversity*, Routledge & Kegan Paul.

Wallace, H. (1986) 'The British presidency of the Council: the opportunity to persuade', *International Affairs*, vol. 62, no. 4.

CHAPTER 3

The Soviet Union and Eastern Europe

MICHAEL CLARKE

One of the perennial questions in the study of British foreign relations is the degree to which any given Prime Minister affects the substance of policy. On the face of it, Mrs Thatcher seems to have had a strong impact on British foreign policy. As a right-wing leader who approves of 'conviction politics', the arena of British–Soviet and British–East European relations would seem to be an obvious sphere where personality has made a difference. Indeed it has; but only within certain limitations which are dictated by the flow of policy over a long period. A more careful look at the nature of those limitations and the nature of Thatcherism in this regard, tells us something both about our own foreign policy and the leaders to whom we entrust it.

In order to try to assess the impact of Thatcherism on relations between Britain and the Soviet bloc, it is necessary to analyse the general pattern of British diplomacy towards the East as it had come to exist during the 1970s. In essence, these relations were characterised by distance more than hostility. States spend much more of their diplomatic energies on their friends than their adversaries. And because British governments had never had any doubt that the Soviet Union was its adversary, there has always been a strong tendency to deal with the Soviet Union formally and politely, but seldom with enthusiasm.

Immediately after the Russian revolution in 1917 British governments were clearly hostile to the new Bolshevik state, if only because it had collapsed the Eastern Front in the war against Germany. They became drawn into a fruitless war of intervention against the new state. In 1924 the first Labour government recognised Bolshevik Russia but this did not herald a new approach to Bolshevism. Through the 1920s and 1930s successive British governments, Conservative, Labour and then the National Government, all regarded the Soviet Union with distaste or indifference; certainly they saw no pressing need to include the Soviet Union in Western diplomacy, even when the problem of dealing with the Fascist powers became critical. Throughout these years the Comintern pursued policies – however unsuccessful – to destabilise Western governments and, since Britain was able to read Soviet message codes up to 1927, Comintern intentions had always been well known to the government.

During the Second World War Churchill was never in any doubt as to what he thought of the Soviet Union. Nevertheless, on the eve of the German invasion of Russia in August 1941 he remarked that, such were the imperatives of the anti-Nazi struggle, 'If Hitler invaded hell I would make at least a favourable reference to the Devil in the House of Commons.' And so it was. There was never any doubt that Britain would make common cause with the Soviet Union after the German attack on it, despite the fact that the signing of the Nazi–Soviet Non-Aggression Pact of 1939 had virtually guaranteed the outbreak of the war itself. With America's entry into the war in December 1941 the Grand Alliance came into being, and for three years the Soviet Union was not an adversary in British eyes. Even so, the Grand Alliance lasted just about long enough to defeat the Axis powers and in truth the strains were clearly visible by mid-1944. The American government was determined that there would be no deals with the Soviet Union to carve out spheres of influence before the end of the war. Roosevelt was convinced that he could persuade the Soviet government to co-operate in a great-power directorate, expressed through the United Nations, to manage world affairs. Churchill, and those around him, were always sceptical about this possibility and sought to confine the

Red Army as far East as possible and arrive at a *modus vivendi* with
the Soviet Union. Churchill and the Foreign Office, in fact, seem to
have based their policies on some very shrewd assessments of the
Soviet state. In Washington very few policy makers agreed with
British assessments. Rather, there was a strong suspicion that the
British would like to manoeuvre the US into some sort of deal with
the Soviet Union which would be good for Britain's postwar position
but which would undermine the principles on which the new
postwar order was to be based. In the event, Churchill never did
manoeuvre the US into an explicit deal; but from 1944 to 1947 a
series of incremental decisions, over the treatment of defeated Axis
powers, the demarcation zones between the armies, the arrangements for restoring government to the liberated countries, and the
administration of defeated Germany, achieved, in effect, the same
result. By 1948 the US agreed with the British analysis of Soviet
policy – indeed it extended the logic of it – and from then on
British relations with the Soviet Union and Eastern Europe were
seen always through the prism of the cold war.

The general effects of this on Britain's relations with the East
expressed themselves in a diplomatic approach that was always
correct and polite but never genuinely cordial. Throughout the
postwar period, the multilateral context has been set by the Atlantic
Alliance and the more structural forces of East–West relations.
Britain has always approached the East as a founder member of
Nato, a power with a special relationship with the USA, and a
country with global commitments and a good deal of diplomatic
experience. It has regarded itself, and seems to have been regarded
by the Soviet Union, as something of a *de facto* manager of
transatlantic relations. As an island, Britain does not have the
immediate territorial concerns of a power like the Federal Republic
of Germany; but equally, as an island in the Nato theatre, it is a
vital reinforcement base and centre of operations in the eastern
Atlantic. Britain approaches the East as one of the two European
states with independent nuclear powers, a member of the European
Community, and one of the 'Big Seven' OECD countries. All of this
makes up a powerful and ubiquitous multilateralism through which
Britain handles the most important aspects of its relations with
Eastern countries. As the British government itself has observed,
'the framework of policy towards the Soviet Union is set by the
North Atlantic Alliance's strategy . . . clearly better understanding

between the United States and the Soviet Union is of fundamental importance' (*UK–Soviet Relations* 1986).

Britain's bilateral relations with Eastern countries have varied according to time and circumstance. They involve trade and commerce, cultural exchanges, the normal flow of diplomatic relations, and exchanges of opinions on major questions which affect both parties. Sometimes, bilateral relations have developed almost a momentum of their own and have deepened in periods of détente; at other times they have been cut back to a minimum of contact and been marked by a frosty sense of formality. All bilateral relations, however, are conditioned by the general context of East–West affairs. In a sense, they are determined by the patterns of multilateral relations which exist at any given time. One of the axioms of British policy towards the East since 1944 has been that Western unity – normally Anglo-American unity – is a prerequisite to any policy towards Eastern Europe or the Soviet Union.

Thus, from the 1950s up to the late 1970s, British policy towards the East was at once indirect and yet remarkably consistent. It was indirect because the most important issues had to be handled through the intensive multilateral framework, and the sort of issues under discussion – arms control, disarmament conferences, East–West security arrangements or reactions to particular crises – are by their very nature replete with implications for all of the Western allies. Yet Britain's relations with the East have also been consistent. Indeed the British attitude to dealing with Communist powers has never swung back and forth as much as that of the USA. During the war Britain wanted a *modus vivendi* with the East as a realistic approach to a general problem of the postwar structure. The USA would not entertain this notion because it smacked of corrupt politics. In the 1950s, British officials were quick to spot the possibilities of a détente with the East following the death of Stalin, and also urged the USA to recognise the new Communist regime in China. In these cases the United States was reluctant to agree because by then it smacked too much of the politics of accomodation. Again, during the tense years of 1960–2, Britain was sensitive to the possibilities that existed for détente with the Soviet Union, notwithstanding the tensions that surrounded the crises in Berlin and Cuba. Throughout these decades, the characteristic British official approach to the Soviet Union and Eastern Europe was one of caution and of moderate expectations. Where détente was possible, it was clearly desirable, so long as it was based on the unity of the West and posed no threat of undermining it. Setbacks in the relationship were to be expected, given the volatile nature of cold war politics, but moderate gains could be made for mutual benefit. The likelihood of that, however, depended at least as much as on the Soviet Union itself, and the attitude it took to the issues involved. There was also a recognition that Western–Soviet diplomacy could not be divorced from Western–Eastern Europe diplomacy; indeed, that the former was a prerequisite of the latter. The Hungarian crisis of November 1956 coincided with Britain's embarrassments in the Suez invasion, but notwithstanding that fact, there was no inclination in the government to do more than protest about Soviet actions. And again in the Czech crisis of August 1968, the West learned anew that it did not help Eastern European states to deal directly with them in a way which seemed to bypass the Soviet Union. The road to Prague or Budapest had to go by way of Moscow. Though there have been differences of emphasis between Britain and the USA over the years, and though Britain's relations with the East have fluctuated with the ebb and flow of the cold war and détente, Britain's wariness of Eastern governments, its 'wait and see' attitude to prospects of any change in the relationship, and its firm conviction that allied unity was always the first priority, have provided a high degree of continuity in Britain's Eastern diplomacy.

During the 1970s, therefore, Britain's relations with the East could be cast in this general mould. The early 1970s were the years of optimistic détente. The SALT I negotiations moved to a successful and dramatic conclusion in 1972 and SALT II was in process; the Conference on Security and Co-operation in Europe was moving successfully towards the signing of the Helsinki Final Act in August 1975; the Mutual and Balanced Force Reduction talks opened in Vienna in 1973, and the Federal Republic's *Ostpolotik* was normalising relations between the two Germanies and with the Soviet Union and Poland. East–West relations were in a phase of active diplomacy and the government of Edward Heath was proceeding with the business of getting Britain into the European Community. There was every reason to believe that East–West relations would continue to improve and British policy toward the Soviet Union and Eastern Europe reflected this. Despite the setback caused by the unprecedented expulsion of 105 Soviet personnel in Britain in 1971 and the recriminations that followed, the visits of

Andrei Gromyko to London in October 1971 and Alec Douglas-
Home to Moscow in 1973 were marked by polite communiqués
which were filled with expressions of hope that détente would be
deepened in all areas.

At the point at which Mrs Thatcher entered the arena, however,
when she became Leader of the Opposition in 1975, relations with
the East were showing signs of change. The oil crisis of 1973/4 had a
major impact on the economies of both East and West and certainly
lowered Western expectations of a more fruitful economic relationship between Eastern and Western Europe. The Soviet Union,
however, enjoyed some windfall profits from the crisis, and in 1975
Harold Wilson went to Moscow for a much-publicised summit, the
centrepiece of which was a £1 billion trade and credit package. The
eventual results of this agreement, however, were far less than the
promise. The tempo of détente was slowing down after 1975. The
SALT II negotiations were bogged down after 1974, the MBFR
talks seemed to be fruitless, and the arms race picked up a new
momentum as Soviet modernisation programmes of the late 1960s
began to pay off ten years later. Critics of détente pointed out that
all the agreements had not prevented this Soviet military 'build-up'.
Meanwhile the Helsinki Final Act rather backfired on the Soviet
Union since it elevated issues of human rights within Eastern bloc
countries and acted as a focus for a good deal of Western criticism.
By the late 1970s the realities of détente were proving, at least in
the West, to be rather less than the earlier expectations of it. The
critics of détente were more confident in their criticisms and the
rhetoric of a 'new cold war' began to build.

The Thatcher Style in East–West Diplomacy

As Leader of the Opposition, Mrs Thatcher found herself intuitively
in agreement with the critics of détente, and her own statements on
foreign affairs gave point and political weight to the unease felt by
many observers. She was not well acquainted with foreign affairs in
1975 and her approach to the East was a characteristic mixture of
instinct and calculation. Her instincts were deeply antithetical to
the Soviet Union and the whole nature of Communism; her
calculation was that she could make the existing Labour Government seem weak and gullible by attacking its support for détente

and its attempts to make capital out of Wilson's Anglo-Soviet summit of 1975. In fact, she made relatively few statements on East–West relations during these years: she was sceptical of the value of the Helsinki Agreement in August 1975; on 19 January 1976 she made the speech which earned her the titles of 'iron lady' from *krasnaia zvezda* and 'militant amazon' from *komsomolskaya Pravda* and provoked an official protest from the Soviet ambassador; she revelled in the discomfort her speech had caused, and then in July 1976 returned to her themes in a major policy statement which formed the basis in October 1976 for *The Right Approach*. This document guided the Conservative party's foreign policy until the election of 1979.

In all of these statements she echoed the preoccupations of the 'New Right' in Conservative ideology (Bell 1985, Kavanagh 1987). In this view, détente was just another Soviet tactic to gain influence over the West, and it was working; it was dangerous to cut defence expenditure, as the Labour government was doing, since the threat continued to increase. It was also dangerous to expand credit for trade with the Soviet Union, since this allowed the Soviets to divert even more resources to the military machine. The statements of Alexander Solzhenitsyn, she said, 'go to the heart of any analysis of the balance between Russia and the West' and they were quoted at length and with approval. Human-rights issues were not only important in themselves, but they revealed the essential nature of the competition between freedom and tyranny. The West had become complacent and lacked vigilance in the face of a Russia 'bent on world dominance' and exercising its power in Vietnam, Angola and Portugal. The response should be to increase defence spending and increase forces' pay, to rededicate Britain to the Anglo-American relationship which was the ultimate security guarantee, and to strengthen the 'Anglo-Saxon heritage' with the former dominion countries.

Margaret Thatcher was not the first leading Tory to say such things; Peter Walker and Julian Amery had made similar statements already. But almost overnight, Mrs Thatcher adopted the mantle of Churchill, warning of the dangers and attacking the adversary in vivid language: Britain had a special role to play in helping the United States fight tyranny, and only a vigorous foreign policy would maintain such a role (Riddell 1985). This Anglo-Americanism was also reinforced by an antipathy to the European

Community. To be a 'Eurofanatic' was to be identified with the Heathite wing of the Conservative party. The New Right was opposed to any attempt to settle the Rhodesia crisis by dealing with Robert Mugabe and Joshua Nkomo; the old Churchillian combination of an Anglo-American special relationship, backed up by the white commonwealth, should be the focus of Britain's foreign relations. Undue enthusiasm for the EC or residual guilt over the black former colonies had no place in a radical Conservative vision of Britain's place in the world.

In addition to her anti-Communist instincts, Mrs Thatcher also brought to her perspective on foreign policy a personal distrust of bureaucracy and a scepticism about the role of the Foreign and Commonwealth Office in dealing with the Russians. In part, this was another theme of the New Right, but it was also an intensely individual conviction. For her, the FCO were trimmers and the traditional language of diplomacy, even more of détente, was the language of euphemism and compromise. As Francis Pym has commented rather ruefully, 'her experience was very, very limited', she tended to look, 'at international problems as she looks at domestic problems and has the approach to them of an extremely practical, down-to-earth housewife who wants to get on with the job. This isn't always easily understood overseas' (Young and Sloman 1986). Or in Julian Critchley's more impish comment, 'she cannot see an institution without hitting it with her handbag'. It is hardly surprising that her natural style was at odds with the FCO from the very beginning of her premiership; initially over the question of European Community budgetary adjustments. She demanded 'Britain's own money back', sometimes even 'my money'. This was not the approach of the FCO. As far as the Soviet Union was concerned, she seemed to feel only a suspicion that the FCO's perspective – indeed that of most of Whitehall – would serve to disguise and confound the essentially simple reality that the Communist threat was growing and that Britain must do more about it. She was therefore much more inclined to accept the analysis of the Soviet Union offered by her own personal advisers than to rely chiefly on the FCO's own analysis.

These, then, were the ingredients of Britain's relationship with the East in 1979. The Anglo-Soviet relationship had never been intense and was marked by a wary scepticism. British relations with the East were, in any case, a reflection of the wider context of cold war relations; and in 1979 these relations had gone into a rapid decline after the expanding détente of the post-1963 decade. Mrs Thatcher's own personality, and that of the new conservatism she was attempting to mould, both reflected and reinforced this growing hostility.

The First Thatcher Government, 1979–83

Throughout most of the first Thatcher administration there were very few direct issues to be dealt with between Britain and any of the states of the East. Nor was there much interest on the part of the Prime Minister or her immediate advisers. Some major decisions over defence had a bearing on Anglo-Soviet relations, but in reality the Soviet Union was more a contextual factor – a way of justifying policy – than a direct input into the making of it. The Conservative government had inherited from its predecessor a Nato commitment to increase defence spending by 3 per cent per annum, so its criticisms when in opposition were in fact not so fundamental. Nevertheless, forces' pay was substantially increased, and this item in the defence budget was exempted from cash limits for the first two years of the government's term. More significantly, the question of Polaris replacement arose almost immediately. Officials had a very full dossier already prepared; all the evidence seemed to point to the Trident programme as the Polaris replacement. Senior members of the Callaghan government had discussed the alternatives but deliberately avoided taking a major Cabinet decision on it before the election. The incoming government discussed nuclear matters both in an official committee on Polaris replacement, and more widely in the Cabinet sub-committee, MISC 7. By July 1980 the Thatcher government was prepared to announce its decision to go ahead with Trident. It had also decided in MISC 7 to give its wholehearted support for Nato's double-track decision of 1979 to deploy Cruise and Pershing II missiles in Europe (Bowles 1985).

All three of these decisions were well in the pipeline before Mrs Thatcher came into office and it is difficult to imagine that, at that particular time, any other choices would have been made by another government. Nevertheless, Mrs Thatcher's first year created an image of strength on defence matters. The bipartisan consensus on defence began to break down, and the government's attitude to the

East was clearly revealed in its public justifications of these policies. In truth, all three decisions were fundamentally determined by reasons which were either internal to Britain, or internal to the Atlantic Alliance. Nevertheless, the government defended itself with the rhetoric of robust anti-Sovietism. Humphrey Atkins, speaking for the FCO in the Commons made it clear that if Britain flinched in its resolve 'then the temptation to threaten and blackmail will grow' (*Hansard*, 5 Nov. 1981, col. 720). Peter Blaker made the same point: the threat from the Soviet Union, realistically, was a blackmail threat. Mrs Thatcher's own intuitive stance shone through these debates. In July 1981 she said in the Commons that the British way of life would be put at risk without the nuclear deterrent. On the Jimmy Young radio programme she opined that 'A bully always goes for the weakest. If the Soviet Union ever threatened us we would be in a position to deliver a devastating blow.' The country needed Cruise missiles to restore the balance upset by the introduction of Soviet SS-20s. She found it 'remarkable' that this logic was not crystal clear to a Labour critic (*Hansard*, 27 Oct. 1981, col. 720). In 1983 she still upheld the absolute necessity of installing Cruise missiles because the Soviet Union presented Britain with its greatest threat since Munich in 1938.

In addition to these arguments the US presidential election of 1980 had brought Ronald Reagan to power, and the reluctance of his administration to pursue arms control and his own antipathetic instincts towards the Soviet Union, both supported the Thatcher approach and tended to create a self-fulfilling prophecy by contributing to the general worsening of East–West relations.

Though there were few direct Anglo-Soviet issues of great importance in these years, Britain's own internal defence arguments set a certain tone, and there was plenty in the general context of East–West relations about which attitudes had to be expressed. Apart from the perennial questions of arms control, the crises in Afghanistan and Poland occupied a certain amount of the government's time. Its reactions to these crises, however, also reveal something of the way in which British policy towards the East was being made. On the face of it, Britain reacted more strongly to these crises; was more outspoken than its European partners and more in tune with the indignation of the USA. In this sense, the government reflected the political ideology of Mrs Thatcher's conservatism. Her own statements were unequivocal. In March 1980 the government

roundly condemned the Soviet intervention in Afghanistan in a
House of Commons motion and called on the British athletic
community to boycott the Moscow Olympic games. Denis Follows,
Chairman of the British Olympic Committee, did not agree. Mrs
Thatcher was visibly angry with the BOC and was, in her words,
'astonished' at Denis Follow's statements. She had expressed her
views to him in 'no uncertain way' (Hansard, 6 Mar. 1980, col. 652).
Nor did she lose any opportunity to condemn the Polish government
for its inability to respond sufficiently to the demands of
spontaneous trade unionism. There was a greater governmental
emphasis on human-rights issues. At the CSCE review conference in
Belgrade in 1977–8, the British delegation had always been
reluctant to pursue human-rights issues too specifically since this
was felt to be diplomatically counterproductive. By 1982, however,
at the Madrid review conference, the delegation had been instructed
'from a very high level' to pursue human-rights cases individually
and in detail if necessary. Madrid was, in any case, a bruising affair
which opened to the accompaniment of the Afghanistan and Polish
crises and wound up with the wretchedness of the Korean airliner
shot down in 1983. In all of this the toughness of the Thatcher
government was plain. Indeed, it appears that Mrs Thatcher's
attitude to Britain's standing in the world was, in part, defined by
the strength of her pro-American, hawkish commitment at a time of
growing East–West hostility. Looking back on the Falklands crisis,
Alexander Haig thought it was 'very evident' that she felt this was a
test of Britain's standing in the world and that her action was to
avoid 'a major setback once again . . . in the eyes of the totalitarian
east and the Soviet Union' (Young and Sloman 1986). Nor was
Mrs Thatcher interested in making the most of any diplomatic
opportunities in relation to the Soviet Union. In 1982 she did not
attend Brezhnev's funeral; in 1984 she attended Andropov's but did
not speak, or even shake hands, with his successor, Chernenko. It is
clear that, as a Conservative government, the first Thatcher
administration dealt with the Soviet Union and Eastern Europe at a
fairly high level of political abstraction. Events in which Britain had
no direct interest and certainly no influence demanded reactions;
and the reactions could be tough and very declaratory.

Meanwhile, however, the normal pattern of British diplomacy
with the East, as conducted by officials in Whitehall, seemed to be
relatively undisturbed, though as always it was hardly intense. The

Foreign Secretary visited Rumania, Hungary and Poland in 1980–1, while ministers of state went to the GDR and Moscow in 1981 and 1983, always to discuss the Polish and Afghanistan problems among other things. British diplomatic relations with Czechoslovakia were generally poor as US and British officials operating there were harassed. There were some diplomatic expulsions from both countries and the Czech media remained highly hostile to the West as long as Britain and the USA maintained their concern for Czech dissident groups. Trade and social contact continued in its own low-key way. British trade with the East continued to be worth, on average, less than 2 per cent of Britain's total world trade, half of it accounted for by British trade with the Soviet Union alone (Foreign Affairs Committee 1985–6, Hanson 1981). Personal contacts continued to be almost negligible, and the general scope of diplomatic relations with the Soviet Union was (and is) contained within the terms of the 'Joint Commission', the 'Cultural Agreement' and the 'Joint Maritime Commission' (Foreign Affairs Committee 1985–6, vol. I). There were certainly fewer high-profile cultural exchanges between Britain and the East in this period, since officials are nothing if not sensitive to the political mood of any given administration, but the normal run of bilateral diplomacy was not substantially affected.

In 1982, the imposition of martial law in Poland provided an instructive contrast. Nine days after the declaration of martial law on 13 December 1981, Mrs Thatcher made clear to the House of Commons how much her government 'totally' condemned the 'aggression of the present regime' and 'bitterly and deeply' regretted 'that action is being taken to extinguish the flame of freedom that had started in Poland'; the Polish authorities were 'making an error of historic proportions' (*Hansard*, 22 Dec. 1981, cols. 866–7). And on 1 January 1982 she commended the 'excellent lead' President Reagan had given in his stand on sanctions against Poland. Britain was the first West European state to announce sanctions, just two days after the Nato Council Meeting of 3 February 1982. The reality of British reactions, however, was rather different. Lord Carrington, as Foreign Secretary, chose much more restrained language in outlining the government's initial reactions in the Lords. He stressed that British policy was one of strict non-intervention, he looked to the Polish government to improve its observance of its CSCE commitments and Jaruzelski's own promises of reform. More to the point, the sanctions, when they came, were extremely mild. They were announced on 5 February, not by the Prime Minister but by Humphrey Atkins; and not in the Commons but in an answer to a question. Polish diplomats were to be restricted to movement within a 25-mile radius of London; rescheduling of Polish debts was suspended; officially guaranteed credits which had already been placed were held in abeyance, though with some exceptions. Sanctions against the Soviet Union were also announced. Existing travel restrictions on Soviet diplomats were tightened from a radius of 35 miles from London to 25 miles. Various Anglo-Soviet co-operation agreements were reduced in scope and – something that well-suited the fishing industry – Soviet factory ships would require licenses to tranship fish caught in British waters, and the 1968 treaty on merchant navigation was to be renegotiated. In addition, BBC Polish language broadcasts would be increased from 21¼ to 26¼ hours per week. Certainly it was a package of sanctions, but its reality belied the strength of the political declarations which surrounded it.

In general, therefore, the first Thatcher administration can be characterised as one in which the general context of East–West relations and the intuition of a radical right-wing government set a strident tone towards the Soviet Union and Eastern Europe. But this stridency was not the product of direct or major issues between Britain and the East. Such relations were not in their very nature particularly intense and, though the Government's declarations suggested a significant worsening of bilateral relations, they reflected rather a degree of disapproving indifference to diplomacy with the East. The problems of the Atlantic Alliance and British defence policy were sufficiently absorbing. Relations with the East were dominated by the government's need to react to events; there was nothing initiatory about the policy. Essentially symbolic issues such as human-rights questions were given greater prominence, but below the rhetorical level Britain's bilateral relations with the socialist states ran through normal diplomatic channels and remained very much as they were. In effect, the Thatcher government did not have a coherent policy towards the East.

The Second and Third Thatcher Governments, 1983–88

None of the premises on which Anglo-Soviet or Anglo-East European relations have traditionally been based have altered since

1983. Nevertheless, the substance of those relations is somewhat different now because of a clear and precise change in the Thatcher government's approach which occurred after 1983, creating a new political momentum in relations with the East.

In the summer of 1983 Mrs Thatcher and senior ministers engaged in a major reappraisal of Britain's relations with Eastern countries. They appeared to feel that the Soviet Union was capable of change and was becoming more dynamic. A confidential meeting was held in September with Soviet specialists outside government to offer advice and analysis on how the politics of the Soviet Union and Eastern Europe should be interpreted. Mrs Thatcher was now clearly anxious to consider an initiative towards the East: the FCO believed that a policy of 'differentiation' might be fruitful – to approach the more accessible of Eastern countries and establish some common ground where possible as a way of testing the water. In a sense, Mrs Thatcher was beginning to agree with the natural FCO approach to the East. Strident political rhetoric was less in evidence and there was a greater willingness in top political circles to approach Eastern countries more sympathetically.

Opinions differ somewhat over the origin of this shift of emphasis. One view has it that the FCO simply managed by 1983 to persuade Mrs Thatcher that a more traditional, balanced approach to the Eastern states would be beneficial to the government. Some view it as a natural evolution of Mrs Thatcher's growing self-image at the time as the senior stateswoman of the West; Geoffrey Howe has claimed that it was a natural, timely and independent governmental reassessment of Britain's Eastern relations. Others have seen it as a response to international events, particularly the disarray in Nato after the worst of the INF debates and the growing dismay of the Europeans at the sort of leadership being offered by the United States. In particular, there is some evidence that the West German Christian Democratic leadership were anxious to encourage Britain to take a more moderate diplomatic line (Young and Sloman 1986; Foreign Affairs Committee 1985–6, vol. II; Morgan and Bray 1986).

The exact origin of this reappraisal, however, is not in itself so important. Clearly, there were a number of motives and possible gains. Mrs Thatcher was in confident mood after the Falklands and her election victory, and like most Prime Ministers tends to take more personal interest in foreign affairs as time goes on. The international scene was showing signs of change for both good and bad, and Britain's commercial interests could certainly benefit from some more active diplomacy. In short, there were many good reasons to shift the emphasis.

Having decided to be more initiatory, events moved quickly and the tempo of diplomacy quickened markedly during 1984. Geoffrey Howe, as Foreign Secretary, visited Hungary in September 1983. This was the state which could more fruitfully be 'differentiated' from the monolith of the Soviet bloc, and it cleared the ground for a memorable step for Mrs Thatcher. On 2–4 February she visited Hungary in her first prime ministerial visit to a Soviet bloc state. Anglo-Hungarian trade had risen by around 20 per cent during 1983 and Mrs Thatcher was keen to build on this. Relations with Czechoslovakia remained very poor, however, and the visit was bitterly criticised by the Czech press. Ten days later Mrs Thatcher was in Moscow at Andropov's funeral. Her attitude to the Soviet Union at this stage did not seem to have changed and there was no attempt to use the occasion for active Anglo-Soviet diplomacy.

Nevertheless, Anglo-Soviet diplomacy at a lower level did move into a faster gear. In March Mr Kornienko, the First Deputy Foreign Minister of the Soviet Union, visited Britain, his original visit having been postponed in the wake of the Korean airliner crisis. Paul Channon led a trade delegation to Moscow in May, and in June Sir Geoffrey Howe visited the Soviet Union. At this time, however, constructive talks were overshadowed by disagreements over the American SDI programme. At the end of 1984 a considerable change occurred when, in November, Mr Kinnock led a Labour party delegation to Moscow and, in December, Mr Gorbachev, clearly being groomed for future leadership, led a Supreme Soviet delegation to Britain under the auspices of the Inter-Parliamentary Union. Gorbachev was the most senior Soviet politician to visit Britain since Mr Kosygin in 1967. In part this was a compliment to Mrs Thatcher, since it seems that she was perceived as a stateswoman of experience who might have some useful influence over an American President with whom the Soviets found it very difficult to deal. Gorbachev also brought with him the hope which he expressed that Anglo-Soviet trade could rise by 40–50 per cent and he urged British firms to try to become more closely involved with the next Soviet Five-Year Plan due to begin in 1986. Mrs

Thatcher was clearly impressed by Mr Gorbachev and declared that he was someone with whom she could 'do business' (*The Times*, 18 December 1984). On the face of it, British diplomacy was in full swing. In 1985 Anglo-Hungarian relations developed further to culminate in the visit of Mr Kadar to Britain in November. The Foreign Secretary visited the GDR, Czechoslovakia and Poland in 1985, and Yugoslavia in 1986. Other ministers led particular delegations: Malcolm Rifkind a trade delegation to Moscow, Lord Whitelaw a UK parliamentary delegation to return Gorbachev's visit, Peter Walker a delegation to sign an energy agreement just prior to Chernobyl, and Michael Jopling a delegation from the Ministry of Agriculture Fisheries and Food sometime after Chernobyl.

The government's approach, however, and particularly that of Mrs Thatcher, was much more nuanced than this catalogue might suggest. To begin with, Anglo-Soviet relations were not trouble-free. There had been no diplomatic expulsions in relations between the two states since 1971. But beginning in 1981 a new trickle of expulsions took place every year. In 1985 the number of expulsions from Britain jumped from a few to no less than 31 – a figure matched exactly on this occasion by the Soviets. Generally, the Soviet Union did not respond with absolute reciprocity to Western expulsions; their staffs in the West are very large and they usually expel fewer Western officials from the Soviet Union than have been expelled from the West. But 1985 witnessed the biggest diplomatic expulsion crisis in Anglo-Soviet relations since 1971, and Gorbachev seemed to want to make it clear with his strict reciprocity (which seems to apply across the board to all Western states) that relations could deteriorate as well as improve. There was also tension over the miners' strike in Britain when, in October 1984, the Soviet Union announced that it would suspend fuel supplies to the UK for the duration of the strike 'on the initiative', it claimed, 'of the Soviet trade unions'. The Government protested angrily and Moscow immediately backed down, agreeing that it would honour all existing contracts. In addition to such specific issues in Anglo-Soviet relations, the failure of arms control and the continuing problem of the American SDI still coloured the diplomatic dialogue between London and Moscow. When Mrs Thatcher attended the Chernenko funeral in March 1985, for instance, the occasion was, finally, used for a diplomatic purpose and she and Sir Geoffrey Howe spent an hour with Gromyko and Gorbachev. Their discussions, however, revolved essentially around the problems of SDI and the difficulties of arms control. Mrs Thatcher was, in effect, presenting an unpopular Western diplomatic position.

More specifically, Mrs Thatcher's own attitude towards the East has remained essentially wary and sceptical. She was still notably critical of the Soviet Union in her speeches. She was still apparently incensed by the situation in Poland and personally declined to meet the Polish Foreign Minister in a proposed visit by him to London, which was recommended by the FCO and the Foreign Secretary but then could not take place. There was still an emphasis on human rights in her government's essential reaction to the Soviet Union. Nevertheless, a theme emerging in the Prime Minister's statements which had never been there before was the idea that she could 'deal' with the Soviets. In an important speech to the European Atlantic Group in July 1984 she was keen to pursue a realistic deal with the Soviet Union, despite her criticisms. Speeches by the Defence Secretary, Michael Heseltine, echoed the same theme. She attended the Chernenko funeral in March 1985 hoping, she said, to 'do more business with the Soviet Union', and in the wake of the 31 expulsions in 1985 she declared that she was anxious to 'draw the line under it' and 'get on with a constructive relationship'. In the considered phrase of the Foreign Secretary, the 'three cornerstones' of the Thatcher government's policy towards the Soviet Union are 'realism, vigilance, and an open mind' – very much, one suspects, in that order (Foreign and Commonwealth Office 1987).

This willingness to deal with the Soviet Union and Eastern Europe was also prompted by the development of external events between 1984 and 1986. The Reagan Presidency slipped even further in the esteem of the British public, while the Soviet leadership enjoyed an improving image. The British public has no doubt at all which of the two superpowers it prefers as societies; which culture it feels more comfortable with and admires (Crewe, 1985, Clarke forthcoming). Nevertheless, to judge by a celebrated series of questions asked regularly by the Gallup organisation, the proportion of the British public which 'disapproved of the role the United States is now playing in world affairs' was greater than that which 'disapproved' of the Russian role. In April 1986, for the first time ever, the US earned a higher 'disapproval' rating than the Soviet Union, and this has continued to be the case ever since

(Gallup 1986). This same trend is echoed in many other surveys. The public is still a great admirer of the USA, but it tends to take a cynical view of superpowers as such, has very little confidence in Reagan, is increasingly impressed by Soviet leaders, and seems to perceive less and less moral difference between the actual policies of each superpower.

Apart from this, 1985 began to see the beginnings of some realistic prospects in the realm of East–West arms control. President Reagan became enthusiastic to conclude a superpower deal before the end of his second term of office and the new Soviet leadership under Gorbachev and Foreign Minister Shevardnadze gave a new and sophisticated impetus to Soviet dealings with the West, particularly in matters of arms control. By autumn of 1985 the British press were in no doubt that the new leadership in the Soviet Union had affected not just the style but also the substance of Soviet foreign policy. In May 1986 Gorbachev convened a senior conference of diplomats and foreign ministry officials in Moscow. Almost 40 per cent of the Soviet Union's ambassadors were recalled for it, and it appears that Gorbachev was concerned both to reorientate Soviet foreign policy and to put his own stamp on it. In this context, the British government's reassessment of its Eastern policy in the autumn of 1983 was indeed timely and may well have given Britain a certain amount of diplomatic credit in that it acted as a valuable channel of liaison in the diplomacy before the Reykjavik Summit.

Then too, the defence consensus in Britain continued to be dramatically fractured from 1983 to 1987. The Labour party channelled and moulded a significant minority of anti-nuclear opinion in opposition to the government's defence policy. And though the government won all of the major arguments, the opposition was not negligible; it was always fairly volatile, with the result that the Conservatives had to fight for every point. Under pressure from the opposition at home, and its major ally abroad to move more enthusiastically towards better relations with the Soviet Union and to accept the logic of a European arms-control deal, the government, like other Conservative governments in Western Europe, found itself in the position of being a 'beleaguered majority'; firmly in power and in control of its defence policy, but under a range of pressures to accept a change in its context and to modify it.

In this situation, Mrs Thatcher's approach has become Churchillian

in a different sense. Whereas in opposition she took up the calls of
the New Right to be alert to the dangers of the Eastern bloc, ten
years later, with a good deal of foreign policy experience behind her,
she is the Churchillian politician who has the ability to engage in
realpolitik diplomacy with the East and she draws inspiration from
this more traditional strand of Britain's approach. In a sense, the
Thatcher approach has made a political spectacle out of a trend of
official thinking that is normally implicit, and she has given it the
stimulus of the characteristic vigour with which she pursues all of
her cherished projects. In the Thatcherite characterisation, Britain is
prepared to speak harshly to the East and is not afraid to give
offence; but it is also prepared to engage in *realpolitik*, based on the
diplomacy of tough leaders who command strong domestic support.

All of these strands wove together into a flurry of Anglo-Soviet
activity during 1986–7. In July 1986 Mr Shevardnadze visited
Britain. His visit signified that both the Soviet Union and Britain
wanted to put the diplomatic expulsions of 1985 behind them. It
also took on added significance, not only as a prelude to Mrs
Thatcher's own visit to Moscow but also, as diplomatic sources said,
because no obvious 'back channel' existed between Moscow and
Washington at a time when Soviet–American relations were at a
point of some delicacy. Apart from that, three specifically Anglo–
Soviet agreements were concluded: a ratification of the Anglo-Soviet
Economic and Industrial Co-operation Programme for 1986–90,
which was agreed in February 1986 to replace the 1975 agreement
concluded at the time of the Wilson summit; an agreement on the
prevention of incidents at sea; and, interestingly, a settlement of
outstanding claims from the 1917–24 period, wherein both sides
agreed to waive all extant claims. This was of particular importance
to the Soviet Union since this old dispute had prevented the Soviets
from operating on the London capital markets – something they
may now wish to do (*Financial Times*, 16–17 July 1986).

The first half of 1987 saw a series of visits between London and
Moscow. In January, Soviet jamming of BBC Russian-language
broadcasts stopped after six years of continuous operation. In
February, a new long-term finance and credit agreement was
concluded between Britain and the Soviet Union, to run up to 1990,
in an attempt to stimulate British exports of capital goods. There
were also, significantly, exploratory talks on the prevention of
terrorism. And then from 28 March to 2 April Mrs Thatcher made

her celebrated official visit to Moscow to engage in a summit with Mr Gorbachev that included thirteen hours of talks with him. Much of their discussion was taken up with East–West arms control issues, but many bilateral matters were also discussed. Mrs Thatcher described it as 'the most fascinating and invigorating visit I have ever made abroad as Prime Minister'. The summit resulted in a series of agreements, on the establishment of a London–Moscow 'hotline', on more diplomatic exchanges, on co-operation in space, and on the exchange of cultural and educational information.

Such agreements were predictable. Indeed they are part of the necessary diplomatic packaging of any summit. More significant, perhaps, was the image it created. Here was Mrs Thatcher in her second Churchillian mantle. In a 50-minute Soviet television interview she was critical of Russia and extremely frank. She seemed to get on well with Mr Gorbachev and appeared as a skilful diplomatist – a cross between a head of state and a leader of government. There were sharp differences between the two sides on nuclear issues, and the Prime Minister went out of her way to highlight some individual human-rights cases in the Soviet Union. But the overall impression was of a constructive and hard-headed meeting: 'courteous but robust' as the *Daily Telegraph* commented. The image certainly contributed to Mrs Thatcher's re-election campaign in June 1987 by reinforcing an image of experience and seniority in foreign affairs which turned out to be impossible for the Opposition to dent.

Her liking for Mr Gorbachev and her genuine belief in him as a reformer, was always tempered by her conviction that the most pervasive feature of the Communist system is that 'there is a big bureaucracy' and that the Soviet system will never be 'a real democratic system in my lifetime'. She was able to reap the benefits of *glasnost* without appearing to compromise on an intuitive Conservative scepticism regarding the Soviet Union. Other developments have strengthened these trends. On 7 December 1987, Mr Gorbachev stopped off to see Mrs Thatcher on his way to the INF arms control summit in Washington. It was merely a two-hour meeting during a refuelling stop, but its symbolic value was immense. Here was Mrs Thatcher standing almost in the old style as one of the 'big three', not as a European leader (a fact not lost on European commentators in France and Germany) but as someone who was seen to have influence with Mr Reagan and whose attitude to arms control was seen to be important. This meeting, and the talks which surrounded it, were also symbolic of the attempts to improve practical relations between Britain and the Soviet Union on a broad front, not least in the attempt being made to increase trade between the two countries by 40 per cent by 1990 (*Financial Times*, 8 December 1987).

During Mrs Thatcher's third term in office, therefore, Anglo-Soviet relations and, by implication, relations with Eastern Europe may be seen as both changing and unchanging. They are unchanging in so far as they continue to be less intense than Britain's relations with Western-world states. Anglo-Soviet relations are still contained within formalised frameworks which have to be adjusted before the substance of relations will change. Trade relations may improve somewhat but are unlikely to be dramatic since Britain's share of trade with the Soviet Union has been in steady decline in relation to that of other West European states. There are still very few interest groups – political, economic or cultural – in either society who have an important stake in a deepening of relations between the two countries, and the study of Russian language and culture continues to decline in Britain as the educational system consolidates to meet expenditure cuts. The more vigorous Thatcher diplomacy of recent years has not altered any of these realities; indeed was not intended to. Anglo-Soviet relations *have* changed, however, in so far as they have always been determined essentially by contextual factors, and over the last four years the context has clearly changed quite a lot. Mrs Thatcher's diplomacy is both cause and effect of this. For the first time, Soviet leaders appear to be genuinely able to affect the defence and foreign affairs debates within Britain. Mrs Thatcher has to react to this fact; in part she has created it, by approving of the Gorbachev reform policy. And if European arms control has a reasonable future then negotiations between the Western powers and the Soviet Union will inevitably become more intense.

It is tempting to observe that Anglo-Soviet relations have always tended to be cyclical, where periods of détente are inevitably followed by a worsening of relations. In the present situation, however, the changing Soviet context seems to indicate that whatever 'worsening' might follow the optimism of 1987–8, it is unlikely to fall back into the old mould. East–West relations are changing, no less than are West–West relations. For good or bad, the 'Thatcher era' in Anglo-Soviet diplomacy may mark the end of a long-established pattern, and cover a transition to a new correlation of diplomatic forces between the East and the West. If this is the case, then it will be interesting to measure up the premises of British diplomacy towards the East against the size and nature of the task.

References and Further Reading

The most concise historical accounts of Anglo–Soviet diplomatic relations are to be found in Frankel, J. (1975) *British Foreign Policy, 1945–73*, Oxford University Press; and Keeble, C. (1986) 'The Development of the Relationship between the United Kingdom and the USSR', Appendix A, Second Report from the Foreign Affairs Committee, 1985–6, *UK–Soviet Relations*, Vol. 1, HC 28–1, HMSO, pp. lxxxc–cii.

Bell, D.S. (ed.) (1985) *The Conservative Government 1979–84: An Interim Report*, Croom Helm.
Bowles, N. (1985) 'The defence policy of the Conservative government' in Bell (1985).
Clarke, M. (1985) 'The implementation of Britain's CSCE policy 1975–84' in Smith, S. and Clarke, M. (eds) *Foreign Policy Implementation*, Allen & Unwin.
Clarke, M. (forthcoming) 'Anglo-Soviet relations' in Flynn, G. (ed.) *Domestic Sources of Policy Towards the Soviet Union*, Atlantic Institute, Paris.
Crewe, I. (1985) 'Britain: two and a half cheers for the Atlantic Alliance', in Flynn, G. and Rattinger, H. (eds) *The Public and Atlantic Defence*, Croom Helm.
Foreign Affairs Committee (1985–6) Second Report: *UK–Soviet Relations*, 2 vols, HC28–I, 28–II.
Foreign and Commonwealth Office (1987) *East–West Relations*, HMSO.
Gallup (1986) *Gallup Political Index*, 309, April.
Hanson, P. (1981) *Trade and Technology in Soviet–Western Relations*, Macmillan.
Kavanagh, D. (1987) *Thatcherism and British Politics: The End of Consensus*, Oxford University Press.
Morgan, R. and Bray, C. (eds) (1986) *Partners and Rivals in Western Europe: Britain, France and Germany*, Gower.
Observations by the Government (1986) To the Second Report from the Foreign Affairs Committee, 1985–6, Cmnd 9842, July.
Riddell, P. (1985) *The Thatcher Government*, Blackwell.
Young, H. and Sloman, A. (1986) *The Thatcher Phenomenon*, BBC Publications.

CHAPTER 4

The Middle East

SIR ANTHONY PARSONS

The Historical Background

Throughout the nineteenth century British interest in the Middle East derived from the need to protect communications with the Indian Empire. It was for this reason that Britain responded with military and naval action to Napoleon's invasion of Egypt in 1798; played a leading role in protecting the enfeebled Ottoman and Persian Empires from the expansionist ambitions of Tsarist Russia, France and Imperial Germany; created the Aden Colony in 1839; extended her protection over its hinterland (now the People's Republic of the Democratic Yemen) and over the Arab sheikhdoms of the Persian Gulf (now Kuwait, Bahrain, Qatar, the United Arab Emirates and Oman); and occupied Egypt in 1882 and the Sudan in 1898.

By the outbreak of the First World War in 1914, a second focus of interest had been added to the need to protect imperial communications – Middle East oil. In 1908 oil had been discovered in southern Persia by the Anglo-Persian Oil Company (incorporated in 1909) and, in 1914, the Royal Navy converted from coal to fuel oil, the government taking a 50 per cent share in Anglo-Persian. In the same year the Ottoman Empire signed its own death warrant by joining the Central Powers in the First World War. By 1918,

Germany and Russia had also been eliminated from the Middle East power game by defeat and revolution respectively. Britain and, to a lesser extent, France emerged supreme.

The postwar settlement led to a qualitative increase in British involvement. Previously, apart from Egypt and the Sudan, the British presence had been confined to the thinly populated periphery of the Arabian peninsula. Now, with the assumption of League of Nations Mandates over Palestine, Transjordan and Iraq, Britain became embroiled in the politics of major centres of population. Her task was complicated by the inclusion in the Palestine Mandate of the Balfour Declaration of 1917, under which Britain was committed to the contradictory tasks of encouraging the establishment of a Jewish National Home while avoiding damage to the interests of the 90 per cent Arab population. And, as industrialised Europe turned to petroleum as a major source of energy, oil was discovered in Bahrain, Saudi Arabia, Iraq and Kuwait. British interests had again expanded. To the historical objective of protecting the lifeline to India were added the need to preserve the free flow of oil and the privileged status of the British oil companies, and responsibilities for the destinies of newly emergent states.

By 1939 Britain was in difficulties. Egypt was restive at British control. Palestine was intractable. Iraq was in ferment and had experienced the first of many military *coups d'état*. In Iran the new ruler, Reza Shah Pahlavi, impatient with the British monopoly of influence was turning to Nazi Germany as a substitute. Only in Transjordan and the Persian Gulf was there an apparently tranquil acceptance of British tutelage.

During the Second World War, Britain played the leading part in protecting Allied interests. It was a close-run thing, with threats developing on different fronts. Libya was an Italian colony and Italy was poised to strike at the Sudan from Abyssinia. The German drive through the Balkans threatened the eastern Mediterranean, while the fall of France in 1940 left Syria and Lebanon exposed. The German onslaught against the Soviet Union in 1941–2 menaced Iran, and there were also pro-German elements in Egypt, Iraq and Iran. By 1943, however, the threat had been lifted. The Italians had been expelled from Abyssinia, and German and Italian forces from North Africa. Syria and Lebanon had been occupied by the British, and British forces had invaded Iraq and toppled a pro-German government. Iran was occupied by British and Russian forces. The oil supplies and communications to India and the Far East had been preserved.

In 1945 the British position was deceptively supreme. Britain had been exhausted by the war and two new great powers were looming on the horizon; the United States and the Soviet Union. Moreover the international atmosphere was coloured by the principles of the Charter of the United Nations – self-determination, sovereign independence and the equality of states. Nineteenth-century notions of empire and spheres of influence were under fire. Only two years later, the watershed of decolonisation – the independence of the Indian Empire – was passed.

The first major check to Britain in the Middle East came in Palestine. Following the Nazi massacres, pressure for the establishment of a Jewish state, strongly supported by the United States, overcame British political will to continue the search for a settlement. In April 1947 the government handed the problem to the United Nations, which recommended partition. Fighting broke out and Britain withdrew in May 1948; the State of Israel was born.

This event had a profound effect on the political climate in the Middle East. Britain was no longer invincible and a greater power was emerging. The clamour for British withdrawal from Egypt mounted and in 1951 the Prime Minister of Iran, Mohammed Musaddiq, nationalised the Anglo-Iranian Oil Company, precipitating the Abadan crisis. In 1952 the Egyptian monarchy was overthrown by a group of officers led by an unknown Lieutenant-Colonel, Gamal Abdul Nasser. The Arab world was dominated for the next fifteen years by 'Nasserism' – a call for Arab unity based on republicanism, anti-imperialism, 'positive neutrality and non-alignment' and anti-Zionism. This message was inspirational and the conservative Arab governments, as well as their foreign patrons, were embattled.

For a time British policy looked like weathering the storm. The British government agreed with Egypt on the independence of the Sudan and withdrawal from the Suez Canal Zone. The Americans co-operated with Britain in embargoing Iranian oil exports and engineering Dr Musaddiq's downfall. An Anglo-US oil consortium (40 per cent of the shares owned by British Petroleum) was established in Iran. In 1955, the Baghdad Pact was created as a defence against Soviet penetration and a means of perpetuating a British military presence in the eastern Arab world. Supported by the United States, the members were Britain, Turkey, Iraq, Iran and Pakistan. But the Pact became the object of Nasser's hostility, being seen as a Western attempt to built up Iraq as a counterweight to Egypt. The turning point came at the end of 1956. In 1955 Nasser had excited American hostility by turning to the Soviet Union for military equipment. The second superpower had overleapt the Northern Tier without firing a shot. In 1956 American hostility to Nasser culminated in the withdrawal of financial aid for the construction of the Aswan High Dam (eventually built by the Russians) in Upper Egypt. Britain followed suit and Nasser responded by nationalising the Suez Canal Company. The ensuing international crisis ended with the Anglo/French/Israeli invasion of Egypt in the teeth of international, including American, opposition. The British, French and Israeli forces were constrained to withdraw to be replaced by a UN peacekeeping force.

This adventure cost Britain dear. It was plain that she was no longer a great power and British influence was never to recover. However, Britain still had major assets – control of the Arab shore of the Gulf and of South-west Arabia, a military base in Libya, a close relationship with Hashemite Jordan and membership of the Central Treaty Organisation (CENTO), the successor to the Baghdad Pact after the overthrow of the Iraqi monarchy in 1958. With these she was able to protect her continuing interests in communications (the air route to strategic positions in the Far East), the free supply of oil, and the financial benefits accruing from it. In 1957–8 British forces enabled the Sultan of Muscat to quell a revolt in northern Oman. In 1958 British paratroopers helped to stabilise Jordan. In 1961 British forces landed in Kuwait to deter an Iraqi threat to the sheikhdom. However, British attempts to construct a federation out of the Aden Colony and Protectorates foundered.

The year 1967 was another turning point. Nasserism was in difficulties. The union of Egypt and Syria had disintegrated in 1961. Revolutionary Iraq had become a rival. Egyptian forces were bogged down in a civil war in the Yemen. Then the June War of 1967 destroyed the Egyptian, Syrian and Jordanian armed forces and led to the Israeli occupation of the Sinai peninsula, the Golan Heights, the West Bank and the Gaza Strip.

This disaster for the Arabs generated fundamental changes. Israel came to be perceived as a regional superpower championed by a

global superpower, the United States. Nasserism ebbed as the
revolutionary Arab states realised that they needed stability in the
oil-rich Arab states. A halt was called to the subversion of
conservative regimes. Arab solidarity based on common Arab
interests replaced the notion of pan-Arabism on the Egyptian
model. The centre of power began to shift to the traditional
monarchies and the focus of inter-Arab preoccupation moved to the
Palestine problem, over which the Palestine Liberation Organisation
(PLO) led by Yasser Arafat began to dominate the agenda.
Internationally, although Britain played a useful part in the
negotiation of United Nations Security Council Resolution 242 of
November 1967, Arabs and Israelis turned increasingly to the Soviet
Union and the United States respectively for political and material
support.

In 1967 Britain withdrew from South-west Arabia, ceding power
to a Marxist regime (now the People's Democratic Republic of the
Yemen), and in January 1968 Britain announced that her presence
'East of Suez', including the protective treaties with the Gulf states,
would be terminated at the end of 1971. In 1970 the incoming
Conservative government confirmed this decision. By 1972 Britain,
now a member of the European Economic Community (EEC), had,
apart from the legacy of history and membership of the moribund
(but still extant) CENTO, no foothold in the Middle East beyond
that of any major West European state.

In October 1973 Egypt and Syria attacked the ceasefire lines in
Sinai and the Golan Heights: although the outcome of the war was
inconclusive, Arab military honour was restored and, with the
trebling of the oil price in December 1973, Arab negotiating power
was strengthened. The oil boom had begun. Moreover the shock of
the October War, which had nearly resulted in a superpower
confrontation on the battlefield, galvanised Washington into major
efforts to ameliorate the Arab–Israeli dispute. These culminated in
1978–9 in the Camp David agreements, which led to Israeli
evacuation of Egyptian territory and a deep split within the Arab
world.

Before considering the policies of the Conservative government
since 1979, it is worth summing up the record of British policy
between the early nineteenth century and the termination of direct
British involvement in 1971. Overall the balance must be regarded
as favourable. The lines of communication, first with the sub-

continent and latterly with Western strategic positions in the Far East, were held. In two world wars Britain took the brunt of the fighting, thus protecting her own economic and strategic interests and those of her Allies. The British presence helped to maintain the supply of cheap crude oil which played a crucial role in the recovery of the industrialised world following the Second World War. There is no doubt that the Gulf states, from Kuwait to Oman, would not now exist as independent states under their traditional rulers had it not been for British protection. The pattern of states created mainly by Britain after the collapse of the Ottoman Empire, for all the equivocal undertakings given to the Arabs between 1916 and 1918, has survived. Systems of administration, civil and military structures throughout the region, owe much to British methods and training.

On the debit side, Britain was responsible for the tragedy of Palestine, the cause of much war, suffering and the displacement of peoples as well as posing a continuing threat to world peace. The Balfour Declaration in both its parts was not capable of implementation and the end of the Mandate was humiliating and irresponsible. The Suez affair of 1956 was an aberration which hastened the decline of Britain as a world power. The British departure from South-west Arabia was ignominious and damaging in its consequences. Moreover, it can be argued that British policy during the 1950s was unimaginative in failing to catch the tide of the new nationalism to which Britain was accommodating herself elsewhere in the Empire proper, thus leaving, amongst the younger, politically conscious generation a bitter memory of entrenched opposition to popular forces of change.

Government Policy, 1979–88

When the Conservative party came to power in May 1979, the Middle East scene, and Britain's place in it, had changed in important particulars since the Heath government had been defeated at the polls in February 1974. The dramatic increase in the price of oil at the end of 1973 had made the North Sea deposits commercially exploitable, and North Sea production had risen to a level close to national consumption and was shortly to surpass it. Meanwhile the oil boom had transformed the Middle East into an important export market and source of inward investment. The peace treaty between Israel and Egypt had split the Arab world of which Egypt was no longer the leader. However, in the Arab–Israeli context Britain, except as part of a European consensus, had ceased to be regarded as having a significant role, the United States being in command of the negotiating process. The Gulf states had experienced nearly a decade of independence and the rebellion in Dhofar (Western Oman) had been put down with British assistance. But CENTO, as well as Britain's leading market in the area (Pahlavi Iran), had gone with the Iranian revolution of 1979 which also took with it the privileged position of British Petroleum and Royal Dutch Shell.

Britain still had important interests to protect – the supply of oil as a broader European concern, her own greatly increased export market, and the amelioration of the Arab–Israeli dispute as a major element in regional stability and, indeed, world peace. Moreover, Britain could not escape the burden of history. Middle East governments and peoples still regarded the British as having more power, especially in regard to influencing American policy, than they in reality possessed, and expected more activity from Britain than from other medium-sized European states, particularly over the Palestine problem for which Britain was perceived as bearing the original responsibility.

For the sake of convenience, I propose to discuss the policies of the Conservative governments since 1979 under separate headings although, as will become clear, a fair amount of overlapping is inevitable.

British Exports of Goods and Services and Inward Investment

In 1973, before the oil boom, the Middle East accounted for 4.4 per cent of total British visible exports (and a roughly similar figure for invisibles). By 1978 this figure had risen to about 10.5 per cent and in 1986 it was running at about 9.5 per cent. In 1981 the Middle East accounted for an estimated 15 per cent of overseas earnings on invisibles, such as consultancies, building and civil engineering contracts, and tourism to Britain. In spite of the downturn in the oil revenues of the OPEC membership after 1981, this represented about £6 billion, making the Middle East Britain's largest market in the developing world and the third largest global market after

Western Europe and North America. Moreover, with the decrease in oil liftings, the balance of this trade was very favourable. Nevertheless, in 1985 Britain was only sixth in the league table of OECD exporters, after Japan (15 per cent), the United States (14.5 per cent), Federal Republic of Germany (12.9 per cent), France (11.3 per cent), and Italy (also 11.3 per cent, mainly because of her 33 per cent share of the Libyan market).

The British government has continued the policy of its predecessors in giving maximum support to exporters. In particular relations have been assiduously cultivated with the members of the Gulf Co-operation Council (Saudi Arabia, Kuwait, Bahrain, Qatar, the United Arab Emirates and Oman) by a steady flow of royal and ministerial visits in both directions and a wide range of other promotional activities.

It can be argued that, in so far as state activity is a factor in export promotion, the government has performed effectively. The fact that Britain has not gained ground against her competitors is more a reflection of the relative performance of the British economy than of any inadequacy in government policy. It has of course been claimed that, in the circumstances of the Middle East, politics have a significant effect on trade and that major public- and private-sector contracts are lost or won as much because of the attitude of the foreign government concerned, towards for example the Arab–Israeli problem or the Iranian revolution, as on merit. In some circles in Britain this has become conventional wisdom. I question its validity. Were it the case, would the United States (perceived by the Arab world as the unqualified champion of Israel) still be close to the top of the exporters' league table? There is no evidence that the Conservative government's attitude towards the Palestine problem (see below) has damaged Britain's export performance. It is interesting in this context that, in spite of the total break in relations with Libya following the murder of WPC Fletcher in St James's Square in 1984, the British share of the Libyan market has not declined, while the share of the Iranian market, much smaller since 1979, has remained constant in spite of the anti-British and anti-Western bias of the revolution itself. I am inclined to believe that, as with other parts of the world, the determining factors in the Middle East are price, quality, delivery dates, export promotion and so on, rather than politics and that against this background the performance of the government and of the British public and private sectors in the Middle East has been as good as could have been expected.

Paradoxically Britain may have been fortunate in that firms from competitor countries such as the United States, Japan and Germany won the lion's share of the colossal public-sector contracts in the boom years between 1974 and 1981, while British exports comprised mainly 'bread-and-butter' business. It is now the huge contracts which are being cut back or abandoned, while less glamorous business continues. In fact the only really spectacular contract secured under the present government has been the $7.3 billion project for the supply of Tornado aircraft and associated equipment to Saudi Arabia, a major boost to the British defence industry, which was signed by Michael Heseltine in September 1985 following Mrs Thatcher's visit in April that year.

Oil Production and Pricing

During the period under review Britain became, for the first time in history, a major oil producer. By 1985, North Sea production was 127.5 million tonnes of crude oil a year as against national consumption of 77.8 million tonnes. Britain was not only a net exporter but also the fifth largest producer in the world after the Soviet Union, the United States, Saudi Arabia and Mexico. This development, coupled with a worldwide glut and a consequent sharp fall in oil prices, has substantially altered Britain's relationship with the Middle East. For the time being, there is no longer a threat of oil being used as a 'weapon' for political purposes, thus freeing British policy from a constraint which had persisted from the 1950s. Nor are there major British fixed assets requiring diplomatic protection, with the relegation of the major oil companies, including British Petroleum, to the role of purchasers from national oil companies as opposed to the holders of old-fashioned concessions embracing both production and downstream operations.

Hence the dialogue between Britain and the Middle East producers has been relatively free of political overtones and has focused on price and production levels, as with other non-OPEC producers such as Norway and Mexico. In this regard, the British government has pursued a policy of maximising North Sea production (an inestimable boon to the Exchequer in a time of recession and mass unemployment) and allowing market forces to regulate prices. This has brought Britain into conflict with OPEC price-fixing policies, seldom successfully implemented, which have been aimed at raising and/or stabilising prices by means of voluntary limitation of production levels. Other non-OPEC producers have been disposed to co-operate to some extent but Britain has held firm. In the short term, OPEC has had no means of coercing the British government into modifying this policy and it does not appear that British interests have been damaged. However, in the longer term, Britain would do well to consider the fact that, according to the most reliable estimates, the Middle East still contains 56 per cent of world oil reserves as opposed to the North Sea's 1.8 per cent. By the end of the century Britain's newly acquired independence may be a thing of the past, particularly if there is no restraint on production, and she may again be uncomfortably beholden to Middle East producers, unless of course alternative sources of energy are by that time replacing oil.

The Security and Stability of the Arabian Peninsula and the Gulf

Since 1979 the principal threats to the status quo have been the consequences of the Iranian revolution, and the Iran–Iraq war which began in September 1980. The inspirational effect of the revolution on the Shia' Moslem communities of the Gulf (25 per cent of the population of Kuwait, over 50 per cent of the population in Bahrain and about 300,000 in the eastern, oil-bearing province of Saudi Arabia) has put existing regimes under strain, while the Iran–Iraq war, particularly since the autumn of 1983, has directly threatened the free flow of oil and merchant shipping in the Gulf. In the last few years the possibility of an outright Iranian victory has been perceived as a threat to the integrity of the whole Arab shore of the Gulf, especially Kuwait.

Thanks to Britain's intimate relationship with the Gulf states, the government has been able, in co-ordination with the United States and major European governments, to play an active part in supporting the stability of the area and thus maintaining the free flow of oil to the industrialised world. There are several hundred, perhaps over a thousand, British officers on secondment or under contract to the armed and security forces of the Gulf states, while

British military equipment, including aircraft, tanks and armoured cars, is in widespread use and makes a valuable contribution to British industry and the balance of payments. Britain also contributes by an increased level of naval patrols to the Western naval presence at the southern entrance to the Gulf, and British political advice, especially to the United States, has been an important restraining influence at times of tension, for instance when the Iran–Iraq war first spread down the Gulf with attacks on shipping in the autumn of 1983.

As regards relations with Iran and attitudes towards the war with Iraq, the government's policy has been to conduct 'business as usual' as far as possible with the Khomeini regime and to maintain a strict neutrality in the war. Britain gave full support to the United States over the hostage crisis of 1979–81, although the European Community adopted only some sanctions against Iran in May 1980 out of a feeling of solidarity with the United States. From the outset of the Iran–Iraq war Britain, along with most of the European Community, has adopted a 'hands-off' policy and has embargoed the supply of 'lethal' military equipment to both sides. On the whole this policy has worked. Both sides have complained of Britain's lack of support but relations and commerce have been maintained in spite of a recent run down of representation with Iran to one diplomat on either side.

The Palestine Problem

It is in this area that the British government has been subjected to most criticism for failing to conduct an independent policy, co-ordinated where practicable with her European partners, and for being excessively subservient to the United States. What are the facts?

For the first year Lord Carrington, the Foreign and Commonwealth Secretary, conscious of the need to promote progress towards an Arab–Israeli settlement in the interests of regional and world peace and sceptical that the Camp David agreements between Israel and Egypt would open the way to progress towards a solution of the Palestine sector, worked vigorously to promote a concerted European policy. This culminated in June 1980 in the European Community's Venice Declaration, which included the following principles:

- the recognition and implementation of the right to existence and security of all the states in the region, including Israel, and justice for all the peoples, which implied the recognition of the legitimate rights of the Palestinian people;
- United Nations guarantees for a peace settlement, in which the Nine would be prepared to participate;
- a just solution to the Palestine refugee problem and the exercise by the Palestinian people of their right to self-determination;
- the application of the above principles to all the parties including the Palestinian people, and to the PLO which would have to be associated with the negotiations;
- the rejection of any unilateral initiative designed to change the status of Jerusalem;
- the need for Israel to put an end to the territorial occupation which it had maintained since the conflict of 1967 – the Israeli settlements in the occupied territories constituted a serious obstacle to the peace process and were illegal under international law;
- the renunciation of force or the threat of force by all parties.

When the Nine canvassed this initiative with the parties they met immediate rejection from Israel, a grudging welcome from the Arabs and irritation from the Carter administration. The United States – preoccupied with the Tehran hostage crisis, struggling with diminishing optimism with the post-Camp David negotiations on the Palestine issue and under strong pressure from Israel and the pro-Israeli lobby – was in no mood to commit itself to concepts such as Palestinian self-determination which went beyond the Camp David framework; still less would the Americans consider that the PLO, seen by the Israelis as undifferentiated terrorists, should be involved in any negotiating process. The European initiative drifted and had lost momentum by the time Lord Carrington visited Israel in March 1982, only a week or so before his resignation over the Falklands crisis.

Meanwhile in January 1981 Britain, along with France, the Netherlands and Italy, had agreed to participate, albeit reluctantly, in the Multi-national Force and Observers (MFO) established to police the demilitarised Sinai area on the withdrawal of Israeli forces under the Camp David agreements. The reluctance was due to the divisive effect of Camp David on the Arab world and to Arab and

Soviet opposition which had precluded this peacemaking role being carried out by the United Nations force (UNEF II) already on the ground. The positive decision by the four European states was the result of a belief that to refuse to participate in any initiative related to the furtherance of peace in the region would be incompatible with the spirit of the Venice Declaration.

In June 1981 Israeli aircraft bombed an Iraqi nuclear reactor on the outskirts of Baghdad. Britain played an active role in the subsequent proceedings in the Security Council which led to the unanimous adoption of a resolution condemning the Israeli attack. Also in the United Nations, Britain worked hard with other members of the Council to strengthen the hand of the United Nations Interim Force in Lebanon (UNIFIL) and to help restore Lebanese government authority in the area north of the Israeli border. Britain welcomed the ceasefire negotiated by the United Nations with the PLO in southern Lebanon in July 1981. In December Britain joined in the Security Council condemnation of the extension of Israeli law and jurisdiction to the occupied Syrian Golan Heights and rejected its validity.

On 6 June 1982, in response to the attempted assassination of the Israeli ambassador in London, Israel invaded Lebanon. Her forces brushed aside UNIFIL, dispersed the PLO military presence and quickly reached the outskirts of Beirut. This move created a major international crisis. The Security Council, with British support, condemned the invasion and called upon Israel to withdraw. The Israelis, with tacit American acquiescence, ignored this demand and the United States and Israel refused to agree to the proposal, which was supported by Britain, that a United Nations presence be established in the Beirut area. Instead, following the enforced departure of the PLO fighters from Lebanon and the massacre of Palestinians in the refugee camps of Sabra and Chatila, a multi-national force (MNF) was deployed comprising American, French and Italian contingents, its (never entirely clear) objective being to observe a ceasefire and help to restore Lebanese government authority. In response to American and Lebanese persuasion, Britain, which would have preferred the United Nations option, sent a token contingent of about a hundred men to join this force.

In September 1982, President Reagan announced a fresh peace initiative which, in effect, called for Israeli withdrawal from territories occupied in the June War of 1967 and the restoration of the West Bank to Jordan in some kind of federation. This was quickly rejected by Israel, and also by the Arabs on the ground that it did not meet Palestinian aspirations. It received a lukewarm welcome from the European Community since it fell short of the principles in the Venice Declaration and a slightly warmer bilateral response from Britain. The American administration failed to press their initiative and it soon joined the archive of unsuccessful proposals which had been mounting since 1967.

An Arab summit meeting in the same month at Fez in Morocco produced what became known as the Fez Declaration. This called for total Israeli withdrawal from the occupied territories and the establishment of a Palestine state. But it went a little further in the direction of implicit recognition of Israel's right to exist than had previous Arab statements. The Arab League decided to send a high-level delegation to European capitals to canvass support for the Declaration. This precipitated the first serious difference of opinion between Britain and the Arabs since the Conservative government had come to power.

Historically the Arabs have regarded the British Labour party as being more under the influence of Zionist and pro-Israeli sentiment than the Conservative party, notwithstanding Ernest Bevin's reputation in the last years of the Palestine Mandate when he was excoriated by all pro-Jewish elements, and Anthony Eden's collusion with Israel over the Suez invasion of 1956. They were particularly suspicious of the Wilson governments of the 1960s and 1970s, in spite of the major part played by Britain in the negotiation of SCR 242 of November 1967 which called for Israeli withdrawal after the June war, and were apprehensive that Mrs Thatcher, representing a North London constituency with a substantial Jewish community, would have pro-Israeli leanings. However for the first three years it was the Israelis who complained, about the pro-Arab bias of the government and in particular about the Venice Declaration. The only serious bone of contention with the Arabs was the refusal of the British government to 'recognise' the PLO and to receive its leaders at Cabinet ministerial level, contacts being confined to the official level. This policy was due partly to the refusal of the PLO leadership to accept Israel's existence even on the condition, which Britain pressed, that Israel should reciprocate by recognising the Palestinian right to self-determination, and partly to the government's rejection of high-level contact with any organisation which used violence (terrorism) in order to further its aims.

This situation came to a head in 1983 with the visit of the Arab League delegation which included a representative of the PLO and was received in other European capitals. The British government was not prepared to accept this and a long-drawn-out and ill-tempered exchange followed. In the event, the delegation came to London, with a distinguished Palestinian academic (not a PLO member) representing the 'Palestinians'. They were received by the Prime Minister and Foreign Secretary, Mr Francis Pym, and had an audience with the Queen. The discussions were friendly if inconclusive and no great harm was done; but the memory of the incident lingered on both sides.

However, for the remainder of 1983, all talk of peace initiatives was overshadowed by the Lebanese crisis. The MNF became embroiled in the factional fighting between the Druzes, the Maronites and the Shia 'Amal in and around Beirut. In May tension rose dangerously between Syria and Israel, and Secretary of State Shultz's painstakingly worked out agreement between Israel and the Lebanese government for an Israeli withdrawal from central Lebanon was wrecked by Syrian opposition. The United States moved a naval armada close inshore and air and naval attacks (including the heavy guns of the battleship USS *New Jersey*) were launched against Druze positions in the hills behind Beirut. Vicious, suicidal car bombings were directed against the French and Americans by fundamentalist elements and, at the turn of 1983–4, the MNF withdrew.

Over the next three years the British government, indeed the European Community as a whole, made no further public attempt to revive any of the moribund peace initiatives. There was another abortive delegation visit to London in October 1985 when two senior Palestinians were denied access to the Foreign Secretary because of their last-minute refusal to issue a statement in advance condemning violence. The government concentrated instead on 'quiet diplomacy', i.e. keeping in close touch with the United States and the friendly regional parties, fostering bilateral relationships and combating the terrorist symptoms of the Palestine problem. The government was conscious of its impotence and of the unfavourable conjuncture of forces, with the Americans disillusioned and reluctant to embroil themselves again in doomed negotiating processes, the Arabs in disarray, the Lebanon in chaos and the Israelis with a coalition government paralysed by the presence of the two main opposing political parties. The situation on the ground continued to fester.

During this period Britain deepened its already close relationship with King Hussein of Jordan and gave him every encouragement in his ultimately unsuccessful attempts to reach a common negotiating position with the PLO leader, Yasser Arafat, attempts which were designed to encourage the United States to reanimate peace negotiations. In 1984 the Queen paid a State Visit to Jordan, the first of its kind, and was followed by Mrs Thatcher in 1985. In 1986 the Prime Minister also visited Israel, where she indulged in some public plain-speaking. Close relations were maintained with President Mubarak of Egypt. But in March 1986, King Hussein's efforts with Arafat collapsed and with them any vestigial hope that his initiative might bear fruit.

From 1984 to 1986 the primary attention of Western governments was focused on the most deadly symptom of the Middle East crisis – terrorism. In early 1984 a series of bomb attacks against anti-Qaddafi Libyans culminated in a demonstration outside the Libyan People's Bureau in St James's Square during which shots fired from the building killed a woman police officer, WPC Fletcher. Britain expelled the Libyan diplomats and broke off diplomatic relations. In 1985 a TWA aircraft was hijacked to Beirut and was released only as a consequence of a massive exchange of Lebanese Shia' detainees held by Israel. In September a group of Israelis were murdered on a yacht at Larnaca in Cyprus. Israel retaliated with a bombing raid on the PLO Headquarters in Tunis. In October, the Italian cruise liner *Achille Lauro* was hijacked in the Mediterranean. In November an Egyptian aircraft was hijacked to Malta and, in December, gunmen fired on the El Al ticket counters at Rome and Vienna airports. In April 1986, in response to an attack on a Berlin disco frequented by American servicemen, US aircraft, some of them operating from bases in Britain, bombed Tripoli and Benghazi. In September Jews in a synagogue in Istanbul were gunned down and an American aircraft was hijacked to Karachi. All these attacks and counterattacks – and the above is not a full list – caused heavy casualties, mainly to innocent civilians. In November, an Arab, Nizar Hindawi, was convicted in a British court of trying to smuggle a bomb onto an El Al aircraft and Britain not only broke relations with Syria but persuaded her EC partners and other friendly states, including the US, to adopt certain sanctions against Damascus.

Throughout this period the toll of Western hostages kidnapped in the chaos of West Beirut mounted. Two British hostages were murdered shortly after the American bombing raid on Libya and, although two or three American and French hostages were released, others were seized to take their place. By early 1987 over twenty hostages of different nationalities, including American, British, French and German, were being held, as well as the Archbishop of Canterbury's personal representative, Mr Terry Waite, who had gone to Beirut to negotiate the release of two Americans. This particular kidnap followed the bizarre revelations that the United States administration, notwithstanding its adamantine rhetoric about terrorism, had in fact been trying to negotiate the release of its citizens in exchange for consignments of arms to Iran – what became known as the Irangate affair. By this act it was revealed that the British government stood alone in stating and applying a policy of not negotiating or doing deals with terrorists.

In early 1987 the leader of the Israeli Labour party, Shimon Peres, began to canvass the notion of an international conference as a means of breaking the deadlock on the Arab–Israeli problem. This move, unprecedented as it was in coming from any Israeli political grouping, was strongly opposed by the Likud members of the Israeli coalition; but it gained American acquiescence in a proposal which had previously been resisted by the administration because of Israeli opposition and because a conference would involve all the Permanent Members of the Security Council, including the Soviet Union. The majority of Arab states had already expressed themselves in favour of a conference, notwithstanding the fact that their concept of its functions differed from that of Mr Peres. On 23 February the European Community Foreign Ministers, including Sir Geoffrey Howe, issued a declaration reiterating their adherence to the principles in the Venice Declaration, expressing themselves in favour of an International Peace Conference under the auspices of the United Nations, and undertaking to grant aid to the Palestinian population of the Occupied Territories and to allow certain products from those territories preferential access to the Community market.

However, Mr Peres failed to secure agreement from the Israeli coalition to pursue this initiative and, by the middle of the year, hopes that it might materialise had, at least for the time being, dimmed; the European declaration has not, at the time of writing, been followed up with any vigour.

Meanwhile international concern has turned to the Gulf War. A major Iranian ground offensive petered out early in 1987 but Iraq has continued its attacks on shipping in the Gulf. In May an Iraqi aircraft, presumably in error, attacked an American frigate causing damage and serious casualties. The American response was to threaten military action against Iran, particularly in view of the Iranian purchase of Chinese ground-to-ground missiles which could be used against shipping. It should however be noted that Iranian strategy, the reverse of that of Iraq, has throughout been to localise the war and to do nothing to provoke the involvement of outside countries, particularly the superpowers; it was Iraq which initiated the attacks on merchant shipping in 1983 while Iran has confined itself to retaliatory reaction. It is, after all, Iran which needs to keep the Gulf open for the transportation of her own exports and imports, whereas Iraq can afford to see the waters of the Gulf turned into a battlefield since her oil is now carried entirely by pipeline across Saudi Arabia and Turkey and her imports enter the country by road mainly from Jordan and Kuwait.

Notwithstanding this background, American pressure on Iran is mounting and it seems that the US administration has been trying to persuade the Western allies, including Britain, to play a more active part in the protection of shipping. The Soviet Union too is becoming involved. Soviet warships have entered the Gulf and Kuwait has brought superpower involvement closer by inviting the Soviet Union and the United States to charter its oil tankers as a deterrent against Iranian attack. This move has naturally aroused the competitive instincts of the US administration. So far as can be judged from public comment, Britain is playing a restraining role, refusing to draw closer to a military confrontation with Iran or into quasi-alliance with Iraq. British warships continue to be available to reassure and, if necessary, to offer assistance to British registered merchant shipping and Britain is working with other members of the Security Council on action designed to promote negotiations between the two parties, possibly to inhibit supplies of military equipment to Iran if she maintains her refusal to negotiate. As was the case at the outset of the attacks on shipping in 1983, Britain appears to be counselling prudence on her more erratic ally. It is therefore unfortunate that the British government should have

simultaneously become involved in a factitious row provoked by the
government in Tehran which has led to a virtual breach of
diplomatic relations between the two countries.

Conclusions

It is difficult to compare the effectiveness of Conservative Middle
East policy between 1979 and 1987 with that of other postwar
British governments of either party. All previous governments have
had more at stake and deeper involvement in the area – whether in
the form of military bases, or membership of a regional defence pact,
or responsibility for mandated territories, a colony, an array of
protected states or for fixed British economic assets, or in the need
for Middle East supplies of crude oil. The present government has
from the beginning been free of all such entanglements as well as
being a net exporter of crude oil. Moreover it found on coming to
power in 1979 that it had ready to hand a fully developed practice,
dating from the Heath government, of British participation in
European Community political co-operation on the Middle East,
and that a major expansion of the Middle East as a British export
market had taken place during the Wilson and Callaghan
governments between 1974 and 1979. Hence the Thatcher
government has been in a position to consolidate the work of its
predecessors in calmer and less reef-infested waters than those
experienced by its predecessors. In a nutshell, drained of her power
and special responsibilities, Britain has sunk lower in the priorities
of the regional governments and the Middle East has similarly
declined in importance to Britain except in the contexts of
commerce and the endemic threat posed by regional crises to world
peace. Mrs Thatcher has involved herself personally in the
promotion of exports and with one state at least, Oman, a 'special
relationship' has been maintained and indeed developed.

In general the Thatcher government will be remembered for its
assiduous cultivation of the oil-rich and politically moderate Arab
states as well as for improving the British relationship with Israel.
Within Britain, Jewish opinion has assiduously cultivated the Prime
Minister and drawn encouragement from her opposition to terrorism. In Arab folklore, an important ingredient in the formulating of
Arab policy, it will be regarded as having been excessively

subservient to the United States – scarcely a fair charge as I have tried to demonstrate in this chapter – and for failing in consequence to exploit the initiative on Palestine which it launched under the Foreign Secretaryship of Lord Carrington.

In particular, certain policies and incidents will stand out in the minds of economic and political historians – Britain's uncompromising stand against state involvement in the determination of oil prices and levels of production, the convergence of rhetoric and action *vis-à-vis* terrorism, the refusal to recognise the Palestine Liberation Organisation and the fact that, through no fault of her own, Britain ended the eight-year period in question with diplomatic relations either severed or virtually non-existent with no less than three Middle East states, Libya, Syria and Iran. However, notwithstanding such ups and downs, which are inseparable from involvement in the Middle East scene, the past eight years have been the most tranquil that Britain has experienced since the end of World War II in terms of the formulation of her Middle East policies.

References and Further Reading

Carl Brown, L. (1984) *International Politics and the Middle East: Old Rules, Dangerous Game*, IB Tauris.

Monroe, E. (1981) *Britain's Moment in the Middle East, 1914–71*, Chatto and Windus.

Parsons, A. (1984) *The Pride and the Fall – Iran 1974–79*, Jonathan Cape.

Parsons, A. (1986) *They Say the Lion – Britain's Legacy to the Arabs*, Jonathan Cape.

CHAPTER 5

Southern Africa

JAMES BARBER

On 21 December 1979 Lord Carrington, on behalf of the British government, and three black nationalist leaders (Robert Mugabe, Joshua Nkomo and Abel Muzorewa) signed the Lancaster House Agreement. That agreement was to transform the British colony of Rhodesia into the independent state of Zimbabwe.

For Margaret Thatcher's new administration it was a diplomatic triumph. It was also a surprise. Before she came to power Mrs Thatcher had made clear that she favoured recognising an internal agreement negotiated by Muzorewa and Ian Smith, the recalcitrant leader of Rhodesia's whites. A confrontation between Britain and black Africa (backed by the rest of the Third World and the Communist bloc) seemed imminent, and the venue for the initial clash was set for the Commonwealth Conference at Lusaka. In the event Mrs Thatcher disarmed her Commonwealth colleagues by agreeing to make a final attempt to negotiate a settlement. She was persuaded to that view less by the anticipated outrage of the Africans than by the advice of her Foreign Secretary, Lord Carrington, and Western leaders such as President Jimmy Carter and Malcolm Fraser of Australia. Yet, even when the delegates subsequently assembled at Lancaster House, the chances of agreement seemed poor because of the bitterness and distrust between the Zimbabwe factions. However, agreement was secured, partly because of the difficulties faced by the protagonists – a protracted guerrilla war with no

obvious end in sight, and external backers who were weary of the
conflict – and partly because of the skill and tenacity of Lord
Carrington and his FCO colleagues and officials (Davidow 1984).

The Southern African Inheritance

For the government Lancaster House was a success both in the
positive sense of enhancing its diplomatic prestige, and in the
negative sense of removing from Britain's international flesh the
long-embedded Rhodesian thorn. It also marked the formal end of
Britain as the 'imperial factor' in southern Africa, but that did not
mean the end of involvement. Extensive British regional economic
interests remained, as did residual ties with the old colonies and
protectorates (Zimbabwe, Zambia, Malawi, Botswana, Lesotho, and
Swaziland). For example in 1984 Britain gave £87 million aid to
Commonwealth countries in the region. Significant bilateral
relations continued with these new Commonwealth states, and later
Britain developed important contacts with Mozambique. However,
above all, and inextricably linked to relations with the black states,
was the problem of South Africa. In that Mrs Thatcher inherited a
situation which had taxed all previous governments – Conservative
and Labour alike – as they sought to balance Britain's interests in
the Republic with those elsewhere in the region, and to judge the
impact of South African policy on relations with neighbours.

At home South Africa had become ingrained into British politics:
creating divisions between and within the political parties;
nurturing powerful pressure and interest groups (like the Anti-
Apartheid Movement and United Kingdom–South Africa Trade
Association); capturing the attention of churches and universities;
prompting large-scale demonstrations; and gaining extensive media
attention. The intensity of the moral debate and the degree of media
attention singled out South Africa from other foreign policy issues,
and as it became part of the domestic scene it passed though the
prism of British political values and interests to emerge in forms
which South Africans (black and white) sometimes found hard to
recognise. While South Africa became a regular feature of British
politics it gained greatest attention when there was open conflict
within the Republic between the government and blacks. That had
happened at the time of Sharpeville in 1960, and again in 1976–7
following the Soweto risings and the death of Steve Biko, but when

Mrs Thatcher came to power Pretoria had regained its security grip and was enjoying a period of relative confidence (Brewer 1986).

The international setting has been equally taxing for British governments. In the bilateral relationship with South Africa there is a large and complex flow of contacts and transactions — with goods, people, information and ideas moving in both directions. That is reflected in the size of South Africa's London Embassy, her largest post abroad, and in the estimated 800,000 residents of the Republic who can claim British citizenship. However, diplomatic relations between the two governments have been ambivalent. The British are keen to foster economic links, but diplomatically to keep Pretoria at a distance, both to demonstrate opposition to apartheid and to avoid 'guilt by association' (Tinker 1977). On its side Pretoria has resented the British government's coolness, the flood of criticism of apartheid, and what it regarded as British appeasement of black states. There have also been strains over particular issues, such as arms bans and Rhodesian sanctions.

However, the strongest international criticism has come from those who believed that because of her extensive economic stake in South Africa Britain has sheltered Pretoria. At meetings of international organisations criticism has been directed at Britain individually and as part of the Western capitalist bloc, which is accused of upholding the apartheid state. She has been accused of defending white regimes, in Rhodesia as well as South Africa, by casting UN Security Council vetoes. The British government argued that these were to protect its own interests and to counter wild proposals, but in radical eyes they were shields protecting white racists. Similar criticism arose in the Commonwealth, which South Africa had been forced to leave in 1961. There Harold Wilson faced bitter attacks for his handling of Rhodesia, and Edward Heath for his decision to resume arms sales. Under such pressures, and before Mrs Thatcher came into power, Britain had agreed to limited steps against South Africa, including the 1976 Commonwealth Gleneagles Agreement to discourage sporting links and the 1977 mandatory UN arms ban.

Policy Objectives

That was Mrs Thatcher's inheritance. Its characteristics and constraints have persisted, and it is within the continuing interplay of domestic and international pressures that the government has pursued its objectives. At times these have concentrated on regional affairs – such as the Zimbabwe settlement and, later, aid schemes for the region's black states – but Britain's main attention has been given to South Africa, and in this case the objectives were succinctly expressed by Sir Geoffrey Howe in 1986, as: 'to promote an early and peaceful transition to a genuinely non-racial democracy and to further British interests in South Africa' (Foreign Affairs Committee, 1985–6). Such a broad statement leaves problems of interpretation, but the main criticism of the government has been less about its objectives than the methods by which it seeks to achieve them. The disputes have usually boiled down to two main questions: Is reform of apartheid more likely to be achieved by contact with or by ostracising Pretoria? Do British economic links further apartheid or help to undermine it?

In responding to those questions the arrival of the Thatcher government marked a shift of emphasis if not direction in British policy. From the beginning Mrs Thatcher made clear that she believed in diplomatic and economic contacts, whereas the preceding Labour government had started to stress the problems and uncertainty of links with South Africa (although it had not broken those links). Shortly after taking office Mrs Thatcher told the US Foreign Policy Association that 'there is now a real prospect that the conflicts on South Africa's borders, in Rhodesia and Namibia, will shortly be ended. This combined with welcome initiatives in South Africa's domestic policies offers a chance to defuse the crisis which was potentially of the utmost gravity and to make progress towards an early ending of the isolation of South Africa in world affairs' (Daily Telegraph, 19 December 1979).

Despite subsequent pressure Mrs Thatcher did not change her views. She made this clear in response to criticism of her meeting at Chequers in 1984 with P.W. Botha, when she pointed out that she was always being urged to make contact with governments, like the USSR, with whom Britain had differences. Meeting Mr Botha, she said, in no way implied approval for apartheid. 'My talks are part of the process through which we and other Western and African countries must continue to press for the sort of changes we all want to see' (The Times, 6 June 1984). Sir Geoffrey Howe, the Foreign Secretary, was equally adamant. In October 1985 he told Parliament: 'Nothing could be less constructive than disengagement in the present situation in South Africa' (*Hansard*, 23 October 1985, col. 305). In the following year he reiterated the point, saying: 'If we are to have a chance of influencing the policy of governments we need to have contact with them . . . It is right for us to have contact with the South African Government' (Foreign Affairs Committee 1985–6). Alongside contact the government has pursued 'positive' goals towards the ending of apartheid, such as training schemes for blacks and codes of conduct for companies. This was recognised as an unglamorous option but one which the government claimed would eventually be more effective.

While there has been broad agreement within the government over the objectives being sought, from time to time there have been differences between the Prime Minister and the Foreign and Commonwealth Office over the appropriate response to external pressure, and over policy presentation. In style the FCO is conciliatory, and has emphasised the dangers of imposing international isolation on South Africa, whereas Mrs Thatcher dislikes fudged compromises and her strong convictions lead her to accept confrontation, and if necessary isolation. Thus while, on occasions, the FCO has favoured 'symbolic' sanctions to avoid alienating other Western and Commonwealth countries, Mrs Thatcher has stood firmly against them. Mrs Thatcher also responds fiercely if provoked. In 1987 she branded the African National Congress a 'terrorist organisation' when there were reports that it might attack British companies because the government would not apply sanctions. Yet the FCO continued to foster the contacts it had already established with the ANC.

The Domestic Setting

Domestic concern about South Africa has continued throughout the Thatcher years. The government has had to cope with conflicting interests and values, powerful pressure groups, persistent media attention, and the entrenched belief that Britain has a special role to play in southern Africa. Newspaper editors, television producers, church and student leaders, as well as politicians, share that belief. In 1986 the Commons Foreign Affairs Committee argued that Britain could ignore neither her 'interests and obligations' as the former colonial power nor her current 'pivotal diplomatic role'

which means that her decisions are 'likely to have a decisive
influence on the actions and policies of the world community
towards South Africa' (Foreign Affairs Committee 1985–6). The
government has not questioned that there is a role to play, and
that Britain is more vulnerable to instability in South Africa than
other Western states. She has the greatest economic stake (taking
trade and investment together) and her other links are not only those
of sentiment and culture but contain the potential problem of a large
influx of passport holders if order were to break down. Yet the
government believes that at home and abroad Britain's capacity to
influence events is often exaggerated.

As in the past political activity related to South Africa has reached
its peak when blacks have mounted serious challenges to the
government in Pretoria. During the prolonged black risings from
mid-1984 to late-1986, the British government came under great
pressure at home and abroad to support UN mandatory economic
sanctions. At the same time the AAM intensified its campaign
against business and financial links, ensuring that companies were
aware of the 'hassle factor' involved in contact with South Africa.
Within its campaign the AAM continued to identify particular
targets. Prominent among these was Barclays Bank, which had first
been selected for special attention in 1970 and which the AAM
noted in 1978–9 was still 'one of the most popular in the field'.
The pressure on Barclays was so intense in the mid-1980s that it
played a part in the bank's decision to withdraw from South Africa
in 1987. Explaining its decision, Barclays pointed not only to the
Republic's current economic difficulties but also to the reduction
in student accounts in Britain which followed the anti-apartheid
activity.

The intensity of anti-apartheid campaigning created other
domestic problems for the government. While previously demonstrations against sports teams had raised public order problems,
under Mrs Thatcher the issue was freedom of speech, or more
precisely the right to express views favourable to white South Africa.
For example, John Carlisle, a Conservative MP, ran into fierce
opposition at universities where he was shouted down, denied access
under the NUS's 'no platform' for alleged racists policy, and even
assaulted. Both Mrs Thatcher and Sir Keith Joseph (when Education
Secretary) publicly defended Carlisle's right to express his views,
and, along with others, his case played a part in the introduction of

legislation seeking to ensure freedom of speech in universities. Similar issues arose in other private organisations. For example, Equity (the actors' union) continued to be deeply divided about its members' right to perform in South Africa even to mixed-race audiences. In another case there was a bitter dispute when the 1986 World Archaeological Congress meeting at Southampton University excluded South African delegates, although two were black and the whites had opposed apartheid (*Times Higher Educational Supplement*, 21 February 1986).

Yet, despite the disputes and the media attention, South Africa has not been an issue in any of Mrs Thatcher's three elections as Conservative party leader. There may be a chance element in this, for the major troubles in the Republic have fallen between elections. However, southern Africa has not been prominent in any British election — including 1966, which came shortly after Rhodesia's UDI, and 1970, when bitter controversies were raging about South African sports tours and arms sales (Barber 1983). What explains the paradox between electoral neglect and vigorous political activity at other times? Perhaps the answer lies in the occasional public opinion polls on southern African issues. These reveal a clear division of opinion and, despite the media coverage, a high 'don't know' response. Both these features create difficulties for electioneering. The division of views means uncertainty of support if a party were to make South Africa a prominent election issue, and the 'don't knows' indicate that although South Africa is a matter of considerable concern to the 'attentive public' there is much less concern among the general public.

The International Setting — the Bilateral Relationship

Even in the Thatcher years the government has tried to keep Pretoria at diplomatic arm's length. However, in an international setting in which South Africa has few friends, Pretoria has attempted to retain good relations with London and there is respect for Mrs Thatcher as a forceful, determined leader, both because of the influence she carries among other Western leaders and because of her firm opposition to sanctions against the Republic. That respect grew as she resisted calls for more sanctions while other Western states, including the USA, bowed before domestic and international pressure. Most particularly it grew during her defiant stands at Commonwealth conferences.

Yet, from time to time there has been tension. In 1984 there was mutual recrimination over two events. In March, four South African officials were arrested in Coventry for illegal arms trading. After a period in custody the 'Coventry Four' were released on bail and allowed to return to South Africa when a First Secretary at the Embassy waived his diplomatic immunity, stood surety in the sum of £50,000 each, and gave an undertaking on behalf of Pretoria that the men would be returned when summoned. The four returned for a brief court appearance in June, but failed to reappear when summoned in October, by which time the First Secretary had been moved from London. The FCO was incensed. On its side Pretoria claimed that it had been absolved from its undertaking because of an incident in South Africa. There, in September, six political opponents of the government for whom warrants had been issued took refuge in the British Consulate in Durban. The British government asked the 'Durban Six' to leave and made it clear that it did not support their action, but it refused to evict them against their will or allow the South African police to enter the Consulate to make arrests. The 'Durban Six' gained considerable international attention, and Pretoria claimed that because the British were obstructing the enforcement of South African law the 'Coventry Four' would not be returned, as an act of legitimate reprisal. London deplored the South African action, and refused to accept that there was 'any justification for linkage of the two cases' (*The Times*, 26 September 1984). However, the South African government refused to change its position, and while the 'Durban Six' eventually left the Consulate, the 'Coventry Four' did not return to stand trial.

On the few occasions that there have been senior ministerial contacts the exchanges have been blunt. When P.W. Botha visited Chequers in 1984 (the first visit to Britain by a South African Prime Minister since Dr Verwoerd's unsuccessful Commonwealth visit in 1961) Mrs Thatcher was characteristically 'firm and forthright'. In 'candid' discussions she outlined her objections to apartheid and urged a settlement in Namibia, while on his part Mr Botha complained of the ANC office in London (*The Times*, 3 June 1984). There were further differences when Sir Geoffrey Howe visited South Africa in 1986. A somewhat reluctant Sir Geoffrey wandered around southern Africa, like the leader of a lost desert band, trying to

salvage something from the failure of the Commonwealth Eminent
Persons Group (EPG). Among the stated aims of his mission were to
seek the release of political prisoners, including Nelson Mandela,
and to urge the unbanning of the ANC and PAC. At his meeting
with President Botha he met a blank refusal. The President did not
hide his resentment at outside interference and stated that he had
not the slightest intention of taking the steps requested by Sir
Geoffrey.

The two meetings, at Chequers and Pretoria, underlined the
difference of interest and perception between the two governments,
based on their need to satisfy different constituencies. At Chequers
Mrs Thatcher, who was conscious of opposition in Britain to Mr
Botha's visit, was seeking to demonstrate that contact could gain
results. Therefore she wanted to make progress on such matters as
the reform of apartheid and Namibia. For Mr Botha the meeting
itself was more important than anything that would come from
it. A visit to Chequers gave South Africa international status, undermined attempts to isolate her, and enhanced Botha's prestige at
home. At the Pretoria meeting Sir Geoffrey, who went ostensibly
as the EC's representative (Britain was President of the Council of
Ministers at the time) was trying to reduce international pressure on
Britain and to buy time while passions cooled in Europe and the
Commonwealth. In contrast Botha, following the EPG visit, had
decided to turn his back on international pressure and was intent on
showing South Africans – white and black alike – that the government would stand firm against external interference.

Economic links have been warmer. Mrs Thatcher's government,
like its predecessors, has claimed that economic contacts both help
the British economy and undermine apartheid. The claim is that
economic expansion breaks down racial barriers and that British
firms introduce good labour practices. Malcolm Rifkind, then
Minister of State at the Foreign Office, claimed in 1985 that
economic development had produced a growing realisation among
whites 'that apartheid is a system without a future'. That, he said,
'is the overwhelming reason why it is indeed the business
community of South Africa that has been in the forefront of the
process of reform, and why one can say with absolute conviction that
capitalism and apartheid are mutually incompatible'. He added
that, while Britain had taken some measures against Pretoria, a
distinction had to be drawn between those 'which will damage

apartheid and bring pressure on the South African Government . . .
and those which we are not prepared to support - measures designed
to do the maximum damage to the South African economy without
regard for the people of South Africa and for that country's future
economy' (*Hansard*, 23 October 1985, col. 341).

Alongside these arguments the British government has advanced
other reasons for its determined opposition to mandatory economic
sanctions: they would make the South African whites more resistant
to change; they are ineffective politically; they are impossible to
impose efficiently; they would adversely affect South Africa's blacks
and neighbouring states; and they would impose a heavy burden on
Britain by increasing unemployment and restricting markets. Nor
does Mrs Thatcher favour symbolic gestures, which she regards as
ineffective, and she also rejects the view that economic sanctions are
the only effective peaceful means of bringing reform to South Africa.
Far from promoting peace she believes that their implementation
would lead to conflict. In contrast her government favours direct
messages to the whites, and 'positive' steps to help black
development and promote reform. It also argues that external
pressure, whatever its source, has clear limitations, and that when
reforms are introduced by Pretoria they should be recognised.
According to this view, change depends on events inside South
Africa, and especially on the actions of the South African
government. Sir Geoffrey Howe, emphasising the need for internal
political dialogue, said: 'We cannot force change on South Africa
from outside.' Pretoria itself had to be persuaded. 'We cannot
dictate to them. They are more likely to be willing to take such
steps if we are willing to acknowledge what they have done so far.'
As examples, he mentioned the abolition of the Mixed Marriages
Act and the granting of freehold and leasehold rights to blacks
(*Hansard*, 23 October 1985, col. 341).

In opposing economic sanctions the government has enjoyed
strong support from the business community but, while the
government's position has been consistent, economic circumstances
have changed. The South African economy has been in difficulties
since late-1981, suffering falls in real GDP of 0.8 per cent in 1982
and 2.5 per cent in 1983. The recession came from a combination of
factors: the decline in world economic growth after the oil price rises
of 1979, drought across southern Africa, the government's failure to
curb public expenditure and inflation, and business fears about the

role of black unions. The 1984–6 disturbances and the South African government's response to them added greatly to the difficulties. Foreign companies, their economic incentive reduced and domestic harrassment increased, re-examined their commitments. New foreign investment virtually dried up and company withdrawals started. At first it was American companies but they were soon followed by the British. The value of the South African currency plunged and some international banks withdrew their support. Ironically, therefore, the financial and business communities, after fiercely opposing sanctions, took steps which had similar economic effects. The major British examples were the withdrawal of Barclays and Standard Chartered Banks, which had both played major roles in the South African economy, handling respectively about a third and a quarter of the country's commercial business. While Barclays gave a number of reasons for its withdrawal, Standard explained its 'sad but necessary' decision by referring only to the need for extra provision to cover Third World debts. It would be surprising, however, if Standard had not also taken account of the 'hassle factor', and its exposed position as the one remaining foreign-controlled bank in South Africa.

When Sir Geoffrey Howe was asked whether the company withdrawals strengthened the case for sanctions, he replied: 'No. It strengthens the case for understanding the distinction between economic pressures arising from natural economic developments as a consequence of policy, and pressures arising from collectively imposed international boycotts.' He argued that the market pressures make Pretoria question its policies, whereas collective political sanctions would make it determined to resist (Foreign Affairs Committee, 1985–6). Even President Botha, it would seem, bows before the power of the market.

The International Setting – Alliance Management and Damage Limitation

Britain's international concern with South Africa has increasingly been less in bilateral relations than in relations with other states. There is persistent pressure at meetings of international organisations for action against 'the apartheid state'. In its international dealings, therefore, the government has constantly to assess whether opposition to further sanctions is worth the price in terms of the unpopularity and strains it creates with close allies as well as critics. In making that assessment differences have sometimes arisen between the Prime Minister and the FCO, with Mrs Thatcher less ready to seek compromises. Broadly, however, Britain has aimed to co-ordinate policy with her Western allies – both to make that policy more effective and to avoid exposure by seeking safety in the pack. In relations with the Third World and especially black Africa the aim has been damage limitation: to defend Britain's position against adverse reactions. The need for both activities – alliance management (with the European Community and the USA) and damage limitation (at the UN and the Commonwealth) – was most acute in 1985–6, as the international community and anti-apartheid groups in the West focused their attention on the struggle inside South Africa.

For the government, the actions of major international partners and organisations are interconnected and mutually responsive. The pressures on Britain, and her successes and failures within each international setting, has an impact elsewhere. For example, the bitter attacks on Britain at the 1985 Commonwealth Conference spilt over to create problems for the government in the UN and the EC. Yet, while recognising this persistent interaction, for convenience the main relationship will be treated separately.

Alliance Management – the USA

Direct USA involvement in southern Africa followed the collapse of Portuguese rule in 1974–5, and the emergence of Marxist governments in Angola and Mozambique. Concerned at that, and the potential vulnerability of the region's mineral supplies, Henry Kissinger took a direct hand: backing South African military intervention in Angola, and seeking diplomatic agreements in Rhodesia and Namibia. His efforts failed. However American involvement continued, although in a different form, as the new Carter administration targetted southern Africa in its drive for human rights. It also played a leading part in the formation of a Western 'Contact Group' (USA, UK, France, West Germany and Canada) seeking a Namibian settlement, and co-operated with Britain in further vain efforts to find a Rhodesian solution.

However, by the time of the Lancaster House Conference the Carter administration was in its final days, and was only peripherally involved in the settlement.

Shortly after Lancaster House, Ronald Reagan took office. For Mrs Thatcher the timing was admirable. Advised by Dr Chester Crocker, the Deputy Under-Secretary of State, the new administration pursued 'constructive engagement'. This was conceived as a regional policy, aimed at bringing stability across southern Africa, helping the fragile new black states to survive, and promoting reform in South Africa itself. Although rejecting apartheid, the Americans recognised Pretoria's strength. They argued the need to persuade/pressure her to help settle regional problems, to make positive use of her economic power and to introduce reform at home. Like Mrs Thatcher, the Americans argued that these objectives could not be achieved by isolating Pretoria; nor could the country's future be determined by external revolutionary movements. Crocker argued that if the West, and in particular the USA, was serious about promoting stability, encouraging reform and countering Communism, it had to become directly and positively involved. The USA could not afford to stand on the sidelines criticising. Its role should be that of broker, seeking to determine neither the course of events nor their outcome, but to work for peaceful reform while respecting each state's sovereignty and for economic co-operation. It was in this spirit that the USA in 1984 actively supported the Nkomati Accord between Mozambique and South Africa, and a ceasefire in Angola (the Lusaka Agreement). Inside South Africa the Americans welcomed reforms in labour laws and, while recognising that the new 1983 constitution was flawed, they made the point that there was no sense in criticising a franchise restricted to whites and then rejecting its extension to Coloureds and Asians.

The British government supported 'constructive engagement' in its own right, and there was the added advantage that bold American leadership took attention away from Britain after the bruising Rhodesian experience. Britain tucked into the American slipstream. Problems arose, however, in the mid-1980s when the US administration came under pressure at home. Step by step South Africa became an issue of US domestic politics – Jesse Jackson raised it in his presidential campaign, there were organised protests outside South Africa's Washington Embassy, black leaders like Bishop Desmond Tutu came on visits, and television brought the conflict of South Africa's black townships into people's homes. In 1986 President Reagan was forced to acquiesce in further sanctions when Congress overrode his veto. This exposed the British government, focusing attention on its refusal to take further action, and there were demands at home and abroad to follow the American example. However, the pressure eased as Pretoria regained its security grip, and reporting restrictions took South Africa off television screens. Temporarily South Africa slipped down the political agenda and the voices calling for action became less strident.

Alliance Management – the European Community (EC)

The European Community as a body has played a less prominent role in southern Africa than the USA, although individual members (notably Britain, West Germany and France) are deeply involved. In 1977 following a British initiative the Community agreed to introduce a Code of Conduct for firms operating in the Republic (Britain had earlier operated a Code of Practice). The EC code was introduced partly from a genuine desire to improve working conditions and opportunities for blacks, partly to exert pressure on Pretoria for reform, and partly to divert criticism from black states at a lack of action by the Europeans following the Soweto risings and the death of Steve Biko (Barber 1980).

The intense international activity of the mid-1980s again brought South Africa before the Community. The ideal for London would have been united support for the British approach, or at least acquiescence from other members. That did not happen. The EC was divided, not in its opposition to apartheid but on the action to be taken. Britain was in a minority in opposing further sanctions but she was not isolated and few favoured comprehensive sanctions. Various efforts were made to overcome the divisions, including a visit to South Africa in 1985 on behalf of the EC by representatives of three member states – Italy, Luxembourg and the Netherlands. In September 1985 a number of 'positive measures' were agreed, such as support for black training and improved housing. There was also a call for the release of political prisoners, and very limited 'negative' sanctions – withdrawal of military attachés from Pretoria and refusal to grant accreditation to new South African attachés.

However, there were still clear divisions when the European Council met at the Hague in June 1986. Some members – Britain, France, Germany and Portugal – were opposed to further sanctions. Others – the Netherlands, Ireland and Denmark – called for import bans, including wines, fruit and vegetables. A third group, including Italy, argued that while they were not opposed to further sanctions it was pointless to do anything without common agreement. Not surprisingly the meeting finished in confusion. Although consideration was given to further steps – bans on the import of coal, steel, gold coins, iron and new investments – they were not to be implemented immediately and, to the consternation of her colleagues, Mrs Thatcher subsequently distanced herself from the proposals (Lodge 1986).

In the following six months Britain was President of the Council of Ministers and used the opportunity to continue the search for a united stand, and to defend its own position. Sir Geoffrey Howe made his visit to southern Africa as the EC's representative, but it was also a useful delaying and diversionary tactic for London while tempers cooled. In the event nothing came from the visit, and in September bans were agreed on the import of new gold coins, new investment, and iron and steel. The government was reluctant to impose these sanctions but they were not serious for Britain. Proposals which could have had an impact on her, such as cutting air links or banning the import of fruit and vegetables, were not introduced because Britain, with others, was not prepared to support them. At the same time Britain gained agreement for some positive steps such as financial support for black students.

Damage Limitation – the Commonwealth

In 1979 at Lusaka Mrs Thatcher had delighted her Commonwealth colleagues by changing her mind on Rhodesia. In 1985 at Nassau she infuriated them by refusing to change her mind on South Africa. By then the Commonwealth had become the British government's most difficult international setting. Even at the UN Britain could anticipate support on South African issues from a few Western allies. At Nassau Mrs Thatcher was completely isolated. Other members, including the old 'white' Commonwealth, were unanimous in believing that further sanctions were necessary. (In the case of Australia and Canada their moral abhorrence of apartheid may have been reinforced by the economic advantage to be gained if South Africa's mineral and agricultural exports were restricted.) Again the point at issue was not opposition to apartheid but how apartheid could be ended – though the debate was no less bitter for that. Rajiv Gandhi, commenting on Britain's position, said: 'It is not just a question of being alone. It is a question of what we really stand for. What does Britain stand for – for freedom, for human rights? Well, where is it? We don't see it in South Africa' (*The Times*, 11 October 1985). The other members argued that additional sanctions were the only peaceful way to achieve the end of apartheid. Mrs Thatcher responded sharply that they would increase resistance.

The Nassau debate also threw up questions about the nature and operation of the Commonwealth. Pressure came on Mrs Thatcher not only from her fellow leaders but from the Commonwealth Secretariat and probably the Crown. When the Secretariat was first formed in 1965, Arnold Smith, the first Secretary-General, interpreted its task as that of a bureaucratic body to service the institution. 'Sonny' Ramphal, who succeeded Smith, adopted a different approach. He took initiatives and became a political actor in his own right, particularly on southern Africa. He was active during the Lancaster House Conference, in that case working alongside Britain. At Nassau, however, it was clear that a clash was imminent when he outlined his views to the press. In general terms he spoke of 'replaying history' by drawing a direct link between the abolition of apartheid and the earlier abolition of slavery. He saw economic sanctions as a means of exerting continuous pressure on Pretoria, not by imposing the full range of sanctions immediately but by using a ratchetting process – an incremental programme of action if Pretoria did not respond to the demands being made of her. Later, after the unsuccessful visit of the Eminent Persons Group (EPG), Mr Ramphal wrote that 'Sanctions and peace for South Africa have now become one and the same' (Eminent Persons Group 1986). He also said that many people believed, despite the British government's denials, that Britain supported apartheid through her economic links. The government shared neither Ramphal's views nor his interpretation of his office. Lord Home, doubtless reflecting the British view, wrote to warn against the attempt to 'turn the Commonwealth Secretariat into an executive instrument of policy' (*The Times*, 8 August 1986).

The Queen's involvement is more difficult to explore, because of the confidentiality which surrounds her views. She may earlier have played a part at Lusaka in 1979 where, it has been claimed, Mrs Thatcher's 'decision was clearly influenced by her desire not to embarrass the Queen, who had let Mrs Thatcher know that she would not be pleased by disarray or vituperation' (Davidow 1984). At the time of Nassau reports appeared in *The Sunday Times* from 'sources close to the Queen' that she was greatly concerned that Mrs Thatcher's intransigence was endangering the Commonwealth. The Queen had no views about sanctions as such, but thought that a compromise should be sought to avoid a major split. The Queen had no doubts about the Commonwealth's importance and the need to ensure its future. The reports spoke of her concern at the number of states that had protested against Britain's policy by boycotting the Edinburgh Commonwealth games. A 'close adviser' was reported to say that the Queen 'knows more about the Commonwealth than anybody . . . She believes that she inevitably takes a much broader view than the Prime Minister can do' (*Sunday Times*, 22 July 1986). The reports were later denied and even if there was substance in them they did not lead to a constitutional crisis. However, storm cones had been hoisted that two of the Queen's roles – monarch of the UK and Head of the Commonwealth – could conflict.

Under the pressure that surrounded her at the time of Nassau Mrs Thatcher had three options: to abandon her position; to compromise; or to refuse any concessions. She does not abandon a position lightly and for most of the conference she held to the third option, but eventually she gave a little ground. An Accord was agreed. This: a) criticised apartheid and Pretoria's aggression against her neighbours; b) called on her to abandon apartheid, to release Nelson Mandela and to start an internal dialogue; c) reaffirmed the bans already imposed and introduced small additions, such as refusing government funds for trade missions; and d) established the Eminent Persons Group (EPG) of senior politicians to visit South Africa to forward the aims of the Accord. It was also agreed that if no progress were made by the EPG a mini summit would meet in August to consider further steps, including cutting air links and banning agricultural imports. By giving a little ground Mrs Thatcher had gained an agreed position, but she lost whatever goodwill she had salvaged from her Commonwealth colleagues by a patronising television interview in which she disparaged the agreement. Later she was more circumspect in responding to John Carlisle's suggestion that Britain should have stood in 'honourable isolation', and refused to step onto the sanctions 'escalator'. No, said Mrs. Thatcher, she had obtained a very good agreement which was much better than a separate statement (*Hansard*, 29 October 1985, col. 822).

After initial hesitation the South African government agreed to the EPG's visit, probably because Mrs Thatcher made a personal request to President Botha. Momentarily it appeared that the visit might be an astonishing success. The South African Cabinet was said to be split over the EPG's proposals, but in the end the proposals were dramatically rejected as South African forces raided neighbouring states. President Botha made clear that he rejected external interference. Yet when the Commonwealth mini summit assembled later, Mrs Thatcher refused to accept a package of sanctions supported by the other six participants (Australia, Bahamas, Canada, India, Zambia and Zimbabwe). She would only accept a voluntary ban on new investment and tourism promotion, but agreed to abide by whatever decisions were later reached by the EC. The other Commonwealth members decided to impose the package of sanctions themselves. Biting on the bullet, Ramphal claimed that the credibility and integrity of the Commonwealth had been enhanced by this, because the other members had risen above the level of the lowest common factor, acting despite Britain. Yet he and the other leaders knew that only Britain among Commonwealth states has the capacity to make an impact on the South African economy.

That realisation was prominent at the next Commonwealth conference at Vancouver in October 1987. Once more sanctions against South Africa was the most controversial item, but although a 'mini summit' on South Africa preceded the main conference, the tension was less than at Nassau and the issue somewhat less prominent because Mrs Thatcher had already made it known that she would not support further sanctions. There were bitter complaints about this and in the final communiqué five references to Britain standing alone, but no further sanctions were imposed.

There were also less formal accusations that the government was breaking the spirit if not the letter of undertakings it had given.

There have, for example, been persistent complaints about breaches
of the sports boycott, although the government insists that it has
kept to the Gleneagles Agreement. Another complaint, raised at
Vancouver, was about a proposed trade mission to South Africa by
the United Kingdom–South Africa Trade Association (UKSATA) in
November 1987. The government explained that it was not
sponsoring the mission as it had in the past, but critics noted that
UKSATA was one of the Overseas Trade Board's designated advisory
group, and that the mission was to receive briefings and a reception
from British representatives in South Africa (*The Independent*, 17
September 1987).

There is, therefore, still uncertainty about future Commonwealth
action in relation to South Africa, and about the strains that the
dispute throws on to the organisation. If many Commonwealth
members feel resentful at the failure of Britain to act, and accuse her
of placing material interests above moral considerations, there is a
British view that many Commonwealth members are very willing to
trail their moral coats because it costs them nothing. Action would
impose cost on Britain but not on them (although obviously that
judgement would not apply to Commonwealth states in southern
Africa). A complacent British view is that threats against Britain
and/or the future of the Commonwealth are not real, but simply a
means of exerting pressure. *The Economist* concluded that Britain
could take the threats as a 'reassuring compliment', for although in
principle the 49 Commonwealth members are equal, 'in practice
only British actions (or failure to act) are held to be capable of
jeopardising the future of the association' (*The Economist*, 19 October
1985). However, such views are contested in Britain, and not only
by the Anti-Apartheid Movement. The members of the Commons
Foreign Relations Committee concluded that the disintegration of
the Commonwealth over South Africa 'is not to be dismissed
lightly', and if it were to disintegrate it would be against British
interests, for 'membership and leadership of the Commonwealth is
undoubtedly a major diplomatic asset' (Foreign Affairs Committee,
1985–6). For her part Mrs Thatcher does not appear to have
strong sentimental attachments to the Commonwealth, either in
terms of a lingering imperial tradition or as a new-age, multi-racial
organisation. She probably sees its strength in functional activities,
such as technical aid, and through organisations like the Association
of Commonwealth Universities.

A Return to Regional Concerns

By early 1987 Pretoria had largely regained its security grip, and demonstrated that it would resist external pressures. Responding to the situation the British government diverted more attention to the region as a whole. The South Africa issue remained potentially explosive, but the path chosen by the government was to continue opposition to further sanctions, while at the same time taking 'positive' steps to support blacks in South Africa and the black states in the region.

In South Africa itself the steps included the provision of scholarships for black students, and closer attention to the EC Code of Conduct. Outside the Republic, regional aid was extended to the black states. Some went directly to governments and included military aid for Zimbabwe and Mozambique, as well as economic, technical and educational aid. Some was channelled to SADCC, the multinational organisation through which the black southern African states were seeking to build greater self-reliance and to reduce their dependence on South Africa. In preparation for the 1987 Commonwealth summit in Vancouver Sir Geoffrey Howe had talks with Canadian ministers in which he repeated that further sanctions would be unjustified and ineffective, and suggested that a more appropriate role for the Commonwealth would be to increase aid to the front line states. British officials took a similar line in discussions with Commonwealth High Commissioners at a pre-conference meeting in London. At the Vancouver conference itself the British produced a booklet outlining support for the black states: *British Aid to Southern Africa – a Force for Peaceful Change and Development*.

Prominent in this strategy was increased aid for a non-Commonwealth state, Mozambique, whose development was critical for the whole region because of the transport situation. Many of the region's black states which are land-locked had been forced to rely increasingly on South Africa as other routes had closed because of civil war, inefficiency and lack of resources. If the routes to the sea across Mozambique could be reopened the heavy reliance on South Africa could be reduced. With this in mind British aid to Mozambique was increased from £2.6 million in 1980 to £34 million in 1987. According to the booklet, British aims were to eliminate apartheid by peaceful dialogue and to 'promote the peaceful, stable, and prosperous development of all states in the region'. When Mrs Linda Chalker visited Mozambique and Malawi late in 1987, she emphasised Britain's commitment to helping the development of these states and announced further aid schemes.

The British approach was not universally welcomed. Ominously Zambia and Tanzania rejected it, saying that increased support to the front line states was not a substitute for action against apartheid (*The Independent*, 10 September 1987). They and other critics accused Britain of trying to divert attention away from her failure to confront South Africa. The government's response was that it would continue to apply pressure on Pretoria while helping the frontline states in their general development and to gain a measure of economic independence from South Africa, however precarious that might be. Thus, although the British government has committed resources to the black states and would prefer to play a quiet, 'positive' role across the whole region rather than concentrating on South Africa, it seems doubtful that it will be allowed to do so. Until apartheid is ended the international campaign against South Africa and those who have contacts with her, notably Britain, will continue.

References and Further Reading

Barber, J. (1980) 'The EEC code of conduct for South Africa: capitalism as a foreign policy instrument', *The World Today*, vol. 36, no. 3, March.

Barber, J. (1983) *The Uneasy Relationship: Britain and South Africa*, Heinemann.

Blumenfeld, J. (ed.) (1987) *South Africa in Crisis*, Croom Helm.

Brewer, J.D. (1987) *After Soweto: An Unfinished Journey*, Oxford University Press.

Davidow, J. (1984) *A Peace in Southern Africa: The Lancaster House Conference on Rhodesia, 1978*, Westview.

Eminent Persons Group (1986) *Mission to South Africa: The Commonwealth Report*, Penguin Books.

Foreign Affairs Committee (1985–6) *South Africa*, HC I–I.

Lodge, J. (1986) 'The European Community: compromise under domestic and international pressure', *The World Today*, vol. 42, no. 11, November.

Tinker, H. (1977) *Race, Conflict and the International Order*, Macmillan.

CHAPTER 6

Asia and the Pacific

GERALD SEGAL

Britain and Russia were the only two great imperial powers to have a complete concept of Asia. They were also the only two powers to have colonies at the western end of the continent near Iran, and at the eastern extremity near China. Both were to distinguish between what they ethnocentrically called the 'far east' and the far closer south Asia. But 400 years on from the European conquest of Asia, only Russia remains an Asian power.

At its peak, the British Empire was the most-far flung of all, even spanning the Pacific. It was under Henry VIII and then Elizabeth I that Britain sought trade routes to Asia overland across Russia, westward across the north Atlantic and finally eastward around Africa. Drake's first circumnavigation (1578–80) was a superb use of sea power for plunder, and was to tempt Britain into Asia in search of economic prosperity. Britain found such prosperity in Asia, but she found also entangling alliances and draining wars (Kennedy 1988).

Britain's retreat began as early as the eighteenth century with the surrender in North America and continued in the nineteenth century with the granting of self-rule to white settler-colonies. But it was in the last half of the twentieth century that the retreat from empire became a rush. By the 1970s it was a fashionable self-flagellation of the British to remark on the withdrawal 'east of Suez' as the symbol of a faded imperial glory (Lowe 1981).

But is such pessimism proper in the new world of a 'global economy' and the rise of the 'Pacific Century'? Is Britain so irrevocably committed to its European role that it has no place in Asia? There are some signs, however faint, that Asia, and especially the Asia/Pacific region, is once again of increasing importance to British foreign policy. The reasons for the fall and rise of British interest are to be found in an analysis of political, economic and military affairs in Asia, and at home in Britain. The region is diverse and the actors many, thereby making analysis complex. But at least part of the region and some of the actors are important in the modern world, and British foreign policy increasingly understands that it ignores Asia at its peril.

The near-total neglect of the new trend of the revitalised British foreign policy in Asia has a number of causes. First, the revival is relatively recent, and is mainly evident only in the Thatcher period. Second, the new focus on Europe has masked the extent to which Britain, with a recovering domestic economy, is returning to the global economy. That global economy has developed a more vibrant Asian component, especially in Japan, the Newly Industrialised Countries and the more prosperous members of the Pacific portion of the Commonwealth. Thus the old focus on colonial heritages leads to neglect of the new importance of different states, only some of which had a colonial link with Britain. A new British foreign policy, coupled with a changing international environment, requires new views of Britain and Asia.

Britain and the Superpowers in Asia

The superpowers and Britain had been allies of a kind in the Second World War, but only in the last moments of the war were they allies in Asia (Thorne 1978). The entry of the Soviet Union into the war against Japan brought Soviet power back into north-east Asia while the United States slogged its way across the Pacific islands to a dominant role in the postwar order in east Asia. Britain, humiliated in the war in Asia, only returned by the grace of the United States. And an unspoken price for American aid was the promise of future decolonisation.

Unlike the position in Europe, there was no four-power

arrangement for the defeated aggressor – only United States hegemony and Soviet spheres of influence. Of course, in Europe the reality was soon a cold war and bipolarity. In Asia there was a less clear picture of rival blocs. There was only a role for Britain as the retreating empire. While, in Europe, Britain was concerned that the United States be tied into a structure of defence for like-minded regimes, in Asia Britain hoped the superpowers would take a less active part.

The drawing of containment lines in Europe involved Britain as a major actor. In Asia, the lines were left fuzzy, and when this imprecision helped to lead to the Korean War in June 1950, Britain was primarily concerned that the United States would be distracted from the main theatre in Europe. But war in Asia begun by Communist invading non-Communist was not without implications for Europe.

Britain, like many other allies of America, sent a token force to Korea and suffered casualties. Like the other European allies, it learned that war with the Soviet Union after 1945 was much closer than was thought and that increased defence spending on Nato was required. The Korean War also taught that superpowers were not invincible, even in the age of nuclear weapons. Limited war could still be fought in the nuclear age and Communism was a global threat. These were hard lessons, but a more cheering one was that war could be kept limited and that alliances of democratic states could hold. Britain also discovered that it could play a constructive role in moderating American policy, especially by dissuading them from using nuclear weapons in Korea (Foot 1985).

When the attention of the superpowers did swing back to Europe, Britain was satisfied that the wartime alliance had done well in Korea. But when wars in Asia flared again, most notably in 1962 between China and India, it became clear that the risks of distraction from more important disputes remained. But in the Sino-Indian War, the superpowers were still primarily focused on the momentous implications of the near-simultaneous Cuban missile crisis. When attention did finally shift to the Himalayan war, Britain was an even more important actor than in Korea (Segal 1982). As the former colonial power, it was a major arms supplier to India, and friend when needed. The Anglo-American 'special relationship' functioned better here than during any other conflict in the developing world.

The Sino-Indian War was the last time India would lean to the Western side of the cold war, although conflict flared again in the region in 1965 and 1971. On both these occasions, the superpowers were much more directly involved in managing the crises, and Britain was sidelined. Even in 1971, when a Commonwealth state, Pakistan, was dismembered by another Commonwealth state, India, Britain stood more or less idly by. Of course the United States was also unable to save East Pakistan.

Although the superpowers sparred in south Asia, it was southeast Asia that drew most of their attention in the fifteen years after the mid-1960s. The main British worry was that, with the commitment of half a million American troops in Vietnam (more than in Europe), the United States was losing sight of its main priorities. Unlike Korea, in the Vietnam War the United States' European allies were openly critical of American policy and unwilling to support the war effort. Britain's special relationship was strained by Prime Minister Wilson's attempts to play the mediator between the superpowers in an effort to break the negotiating log jam.

Britain as mediator was very different from Britain as ally, but even less successful. Not even the Soviet Union was impressed by Wilson's efforts (Segal 1982). This was truly a time when, as Dean Acheson noted, Britain had lost an empire but not yet found a role. At the very time that Wilson was playing the peacemaker, the Royal Navy was withdrawing from east of Suez. In the ensuing stages of the American retreat from the Vietnam War in the 1970s, Britain under a Conservative government supported the American effort to withdraw, although London's views were of little consequence to either superpower.

With the end of the American phase of the Indochinese conflict, the superpower relationship in Asia became less important. Rivalry now focused on the arcane calculations of naval balances in the Pacific and Indian oceans. Britain under Thatcher was no longer a major global naval power, but it did have some useful outposts of empire: none more convenient than Diego Garcia. This atoll in the Indian Ocean was cleared of inhabitants by Britain so the United States could base its ships and aircraft there, secure in the knowledge that there were no hostile natives. Even Britain did not get in the Americans' way and the British were simply happy enough to remind the Americans of their firm friendship when, as in the

Falklands War, American support in distant waters was required in return.

By the time of the Thatcher administration, Britain's main concerns about superpower relations were that the Atlantic alliance be maintained and détente pursued (Moreton 1987). Few Asian events impinged on these basic principles, although Britain was very aware of the global nature of international security. For example, the 1987 superpower INF arms control agreement almost fell foul of the Soviet demand for extra weapons in the Asian theatre. Britain, like the United States' other major allies, was concerned that the SS-20 was a 'swing' weapon that could reach either Europe or Asia from the Urals. Thus European and Asian security was linked, and an arms control agreement served the cause of peace in both regions. To the extent that Britain was seen as an influential American ally, some Asian states, most notably Japan, made sure to explain to Britain the link between European and Asian security in the hope the message would be passed on. Mrs Thatcher, the longest-serving Western leader in the 1980s, was happy to have her role confirmed and the place of Britain enhanced. Even as a European power, Britain was also still a global power.

Britain and China

Until the Japanese rape of China in the Second World War, Britain held the dubious honour of being the imperial power most hostile to China. Although many powers grabbed territory from the fading Qing dynasty, in 1945 it was only Britain, Portugal and the Soviet Union that held on to the spoils. Of course Britain, like many of the other European imperialists, claimed to be merely interested in securing free trade and an open Chinese door. To that end, Britain supported the pro-Western regime of Chiang Kai-shek in the civil war with the Communists. When Mao Zedong's Communist party came to power in 1949, Britain, unlike most Western governments, accepted the new reality and established relations with the Communists (Boardman 1976).

Britain's common sense during the time of anti-Communist hysteria was driven by a recognition of the weakness of its imperial position. Although nearly all other imperial enclaves in China were surrendered, Britain clung on to Hong Kong. The 1842 Treaty of

Nanjing ceded Hong Kong island to Britain and in the 1860 Treaty of Tianjin, Kowloon was also ceded. In 1898 the 365 square miles of the New Territories were leased for 99 years, rent-free. Although China never recognised the 'unequal treaties', even the Communist authorities were unwilling to force Britain to surrender the territory. Yet China held all the cards, if only because it controlled the water, food and power supplies to Hong Kong. But Britain provided the atmosphere for this strangest of all enclaves of capitalism to thrive, with its by-product of providing the largest portion of China's foreign currency in times of American-sponsored isolation of China.

This classic stand-off of interests was the basis of Hong Kong's remarkable prosperity – one of the great anomalies of the postwar world. Even in 1967, when radical Chinese Red Guards rampaged through Hong Kong, the central authorities in Beijing and Britain co-operated to restore order and confidence. Although the question of Hong Kong's future always loomed over its people, millions of refugees still continued to flood out of China into the relative safety of the colony. Britain took in these refugees from Communism but was reluctant to open its arms too widely. After all, China held one-quarter of all mankind.

China also relied on Sino-British relations as a window on Europe and the West, and Britain prospered as China's main trading partner in the non-socialist world. But the rise of Japan, Germany and France soon diluted the British role and by the 1970s London was merely one of several major Western capitals for Chinese visitors. The development of Sino-American détente in the 1970s was also to lead China to reduce the importance attached to Britain. Of course China remained aware that Britain had served as a moderating influence on America's earlier anti-China line. And Britain remained the second most important English-language country – a not insignificant consideration for a country that decided that English was to be its main language of communication with the outside world.

Britain's almost-special relationship with China had not, however, translated into a growth in business. The West Germans soon dominated Europe–China trade while Britain only dreamed of the potential of the Chinese market. Under James Callaghan there was even a proposal to sell Harrier aircraft to the Chinese airforce but, because of fear of a hostile Soviet reaction, Britain dithered. By the time Britain made up its mind, China had lost interest.

By the Thatcher era, it became fashionable to argue that British trade with China was held back because of the Hong Kong problem. The reality was more prosaic – Britain could not find enough to import from China to balance the trade and British goods were reckoned by the Chinese to be generally inferior to those from Germany, Japan and the United States. The real push for change in the status of Hong Kong came from the mundane realities of leases in the New Territories which could not be renewed beyond 1997.

Sino-British negotiations got off to a terrible start. Margaret Thatcher, fresh from her Falklands triumph in 1982, did not like the idea of giving back territory that was ceded in perpetuity, especially after having fought a war in the south Atlantic where the legal claim was more dubious. As in the Falklands, the citizens of Hong Kong did not want to be returned to the control of the mainland power. In both cases Britain was thousands of miles away.

But, unlike the Falklands, Hong Kong had five million people, non-white, and with a large ethnic community already established in Britain. In the conservative climate of strict immigration controls, there was no chance of taking in large numbers of Chinese, and they would have to be returned to Communism. Despite sharp disagreements within Britain about immigration controls, the shutting out of Hong Kong residents received a surprising degree of cross-party support in the House of Commons. There was not even any significant criticism from the British right wing of the handing back of five million free citizens to the control of Communism. Mrs Thatcher's 'iron lady' image of hostility to Communism no doubt protected her right flank, while the sheer numbers of potential refugees protected her left side. Nor was there any distinct pressure from the 160,000-strong Chinese community in Britain. They, like their fellow Chinese in America, had avoided involvement in politics and were therefore unorganised, even if they had been willing to make themselves heard.

The remarkable human tragedy of handing back so many people to Communism was made necessary by China's firm insistence that sovereignty had to be returned. Britain had proposed a form of lease-back (as it had initially in the Falklands), but China would not hear of it. This more open China was confident that it could put the hearts and minds of Hong Kong residents at ease and thereby set a good example for the takeover of Taiwan. Britain had the uncomfortable task of negotiating the transition to Communism with few real cards to play.

Britain's only significant card was its ability to help ensure that China obtained and maintained a prosperous Hong Kong, and for that China needed to appear reasonable and considerate of the interests of the arch-capitalists in Hong Kong. To the credit of both Britain and China, in December 1984 they reached as good a deal as was possible, short of full independence for Hong Kong or sudden takeover by China. China promised to leave Hong Kong to run all but its foreign and defence policy for a further 50 years beyond 1997 and provided pleasant promises about respecting the Hong Kong way of life. A Basic Law has yet to be drawn up by China, and until then the future of Hong Kong lies in the uncertain rhetoric of 'one country, two systems', as China describes its policy.

In the short term, official confidence in Hong Kong is high. But those who can, have sought or bought passports in the white Commonwealth and the United States. Some have then returned to Hong Kong to make money before the flag is taken down, but few will find refuge in Britain. The House of Commons closed ranks in approving the deal and in preventing anything but a handful of Hong Kong's remarkably industrious population from coming to Britain and feeding Britain's supposed new enterprise culture. In 1997, Britain will have been responsible for the return of more free people to Communist rule than has ever been undertaken before. Attempts to ensure Chinese good behaviour by moving Hong Kong to free elections before 1997 have been slowed by the Thatcher government, and to a large extent the House of Commons has barely raised a murmur of dissent. *The Economist* may have pictured Geoffrey Howe as a doormat to Hong Kong and China (23 January 1988), but in truth the responsibility can be apportioned across the British political spectrum and not merely to the Thatcher government.

It is perhaps too soon to tell whether the Hong Kong deal has done much good for Sino-British relations. The exchange of high-level visits, like that of the Queen to China in 1986, has certainly been made possible. But despite expectations in some sectors of the business community, trade remains weak. In addition, China's new, more independent, foreign policy has taken it further away from strategic co-operation with the West. Sino-British relations are certainly better than they have ever been, but in many respects, despite the Hong Kong issue, they are less important than at any time in several centuries.

South Asia

Britain had, of course, first begun in south Asia to learn about how to decolonise. India had been by far the most important real estate of empire, but it was by just as much the most tragically botched example of granting independence to former subjects. The creation of two states, India and Pakistan, immediately resulted in a huge loss of life. The world has never seen such a large shift of population as took place around partition. Certainly since then, no war has matched the number of deaths that took place in the intercommunal slaughter at the time of the British withdrawal.

It is perhaps unfair to blame Britain for the fact that Hindu and Muslim hated each other so intensely, but some blame must attach to the colonial authorities for allowing the outcome to be quite so horrific (Lapping 1985). Nothing in the wars in south Asia that have followed has been quite that nasty. The 1947 partition was split again in 1971 when Bangladesh was created out of Pakistan, with India as a midwife hostile to the reluctant mother.

Britain watched the wars of 1965 and 1971 from the sidelines. Although it remains the fourth most important power (after the superpowers and China) for all the states of the region, Britain has been unable and unwilling to control the wars. Although there are more immigrants from south Asia in Britain since 1945 than from anywhere else, they have been unable to have anything but the most marginal effect on British policy. These immigrants have discovered, like the Jews before them, that the British system is unreceptive to hyphenated-British, especially when compared to the obvious power wielded by ethnic-Americans. The south Asian immigrants to Britain have also been divided among themselves, reflecting the natural divisions in the subcontinent.

In part because of these ethnic ties to south Asia, Britain has been remarkably aware of the wars fought there (Barber 1986). When Sikh extremists take their terrorism to the streets of London or the air above the north Atlantic, Britain cannot avoid focusing on the causes of the conflict. When Tamils seek refuge in Britain because they are being persecuted by the Sinhalese majority in Sri Lanka, Britain is forced to take a stand. Old scores, based on the original British importation of Tamils into Sri Lanka to work the plantations, may be a cause of the contemporary conflict, but this cuts little ice with modern immigration officials in London. Britain lives more with the bitter legacy of its colonial past than,

remarkably, with the benefits of its fruits. It can take some credit for
having created the world's largest democracy in India, but the
instability of that democracy is still obvious, and even manifest on
the streets of London. The assassination of Mrs Gandhi by Sikh
extremists led to riots in India, and also in Britain.

More widely, the legacy of colonialism has helped bring a potent
mix of racism and entrepreneurial skills to Britain. The transformation of British inner-cities and ethnic composition is seen most
clearly in the experience of the Indians in Britain. The debates over
what kind of multi-ethnic society to create in a country not used to
seeing itself as a melting pot, has led to the internalisation of south
Asian problems within Britain. It is now less an issue of foreign
policy, and more one primarily of the domestic character of modern
Britain.

British trade with the subcontinent has declined as a percentage
of both British and south Asian trade. India has drifted out of the
Western orbit into a leading role in the non-aligned movement and
to the extent that it looks to the West the younger, Rajiv Gandhi,
generation in particular tends to look as much to the United States
as to Britain. Pakistan has drifted into a type of Islamic
fundamentalism and military dictatorship. Bangladesh remains one
of the world's poorest places, and also under military rule. Sri
Lanka, once a jewel of free-market economic prosperity, is split by a
vicious ethnic war.

India remains the most important of these states, if only by virtue
of its size and leadership of the non-aligned. Yet Pakistan has been
vital in the struggle against the Soviet Union in Afghanistan, and is
guardian of that old north-west frontier line against the spread of the
Russian Empire. Britain remains interested in what happens in these
states, but when south Asian events make the headlines in Britain,
it is rarely because of a British foreign policy role. South Asian
crises, like African famines or coups, are seen as the typical event in
the poor South, but they are all of minor and decreasing importance
for British society, economy and foreign role. The contrast with
Britain's attitude towards the more successful and important east
Asians is striking, and represents a clear change in British policy
towards Asia. Overall, the south Asians may have been some of the
first to obtain independence, but they have retained few basic links
with Britain and hardly serve as a model for other developing states.

Yet all but Pakistan are still Commonwealth members, and even

Pakistan would return if only India would lift its veto. For all the complaints from south Asian states that Britain is no longer a power to be reckoned with in the region, they all see some benefit in clinging to this remnant of empire. The Commonwealth is both a forum of North–South dialogue and a more congenial atmosphere in which to press demands for more aid from the developed world. Britain and its white-settler comrades in Canada, Australia and New Zealand serve as bridges to the richer world, and yet another way to bring to life the poorer states' desire for genuine non-alignment. But in comparison with its other children of the empire, Britain is not particularly pleased with its south Asian offspring. The real British interest lies in the more distant east of Asia.

Japan, Australia and New Zealand

Britain and the United States can claim most of the 'credit' for introducing Japan to the Western international system. Japan, that other great island people off the coast of Eurasia, learned both its modern economics and its imperialism from the British example. At various times, London was anxious to nurture Japan as an anti-Russian, anti-Chinese and even anti-American power in order to relieve the burden on Britain (Nish 1977). The Japanese repayment came in the form of Tokyo's humiliating defeat of Britain in the Pacific theatre of the Second World War. Japan shattered Britain's Asian empire and, although Britain returned in 1945, the colonies had to be let go.

Japan and Britain, like Germany and Britain, had some shared historical and modern geopolitical interests, but the postwar world also made them economic competitors. Unlike Germany, Britain was kept out of the shaping of the postwar Japanese order and was not formally allied to Japan in a collective-security pact. Japan, therefore, was left to rebuild itself with huge American assistance, while Britain agonised about its retreat from Asia. Yet Japan soon rose again as the only non-white power to have pulled itself up by its boot-straps to be a highly developed economy. Britain admired this feat of recovery, as did most of the developed Western world. But also, like the rest of the developed world, Britain became concerned with the emergence of Japan as the strongest economy in the capitalist world and a more powerful member of the economic Group of Five than either Britain or France (Frankel 1981).

Japan was clearly an economic competitor, but it was also a vital engine in the Western economic system. Britain, especially in the Thatcher era, established itself as Europe's second most important trader with Japan and eventually as an attractive place for Japanese investment. Japan, like the United States before it, found that direct investment in Europe was a way around national or EEC barriers, even though Japan continued to despise what it saw as the 'decline of Britain' as an economic power.

The Thatcher revolution may have gone a long way to opening Britain up to Japanese investment, but it was not until her second term that the flow of investment increased. Japanese business was pleased with the new attitude of British labour, the new spirit of enterprise, and above all the relatively low costs of operation in Britain. By 1988 Japan had over $5 billion of direct investment in Britain, only 4 per cent of their total but more than in any other European country and more than in all but five others around the world. Britain has more people employed by the Japanese than any country except the United States (*The Economist*, 16 January 1988).

It was not until the Thatcher revolution that the Japanese began to take Britain seriously again. The Prime Minister's special skills in getting on with the leaders of both superpowers, in maintaining an international role for a relatively small island state and in adapting to the new international financial markets were especially prized in Japan. The visit by Sir Geoffrey Howe to Japan in January 1988 was a vivid symbol of the new importance of the Anglo-Japanese relationship (*The Independent*, 8 January 1988).

As Tokyo developed into the third leg of the fast-growing international trade in financial services, London remained the main European equivalent (with New York making the third leg). Japanese trade with Britain has soared in the past 25 years, its exports rising from 0.9 per cent to 5.7 per cent of British imports by 1986. Britain held its own in the Japanese market, and London was the second most vociferous supporter (after the United States) of the need to liberalise further the Japanese markets. Japan accounted for by far the largest proportion of Britain's growing trade with Asia in the decade from 1975. The Japanese influence, whether in cars, cameras, high fashion or food, was making itself felt in Britain (and Europe) as it had in the 1970s in the United States. The relationship with Japan has been the most striking new feature of Britain's Asia policy in the 1980s under Thatcher, and can be considered a major change of emphasis in the overall direction of British diplomacy. Japan, as the most developed part of Asia, was the leader in the new orientation of British policy towards closer relations with the more developed states of the region and a sharper division between the rapidly developing states and the less-developed ones.

But not all developed states in Asia and the Pacific have seen a rise in British interest. The traditional special relationships with the white-settled colonies of Australia and New Zealand have suffered, but then, given the extreme closeness in colonial days, a degree of distancing was inevitable and healthy. The real move to independence has often been traced to the Second World War when Britain and its colonies realised that London could not defend its Commonwealth allies from Japan. The United States filled the role, and American culture and influence followed its military efforts. In the 1950s Australia was still anxious for British immigrants, but by the 1970s it was taking in more Asians.

British trade also declined. Australia accounted for 7 per cent of UK exports and 4 per cent of imports in 1960 but by 1981 it accounted for only 1.7 per cent of UK exports and 0.8 per cent of imports. Although the figures ceased to decline in the Thatcher years, it had been clear for decades that Britain was reorienting its trade to Europe, while Australia was looking to its Pacific partners. A similar, albeit more pronounced, pattern was evident in Anglo-New Zealand relations.

Both Australia and New Zealand remain among Britain's major trading partners in Asia, but no longer for reasons of Commonwealth (Hocking and Warhurst, 1986). They were both developed economies and their trade with Britain came to be based on more solid grounds of inter-capitalist competition. Like Japan, Australia and New Zealand were natural competitors in the international economy.

Of course, the new economic basis of relations did not entirely displace the historical and cultural ties. To some extent the empire was striking back, sending Australian multinationals to buy into the British food and media businesses (to name but two) and even to help enliven the British film industry by positive example. Commonwealth contacts were still mostly a source of unity, except when an Australian Governor-General sacked a controversial Prime Minister and helped raise the cause of republicanism in Australia. But Australia remained the third most important Commonwealth member and often lined up with Britain (and Canada and New Zealand) as gentle supporters of the arguments of the developed North against the dissatisfactions of the Commonwealth South.

Britain and Australia were also members of the only remaining multilateral defence pact in the Pacific – the Five Power Defence Arrangement. Although this was little more than a shell to cover mostly bilateral exercises and fine-sounding expressions of common security, it was evidence that Britain had not fully retreated from east of Suez. In the 1980s, with the demise of ANZUS, Britain could feel somewhat smug about having been kept out of this South Pacific defence arrangement in the 1950s (Williams 1987). But despite Britain's continuing role in the FPDA, the upcoming withdrawal from Hong Kong and the Australians' new defence policy meant that military co-operation in the future was likely to decline.

Even in the 1980s Britain had disagreements over military strategy with Australia and New Zealand, for example when London joined with Washington in refusing to sign the South Pacific Nuclear Free Zone treaty. It was true that Britain no longer contaminated the Australians with its nuclear tests, as it had done in the 1950s, but as an American ally, Britain was concerned that the New Zealand 'disease' of unilateral nuclear disarmament might catch on in Europe.

In the security sphere, as in economics, Britain remained an important actor in Asia because it was an important actor in Europe and the Atlantic world. In security and economics, as in culture, the world was a smaller place than in the 1950s. Britain had retreated from Asia, but greater international interdependence was bringing Britain back into closer contact, especially with the most developed states of east Asia and the Pacific.

Developing East Asia

Britain's return to Asia and the Pacific in the Thatcher administration has been mostly driven by the new economic priorities at home, and new international economic relationships. Given such sources of policy, it is not surprising that it is the most economically prosperous former colonies that hold the greatest attention of British traders and diplomats in the region. Britain, like other developed economies, is adapting to the fact that, as the idea of a single Third World dies, special attention is paid to the most rapidly developing states of Asia.

Although Japan shattered the former imperial unity of Britain's Asian empire in the 1940s, Britain at least tried to hold bits of east Asia. But unlike France, Britain soon realised the need to manage the transition to independence. Like France, Britain became involved in a nasty guerilla war (in Malaysia) and the uncomfortable regional politics (surrounding the creation of independent Singapore). But unlike France, Britain emerged from the process with friends in independent Asia and managed not to decolonise Hong Kong for decades. While British colonies often prospered, nearly everyone else's fell into war and poverty.

Clearly there was no simple secret why British colonies in east Asia prospered in independence. Singapore and Hong Kong emerged as the two most prosperous Newly Industrialised Countries and Malaysia was the closest to them among the states of the Association for Southeast Asian Nations (ASEAN). Certainly these three did not prosper because of their close economic ties with Britain. They, like the Australians, saw their proportion of trade with Britain cut by three-quarters in the 25 years from 1960. With the important exception of Hong Kong, their prosperity had more to do with a pluralist political system. But all also had highly interventionist central governments and none had a democracy as understood in Britain.

The two other NICs, Taiwan and South Korea, owed their growth to massive support from the United States, but unlike the city-states of Hong Kong and Singapore, their development was a more complex and ultimately more powerful economic process. Neither Taiwan nor South Korea became as important for British economic interests, although Britain was at times involved in their postwar history. British troops fought to defend South Korea in the early 1950s, while Britain was a voice for moderation when the Taiwan Straits crises later in the decade threatened to escalate to a superpower and/or nuclear confrontation.

But it was the economic development of the NICs and the proto-NICs of ASEAN that made east Asia of importance for Britain. As with the development of Japan, these states became more normal parts of the international capitalist economy and thus were more important traders with Britain as part of their entry into the general international economy. By the Thatcher years, South Korea was exporting cars and ships to Britain and Singapore was selling computers. Even Malaysia, which once urged its population to 'buy British last', was looking to Britain to help gain entry to the European market and was taking an increasing share of British investment in Asia (Kershaw 1983). It was in east Asia that new trade partners for Britain were to be found, and they were not always former colonies.

The poorest states of the region remained virtually beyond the interest of Britain except as places of tension and instability. Indochina was at first mainly a French problem and then a sap on American willpower to defend Europe. The exception to this benign neglect was the unwanted, but necessary, process of managing decolonisation in the smaller Pacific states.

By the 1980s Britain had given up all its Pacific islands except the Pitcairn Islands (with a population of 57) while the United States and France held on to more important territory. Most of the islands were poor but independent, and all were far removed from British interests. Some had a difficult birth, like Vanuatu in 1980, where Britain had to send troops to make this union of French and British territories work. On Fiji, an island where the native Melanesians were outnumbered by an Indian population imported by Britain to staff the plantations, the legacy of colonialism came back to haunt the Thatcher government: in 1987, a Melanesian coup destroyed democratic government and took the island out of the Common-wealth.

These south Pacific disputes were primarily within the sphere of influence of the dominant power in the region, Australia. Yet the desire to keep order and retain democracy led some to consider military action (as in Grenada) to restore democracy. Britain, along with Australia, New Zealand and India, was anxious to find some concerted action that would undo the new racist policies. But the Melanesians had support from other Pacific islands and from Commonwealth states which had similar ethnic problems left over from British colonialism, and so the hand of the interventionists was stayed. Britain, with the policy of opposing sanctions against South Africa fresh in Prime Minister Thatcher's mind, did not openly join the interventionists. Thus the Commonwealth failed to act, although even in its inaction Britain was still very much involved in the crises of the south Pacific.

Britain Comes Back

It is fashionable, even among British scholars, to highlight the descent from imperial power, the failure of the colonial legacy and the retreat to the fringe of Europe. But even if the image was once accurate, by the Thatcher years of the 1980s it was certainly wrong. Britain is back in Asia, not as an imperialist power but as an active leader of the international capitalist economy and a supporter of its multilateral security arrangements. Britain's interest is not always with all its former colonies, but with those that prosper. Its main interest is in the international market economy.

In international economic terms, Britain now does more trade with Asia than anywhere bar Europe or North America. Although its trade with Asia is well down from the heights of colonial days, it is now more important for Britain than at any time in the last fifteen years (see Figure 1). It is true that in 1960 British trade with Germany was one-quarter of its total trade with Asia, whereas now Asian trade is worth only three-quarters of Anglo-German trade. But trade with Asia is now worth more than the supposedly 'special' Anglo-American trade. In 1980, Anglo-Middle East trade was twice that with Asia, but by 1986 trade with Asia was one-third higher. By the late 1980s, Asia was allocated nearly a quarter of Foreign Office resources and its percentage was increasing, particularly for the coverage of Japan and China.

The explanation, of course, is that a more prosperous Britain, and one with the market orientations of the Thatcher administration, likes to trade with developed states. When freed of colonial obligations, it has concentrated on the nearby markets of Europe or the developed economies of North America. When the Middle East offered good markets, they too were exploited. But now it is the turn of east Asia to develop and, unlike the shallow boom of the Middle East, east Asia and its NICs are likely to draw increasing amounts of British business.

The obvious prime example is Japan, now the most important Asian actor for Britain. Asia, and especially east Asia, is seen primarily in economic terms. With fewer wars in the region and the failure of south Asian states to develop, Britain, like much of the rest of the developed world, is coming to think of Asia as east Asia, and developed east Asia at that. The developing world, especially as seen in east Asia, is far more complex than described in the images

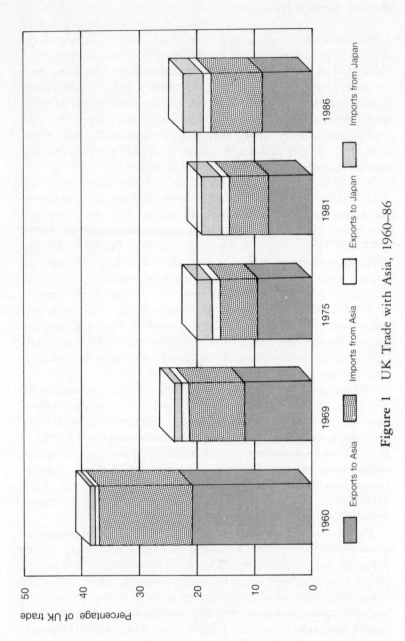

Figure 1 UK Trade with Asia, 1960–86

of dependency theory. The challenge for Britain in the 1980s and beyond is how to keep its economy vibrant enough to compete with its new partners in the international world.

In terms of international security, Britain's interest in Asia has changed, but has not been eliminated entirely. Britain is still a member of the only multilateral regional security scheme and sends ships to exercise in Asian and Pacific waters. Britain certainly recognises, as the 1987 INF agreement makes clear, that the security of Asia and the security of Europe cannot be separated. One of the most important implications of the nuclear revolution – genuine international security – has helped shape British security policy.

Even in the realm of ideas and culture, the Asia and Pacific region and Britain are closer than ever. Britain is now urged to learn management skills from Japan and new economic principles from the NICs. The British certainly have a better cuisine as a result of the Chinese, Indian and Malay immigrants. The arts are enriched by Eastern images in film, literature and modern design.

The new relationship is recognisably different from the imperial model. Especially in the Thatcher years, new ideas and analyses are required of the very different British foreign policy. While British companies sell in Asian markets, so Asian multinationals penetrate British markets and employ British youth. Capital also flows both ways. Of course all these changes mean Britain is less militarily powerful in Asia than it once was, but then all Europeans, and even the superpowers, have suffered that fate. The new power in booming east Asia is more economic and financial. The new Asia is also more challenging, but in a fair fight with its competitors Britain is already showing it has a great deal to contribute to, and gain from, Asia.

References and Further Reading

Barber, J. (1986) 'Britain and India', *The World Today*, December.
Boardman, R. (1976) *Britain and the People's Republic of China*, Macmillan.
Foot, R. (1985) *The Wrong War*, Cornell University Press.
Frankel, F. (1981) 'British–Japanese relations', *The World Today*, August–September.
Hocking, B. and Warhurst, J. (1986) 'Australia and Britain', *The World Today*, December.

Kennedy, P. (1988) *The Rise and Fall of Great Powers*, Unwin Hyman.

Kershaw, R. (1983) 'Anglo-Malaysian relations', *International Affairs*, vol. 59, no. 4.

Lapping, B. (1985) *End of Empire*, Granada.

Lowe, P. (1981) *Britain in the Far East*, Longman.

Moreton, E. (1987) 'The view from London' in Gordon, L. *et al.*, *Eroding Empire*, Brookings, Washington.

Nish, I. (1977) *The Anglo-Japanese Alliance*, Greenwood.

Segal, G. (1982) *The Great Power Triangle*, Macmillan.

Thorne, C. (1978) *Allies of a Kind*, Hamish Hamilton.

Williams, J. (1987) 'ANZUS: a blow to British self-esteem', *Review of International Studies*, vol. 13, no. 4.

CHAPTER 7

Anglo–Argentine Relations and the Management of the Falklands Question

WALTER LITTLE

The origins of the Falklands War of 1982 are well-known. On the British side, governments of both parties had sought a negotiated settlement with Argentina in which the Argentine claims for sovereignty would be met and the desire of the islanders to retain a British way of life safeguarded. A formal transfer of sovereignty with a 'lease-back' of the territory to Britain for a long period was the preferred solution. However, parliamentary opposition to such a deal was strong and the diplomatic negotiations were never completely tied up. Pressure within Argentina for a military solution increased. The British government misread the signs and compounded the error by deciding to withdraw the naval presence of HMS *Endurance*. Argentina concluded that a *coup de main* would succeed: in 1982 Argentina invaded the islands and overcame the tiny British military presence.

The fighting in the south Atlantic in 1982 was real enough but in their war of words Britain and Argentina referred merely to 'engagement', 'hostilities', 'conflict' and even the supremely vague 'events'. To many this opaque language seemed surreally at odds with the reality of death and destruction but under the particular circumstances it was quite a rational thing for them to do.

It was clear that neither nation's basic survival was at stake and, though each government enjoyed a momentary boost in its public standing, neither was particularly popular at the time and neither wished to have to confess to its citizens that its miscalculations about the other's intentions had led the nation to war. Furthermore, though each side made great play about the inflexibility of the other, neither wanted to be branded an aggressor in the eyes of third parties. Thus Argentina stressed not only its legal claims but also the 'peaceful' nature of the islands' seizure and the 'disproportionate' nature of the British response. Britain, on rather more solid legal grounds, cited the self-defence provision of Article 51 of the UN Charter. What neither was prepared to admit publicly was they were formally at war.

Their preference for what many felt were weasel words was also a reflection of the need each felt for flexibility in the management of the crisis. Neither could be certain about battlefield outcomes and neither was in a hurry to abandon the diplomatic option, and to have entered into a state of war would have meant its precipitate foreclosure and with it political isolation. And even after the fighting had started in earnest neither combatant wished to have its hands tied more than was necessary in respect of rules of engagement, the disposal of enemy assets, the treatment of enemy aliens and the neutrality of third parties.

But it was above all a reflection of a tacit agreement that their differences were to do with the islands and that they should not be allowed to overspill into other areas. Thus while Britain may have had observers on the Argentine mainland there was never any question of them taking any military action; and for its part, Argentina refrained from attacking Britain's extended supply line. Similarly, though each side suspended trade and restricted the operation of the other's economic assets, none of the latter were seized and neither state harassed the citizens of the other. Both sides accepted that their ends were limited along with the legal corollary that the means used to obtain them should be proportionate. Indeed, the Belgrano affair became a *cause célèbre* precisely because it seemed to breach this principle of proportionality and, with it, Mrs Thatcher's moral armour. Privately, many Argentine diplomats regard the debate over it in the UK as an unhelpful diversion from the main issue.

Convenient and necessary though it was for everyone to regard the dispute as somehow falling short of war, this self-limitation implied that regardless of how the fighting turned out there could be no 'winners' and 'losers' in the normal sense. Hence whilst Argentine troops laid down their arms their government did not admit defeat and no armistice was signed or peace treaty negotiated. The status quo ante had to a degree been restored and with it the immediate question of continued possession or recovery had been resolved — but the basic problem of who should exercise sovereignty over the islands remained as intractable as ever.

This helps to explain why it is that some six years after the fighting stopped Argentina and Britain remain at loggerheads over the future of the islands. There has been some relaxation of control in respect of investments and visas and there have been talks over other issues such as the Antarctic and the rescheduling of Argentina's debt. But trade remains vestigial and diplomatic contact tightly constrained. Moreover, though there have been no military clashes, talks to normalise relations have not only failed to close the gap between the two sides but may even have exacerbated their differences.

Stalemate

Once the fighting had stopped the immediate question of the cessation of hostilities came to the fore. Here the pressure was felt most acutely on the British side since local logistical difficulties and strategic imperatives elsewhere meant that the Task Force could not be kept for any length of time on the islands. Consequently there was a need for some assurance that any relaxation of a state of maximum alert would not increase the likelihood of Argentina resuming military action. Even minor sorties (which were well within Argentine capabilities) would serve to confound reconstruction and withdrawal.

This strategic weakness was of course not lost on Argentina, which from the very outset perceived the British desire for a formal ending of hostilities as a bargaining card not to be lightly thrown away. Agreement of a sort was reached in July 1982 but it was on the understanding that hostilities had only ceased in the *de facto* sense. This compromise was perhaps the best that could be expected. After all, war had never been declared in the first place

and if discussions formally to end hostilities ensured their
continuance then clearly a fudged resolution was to be preferred.
But the fact that there was no treaty, no reparations, no resumption
of diplomatic relations and no lifting of the exclusion zones or of
trade restrictions indicated that the fighting had done nothing to
resolve the broader dispute.

In the months that followed, although the British repeatedly
stressed their desire for a return to normal relations, it also seems
that they sought to present what were insubstantial adjustments to
the situation as if they were concessions to which Argentina ought to
have responded. For example, when the 200-mile exclusion zone
around the islands was replaced by a 150-mile protection zone to
which Argentine vessels might have access this was advanced as an
earnest of good intent. The fact that the move reflected logistical
rather than diplomatic imperatives and that any Argentine access
would require prior British permission (and hence could be
interpreted as constituting recognition of sovereign rights) was not
lost on Argentina. The distinction between exclusion and protection
has never led to access being requested or granted.

A similar fate befell the suggestion that if Argentina were
formally to declare an end to hostilities then it might be possible to
reduce the size of the garrison and so contribute to the demilitarisa-
tion of the region. As reconstruction progressed and new defence
arrangements were introduced it was inevitable that the number of
troops deployed in the islands would fall. The fact that Britain
wished to reduce troop levels and that this would not significantly
diminish defensive capability was not lost on the Argentines, who
continued to argue that the British were in fact militarising the
region.

It has sometimes been suggested that a different attitude on
Argentina's part might have forestalled this decision. Throughout
1982 and 1983 the interim military regime refused to accede to the
British request to end hostilities formally. Officially this was on the
ground that since hostilities had never been declared in the first
place it was not necessary, but the refusal seems to have had other
motivations. One was pique on the part of the beleaguered military
at having experienced defeat in the area of national defence from
which they had always sought to draw legitimacy. Secondly, there
seems to have been a feeling (legally incorrect) that formally to end
hostilities would in some way constitute a recognition of the

'rightness' of the British military response and hence of their sovereign claim. Thirdly, the junta appeared to believe that by refusing to end hostilities they could significantly increase the cost of defending the islands and that in the long run this would bring the British to the negotiating table. To have formally ended hostilities would not preclude their future resumption but would, they felt, let the British off the hook.

However, there is no reason to doubt the sincerity of Britain's desire to normalise relations with Argentina. Such a step would have justified the recovery of the islands, lowered the cost of maintaining them and reduced the diplomatic embarrassment of defending their colonial status. But equally, the British recognised that their insistence that sovereignty could not be discussed as part of a normalisation package (or indeed, in any other context) meant that it would not come about. The most that could be said for this policy was that the presently unattainable might at some point in the future become attainable. More concretely, the British felt that in view of the state of domestic political opinion and the discredited and divided nature of the junta it was best to wait for the return of civilians to power. The hope was that a new government, untainted by defeat, might be sufficiently flexible so as to allow at least for some improvement in atmosphere.

Indeed, at first it seemed as though this might be on the cards. Although in the pre-electoral period Alfonsin had taken a fairly hard line this was soon dropped. Within days of his inauguration he spoke favourably of the idea of lease-back and argued that 'where there's a will, there's a way'. Though the British continued to insist that sovereignty was not for discussion, there was a distinct thaw in the attitudes and public statements of both sides.

In the months that followed Argentina assumed the initiative previously held by the UK. At a public level Alfonsin's personal initiatives (involving, for example, UN mediation, a special statute for the islanders, and so on) seem to have been designed principally as ways of distinguishing his government from its predecessor especially in the eyes of third parties, but privately the Argentines were pushing more concrete proposals. As early as January 1984 they indicated their desire to establish direct communications and their willingness to downgrade the sovereignty issue in order to allow this to take place. This downgrading involved the following formula: the formal cessation of hostilities; the lifting of the protection zone; the restoration of diplomatic and commercial relations; and the reduction of the garrison. Once these steps had been taken open talks could resume.

The British response was considerably more muted. Convinced that Argentina regarded normalisation not as an end worthy in itself but simply as a means of restarting talks on sovereignty, it was restricted to the possible return (they were careful to avoid the loaded term 'repatriation') of Argentine war dead to the mainland, the resumption of trade, financial and commercial links, and the restoration of direct diplomatic contacts. Argentine suggestions of third-party involvement, garrison run-down and open agendas were clearly not acceptable. To the Prime Minister at least it seemed as if the Argentines were refusing to acknowledge that things had changed as a result of their seizure of the islands. To the Argentines it seemed as if the British were incapable of understanding the changes that had taken place in Argentina. The extent to which governments can be held accountable for their predecessors' actions is moot. Foreign Minister Caputo has rejected the view that Argentina must 'atone' for the military's use of force which his government has since condemned and foresworn.

The position was thus that the British were prepared to discuss everything except the one thing that Argentina wanted. Argentina, for its part, was interested primarily in discussing the one thing that the British had declared they could not discuss. Several months of bad-tempered exchanges followed and it was not until July of 1984 that a way out of the dilemma was found. This consisted of the formula that if a normalisation meeting was held the Argentines could raise the sovereignty issue, the British would then decline to discuss it and so face would be saved on both sides. Unfortunately when the two sides met in Berne in late July this delicate formula broke down almost immediately with each side accusing the other of having reinterpreted the formula at the last moment. Whatever the truth of the matter it indicated that the dispute was one of substance that would not be readily resolved. It also meant that each side learnt that ambiguous language could not disguise the fact that each regarded sovereignty as indivisible and hence non-negotiable.

Since this débâcle at Berne the gulf between the two sides has, if anything, widened. There have been gestures – in July 1985 the UK lifted the trade ban and Argentina responded by offering an end to hostilities in return for talks – but they have been generally unilateral in character and dismissed by the other side as window-dressing. Both sides seem to have resigned themselves to the fact that nothing can be done even in the medium term and that this stand-off is preferable to another failed *rapprochement*.

There have also been objective changes to the situation with the passage of time. The British reconstruction of the islands' defences has been completed and their costs have fallen, if not by as much as is officially claimed. The islanders have a greater degree of self-government, and influence within their community is now more diversified than previously. Above all the declaration at the end of October 1986 of the Interim Conservation and Management Zone around the islands has created a new prosperity and a new self-confidence about the long-term viability of island society and economy. Accordingly, there is significantly more interest vested in the status quo than used to be the case.

The failure of Britain and Argentina to agree to the multilateral management of marine resources around the islands is a clear indication of the distance between them. For several years the Foreign Office resisted efforts by the islanders to declare a licensed fishing zone and sought instead agreement with Argentina under the auspices of the Food and Agriculture Organisation of the UN. This came to nothing because of the Argentine conviction that any such agreement would amount to a weakening of their claim to sovereignty and would constitute an unacceptable precedent. The result of this impasse (an Argentine–Soviet fishing agreement followed by a unilateral – albeit interim – British declaration of an exclusive zone) has been to render the dispute more intractable than at any time since 1982.

It has been suggested that poor communications may be to blame for this state of affairs. It is true that the language deployed by each side differs (Argentina adopting a juridicial style, Britain a pragmatic one) and that channels of communication through the protecting powers (respectively Brazil and Switzerland) are clumsy. It is also true that each side generally has a weather eye open for third-party opinion both domestic and foreign and this can confuse messages. But against this must be set the fact that private channels do exist, that each side is aware of the other's constraints and that each knows the other's arguments to the point where every nuance is not merely familiar but tedious. A communications problem may well have existed prior to 1982 but now the problem is an objective one concerning sovereignty.

The Sovereignty Issue

Sovereignty has proved to be a major stumbling block because each side has taken sovereignty to be indivisible and absolute; that is, something to be enjoyed to the full or not at all. When title is undisputed or has a clear legal basis no difficulties arise (at least in law) but this is manifestly not so in the case of the Falklands.

The Argentine case rests essentially on the following propositions: that Spain enjoyed sovereignty in the eighteenth century; that this was inherited by Argentina (*uti possidetis juris*); that acts of occupation and administration were performed in the 1820s; that the British used illegal force in 1833; that Argentina subsequently protested; and that the islands are, through contiguity, an integral part of the national territory. The British case comprises the following: that the islands belonged to no one (were *terra nullius*) after 1811 when the Spaniards withdrew; that Argentine acts in the 1820s did not constitute effective occupation; that their occupation in 1833 was not illegal at the time and that the doctrine of intertemporal law should apply; that prescriptive rights were acquired in the 149 years of peaceful and effective occupation that followed; that the Argentine action of 1982 was clearly illegal; and that the principles of self-determination enshrined in the UN Charter apply to the Falklands.

The subordinate arguments that have been cited – concerning discovery, the nature of effective protest in the 1820s, the Nootka Sound Convention of 1790, settlement between 1766 and 1774 among others – are nowadays rarely deployed seriously. As international law doctrines have themselves evolved, so the kinds of argument used have shifted. This does not stop the parties disputing what constitutes effective protest and the like but it means that the main principles invoked today are those of territorial integrity and self-determination.

Unfortunately international law is necessarily vague about these essentially political principles. Applied crudely, territorial integrity has profoundly destabilising implications. For its part, self-determination raises unanswerable questions as to what constitutes a 'people'. The dispute may not in fact be justiciable. Neither side has an iron-clad case – though Argentina's claim to the Falkland Islands Dependencies of South Georgia and South Sandwich has no basis in international law – but neither will admit it (Goebel 1982, Foreign Affairs Committee 1983).

An illustration of the shortcomings of the absolutist approach to sovereignty might be useful. If Argentina is in the right then it has enjoyed sovereignty over the islands since Spain left them in 1811; the fact that it has only exercised it briefly prior to 1833 and in 1982 does not affect this right. If the UK is in the right then it has enjoyed sovereignty since 1833 apart from a brief interlude in 1982. However, if sovereignty is a function of power rather than of right then it was enjoyed by Argentina before 1833, by Britain between 1833 and 1982, by Argentina again in 1982, and by Britain yet again since then. These are logically consistent ways of looking at the matter but they are not helpful in resolving the very real problem which exists.

The British Political Context

Repeated polls have shown that the British public is generally unhappy about the present impasse and would like to see it resolved, but has no clear idea of how this might be done or what kind of political future the islands should have. A majority believes that the islanders' interests must be safeguarded and their wishes taken into account, but in a 1986 poll only 38 per cent believed that the best way of ensuring this was through continued British sovereignty. When asked what was the best long-term solution, a further 10 per cent opted for devolution to Argentina, 6 per cent for lease-back, 13 per cent for joint control and 19 per cent for UN administration.

In general, Conservative sympathisers are more hardline than those of the Liberal and Social Democratic parties, who in turn are less conciliatory than Labour supporters. However, all groups are concerned about cost – a clear majority disbelieves that they are indefinitely sustainable – and all party groups are internally divided. The fact that around a third of Labour supporters are hardline while an equal proportion of their Tory counterparts are conciliatory is important because it blurs the message being sent to decision makers. Quite apart from low salience – MPs are hardly inundated with letters on the subject – no set of party sympathisers is unequivocally identified with a particular view. Given the high centralised nature of executive power in Britain and the size of the present government's majority, it is inconceivable that any doubts the electorate might have will impinge on policy making. Indeed the reverse is more likely, for those who do have reservations are divided as to the future they would like to see, while the hard core of 30–40 per cent who oppose compromise not only have a clear preference (the status quo) but also seem to feel strongly enough about it to make their views felt in the event of their being questioned.

Yet within the Conservative party there is considerable dissent, at least at Westminster. Ministers, of course, toe the official line but not with any enthusiasm. On the back-benches there are roughly three groups with a clear view: those who seek to outdo the Prime Minister in their support for the islanders, those who have reservations about the cost of the policy, and those who actively urge some accommodation with Argentina.

The hardliners have a particularly coherent position. Firstly, they argue that there is no certainty that democracy will prosper in Argentina and that even if some agreement is reached it could well be ignored by some future military government. Every detail of human-rights abuse that emerges thus strengthens the hands of those who argue that the islands must on no account be exposed to the sort of risks that Argentine citizens have run in the past and may do in the future. Secondly, they claim that the major costs have already been incurred (and cannot be recovered) and that Britain is now in a position to exploit the natural resources and strategic potential of the area. But the real strength of their position is emotional. The recovery of the islands, they claim, restored national honour, unity and sense of purpose. After decades of drift and compromise it showed the world that Britain was not to be trifled with.

Critics within the Conservative party are in a more difficult position. Their arguments about cost and the distortion of defence priorities have some strength but they are weakened by the fact that they are unable publicly to embrace the logic of abandonment. Though generally complimentary about the new Argentine government they have no clear idea of how the sovereignty issue might be resolved. They are consequently limited to the anodyne position that the parties should sit down and talk, a strategem that has failed once already.

Nor have the opposition parties been able to contribute very much to the debate. They have made it clear that they would enter into talks and that sovereignty would be on the agenda. But at the same time they have been forced to acknowledge that they would not accept any preconditions as to the ultimate location of sovereignty. The islanders' wishes cannot be paramount but they cannot be ignored either. Liberal and SDP speakers have been more explicit than Labour in suggesting that the UN should be involved, but they too perceive that the issue could generate popular nationalism which may work to their electoral disadvantage.

Extra-political associations have not had much impact either. Church groups in particular have been critical of British policy but are open to the charge that, as a secular matter, it is none of their business. Business groups hurt by the loss of trade are reluctant to criticise a government that has done so much for them in other respects. The financial sector has found that it is business as usual.

Lastly, doubts within Whitehall about the wisdom of Falklands policy have failed to have a moderating influence. It is clear that officials in the Foreign Office and Ministry of Defence regard the present situation as a costly diversion from the core commitment to Europe and the Atlantic Alliance. The Treasury is unhappy about costs and the Overseas Development Agency about the disproportionate amount of development aid being channelled to the islands, while the Department of Trade regrets the loss of Britain's commercial links with Argentina. But none feels especially intensely about the matter and none has risked the Prime Minister's wrath by advocating alternatives.

As a result Mrs Thatcher has enjoyed a free hand in making policy and there is no doubt that it is her creation. While she has repeatedly expressed her desire to normalise relations, she has made it clear that she does not expect normalisation to be forthcoming. She recognises Argentina's reluctance to exclude discussions about sovereignty from any normalisation process and is dismissive about attempts to introduce it in a different guise. For example when in 1985 the Argentines used the code phrase 'all aspects' to subsume the question, she retorted, 'Anyone who thinks "all aspects" does not contain sovereignty must be bonkers' (*Hansard*, 28 November 1985, col. 1009).

Nevertheless, the stridency of her language has to some degree obscured her real position. Though constantly stressing the applicability of the principle of self-determination and her conviction that the islanders' wishes should be honoured, she has acknowledged that they are in no way paramount. The likelihood of the islanders changing their 'wishes' is non-existent for so long as she promises to respect them, but there is no reason to suppose that she would not welcome a change. The problem arises out of the fact that she has painted herself into a corner. Believing, perhaps incorrectly, that her election victory in 1983 was in part due to the Falklands factor (Sanders *et al.* 1987) she has become a prisoner of her past actions and the rhetoric that has followed them. For her to change policy now would be tantamount to admitting that she had let British troops die in vain and this is politically and personally impossible. For so long as she is in power no change can be expected in British policy.

The Islanders and their Lobby

The popular image of the Falkland Islands, deriving perhaps from a superficial similarity with the Shetlands, is one of a sturdy crofting community. This belies the complexity of a society which is based on large-scale sheep ranching (of an Argentine character) and which has been thrust into the forefront of world opinion. Despite its small size, its community is surprisingly diverse. Government employees, contract expatriates, Falkland Island Company employees, independent farmers, farm managers and labourers have distinct if overlapping interests. This is compounded by the differences between Stanley and camp residents, in income levels (higher expatriate salaries are much resented by locals), education, and personal and family reputations. It is not, then, as homogenous a society as it might seem.

However, the sense of threat which the islanders have felt since Britain began talking in earnest with Argentina in 1968 has had a unifying effect at the political level. Their small numbers and reliance upon (easily eavesdropped) radio communication makes for the rapid spread of information (and disinformation) and the threat of ostracism encourages circumspection. Though privately often deeply critical of the British government, they are reluctant to seem ungrateful or divided in their views.

Of their first preference there is no doubt. The vast majority wish to see continued British administration. Individual hardliners have at times argued for greater autonomy (not unlike the Channel

Islands) but always with the proviso of a British defence umbrella. At the same time there are undercurrents of fear and insecurity. Islanders are well aware that for years the Foreign Office sought to persuade them to accept an Argentine presence and they suspect (rightly) that this is still its preference. For example, when Foreign and Commonwealth Office staff visited the islands in late 1984 to discuss the draft constitution they were greeted with slogans of 'betrayal'. One islander told me, only half in jest, that the FCO was a greater threat than either Argentina or the UN. They are also acutely conscious of the fact that the opposition parties are committed to talks and regard their reservations as mere window-dressing. They are above all aware that they have few friends in the world and that Mrs Thatcher will not be Prime Minister for ever.

In another respect the image of a simple society is misleading. Many of the better-educated islanders are politically sophisticated and since 1968 have conducted an impressive lobbying campaign in the British press and Parliament. Indeed some of their influence stems precisely from the skill with which they have been able to present themselves as a small people caught in the millstones of power politics. But most of all it comes from the clarity of their goals and the single-mindedness with which they pursue them.

They have been assisted in this by the more chauvinist popular press in moments of crisis and more routinely by the establishment press which gives space for lobbying campaigns, such as the recently successful fishing zone lobby. They have also been helped by conservation-minded peers such as Lords Shackleton and Buxton who are often ready to help set the political agenda to their advantage. At present the lobby comprises the Falkland Islands Committee with branches in London and Stanley, the rather better financed but less political Falkland Islands Association, and a cross-party group of some 30 MPs.

Up to now the islanders have not been asked to make hard choices. The status quo has brought prosperity and more security than they have enjoyed for any time in the last twenty years. More, the greater representation available under the new constitution of 1985 – though it falls far short of anything like the home rule that some would like – and the financial viability created by fishing licensing has given the islanders a new confidence about their future. Even more than in the past, then, they are a party to the dispute.

Argentine Opinion

Many in the UK do not understand why the Argentines should want such an apparently marginal and unattractive piece of territory as the Falkland Islands. Those professionally concerned with the issue do recognise the strength of Argentine feeling on the matter and assume that any Argentine government which made serious concessions over sovereignty (or could be represented by its opponents as having done so) would not only run into serious political trouble but would be likely to fall and be replaced by a much more intransigent and irredentist one. In this sense even if some agreement could be fudged it might be short-lived and perhaps seriously counterproductive.

How well founded is this assumption that Argentine opinion is so monolithically and passionately concerned to recover the islands? Firstly, the islands have a low salience. A recent poll conducted by the Aftalion, Mora y Araujo and Nogera firm in Buenos Aires reported that only 1 per cent of those questioned considered it to be Argentina's main problem, with only a further 7 per cent identifying it second or third in terms of seriousness. Moreover, when asked whether Argentina should consider pursuing the dispute by means of force, only 4 per cent were in agreement, while some 64 per cent favoured the restoration of diplomatic relations with the UK.

However, this low salience is accompanied by overwhelming agreement that the islands belonged to Argentina, were stolen by the British and should be recovered. When asked by what means they might be recovered some 34 per cent of those polled replied that Argentina should unilaterally demand their unconditional return. Forty-seven per cent were prepared to see their government negotiate the issue of sovereignty (with a view to its return to Argentina) but only 15 per cent were prepared to countenance negotiations without explicit reference to the sovereignty issue. Thus while passions may not be quite as high as is sometimes claimed it is clear that the vast majority of Argentines remain convinced of the rightness of their claim.

When the issue of long-term solutions was raised a broadly similar spread of views seemed to be evident. Around 26 per cent of those who responded were able to accept the idea that there might be some future 'sharing' of sovereignty with the UK but, unlike those who wanted exclusive sovereignty, they did not feel especially committed to the idea. Lastly, when asked about what role the islanders might have to play, only 16 per cent acknowledged that they might have a major say whilst no less than 36 per cent said that they had no status at all in the dispute.

Amongst the political class in Argentina there is a rather different attitude. Government and opposition leaders now realise the importance which the islanders have for Britain. Over the last three years and with increasing frequency they have stressed their willingness to guarantee their way of life and have offered specific concessions – including language, maintenance of law and custom, local fiscal and tax autonomy, but falling short of control of immigration and land purchase – which would never previously have been acceptable. For obvious reasons, however, they cannot accept that the islanders' wishes as distinct from their interests should be the decisive factor.

However, a striking element in the new democratic system is the extent to which it is perceived locally as not merely a re-run of democracy but something qualitatively distinct. For the first time in Argentine history, political opinion accepts that democracy has both rules and costs and that consensus is in the long run preferable to partisan extremism. This has yet to be translated into effective and concrete policy making – though it was clearly evident in the way all shades of opinion rallied in support of Alfonsin when the military revolted in Easter of 1987 – but there is undoubtedly a new pragmatism and openness in Argentine political life.

There is evidence of this in respect of the Falklands both at popular and élite level. For example in the period from June 1984 to April 1986 the proportion of those polled who favoured a unilateral demand for the islands' return fell from 52 to 34 per cent while those who preferred negotiations to that end rose from 42 to 62 per cent. This softening of attitudes towards means (if not ends) is a reflection of a general awareness that Argentina needs to become a fuller member of the international community as a third-level but respectable actor.

These attitudes are especially pronounced within the government. President Alfonsin and Foreign Minister Caputo are well aware that under the military Argentina had become not only isolated but even something of a pariah as a result of its human-rights record, its unsavoury activities in Central America at the behest of the USA and

its invasion of the islands. The Argentine government's high profile
in regional North–South and EC–Latin American affairs reflects
their conviction that foreign policy has a part to play in the
consolidation of democracy. In particular, co-operation with
neighbours – there has been a major *rapprochement* with the
traditional rival Brazil in recent years – is an essential part of the
government's wish to deny political space to the military.

Though priority in foreign affairs is inevitably given to the
question of debt, the issue of the south Atlantic still looms large.
The Argentine contention, and it appears to be sincerely held, is
that the area has become militarised and that it consequently has a
potential to become unstable. Such a view should not be
discounted – though it generally is in the UK – simply because it is
a convenient one for Argentina to adopt. The fact remains that even
a liberal government like the present one cannot compromise the
principle of Argentine sovereignty over the islands.

Security Issues

Within a year of the Argentine surrender the British made the major
decision to restructure the defence of the islands. Prior to the war
this had consisted of a handful of marines who were intended to act
as a tripwire deterrent. Clearly this had failed and it was generally
agreed that any future defensive capability must be substantive and
not merely symbolic. The new arrangements involved the construction of an airfield capable of taking long-haul aircraft so as to allow
rapid reinforcement in time of need, an early-warning detection and
interception capability, ground-to-air missile defences, and enough
rapid-response capability to be able to contain minor landings.

Though the Argentine attitude was sometimes cited by the
British as a reason for the defence restructuring it is moot whether it
actually made much difference. What probably did make a
difference was the fact that in the intervening period before civilians
returned to office the Argentine military, well aware that they were
on the way out and that budgets were likely to be cut in the future
more than made good the losses they had suffered. Secondly, it was
clear that defence commitments elsewhere prohibited the maintenance of a conventional garrison sufficient to deter any repeat
invasion. Restructuring would not only meet perceived defensive

needs but do so at a much reduced cost in the long to medium term. It would also, of course, significantly increase the British commitment to the islands. Though the British have repeatedly stressed that their purpose was wholly defensive – ministers and officials make a point of objecting to the use of the term 'Fortress Falklands' – it does represent an investment which may make an eventual agreement more difficult than it might otherwise be.

At present the likelihood of any military confrontation in the area is minimal. Britain and Argentina accept that this would be in no one's interest and have successfully agreed on measures to ensure that the recently installed fishing conservation zone does not lead to clashes which might escalate into something worse. But the potential for armed conflict undoubtedly does exist.

It is clear that one of the reasons why Argentina lost the 1982 conflict was because they never expected to have to fight for the islands at all. Their assumption was that the invasion would be reluctantly accepted by the British as a *fait accompli* – the invasion was even referred to as 'Plan Goa' – and that some face-saving diplomatic solution involving temporary Argentine withdrawal would be reached. Consequently, when it came to fighting they found that they were seriously deficient in a number of areas.

These deficiencies have now been made good. In 1982 Argentina had 130 interceptor/strike aircraft; by 1985 it had 160, many of them close to state-of-the-art. In 1982 it had two modern submarines and five modern escorts; by the late-1980s it will have eight submarines and fifteen escorts. In the same period the stock of Exocet-type, air-to-surface, anti-shipping missiles has increased five- or sixfold. Finally, the Argentine armed forces have acquired air-to-air refuelling capabilities, anti-runway munitions, some over-the-horizon, strike-direction capacity and improved anti-submarine warfare aircraft.

The British justification to Parliament for defence reconstruction stressed the savings to be made. In the period 1982–7 some £3,010 million have been spent and the official estimate of annual garrisoning costs from 1988 onwards amounts to around £100 million per year. When compared with expenditure in 1984–5 of nearly £700 million, the case would seem to have been made. However there are a number of dimensions to this apparently reduced commitment which need to be stressed more than they have been.

First, the figures are based on marginal rather than full costs. Here the argument is that troops have to be paid, fed and clothed regardless of where they are based and, in view of the good training facilities in the islands, they might as well be there as elsewhere. Such an argument, however, does not meet the objection that if they are there they cannot be elsewhere – that is, either troop levels for European defence are too high or there are shortcomings in that defence. Precisely the same objection can be raised in connection with naval deployment in the south Atlantic. Secondly, the garrison generally requires state-of-the-art equipment which is both expensive to maintain and requires higher than normal complements of skilled (and consequently scarce) manpower. Lastly, it is far from clear to what extent the official figures include domestic and other (i.e. Ascension Island) support costs.

What is clear is that the south Atlantic commitment (when coupled with that of the Gulf and that of Belize) has imposed a very considerable burden on Britain's defence role within Nato. Two years after the completion of the airfield some three thousand troops are still deployed at a probable real cost of several hundred million pounds per year. Up to now these costs have been met outside the main defence budget but from the end of the decade they will be subsumed within it. In the context of major projected cuts in non-nuclear defence spending over the next few years, Falklands expenditure is likely to come under much greater scrutiny than has been the case in the past. But this is not to say that it will not continue. Though defence analysts and the army are far from happy about what they privately regard as a diversion from Britain's real priorities – the navy, having been 'saved' by the war is less discontented with out-of-area commitments – their reservations are not likely to bring about major change. For so long as the political will to continue paying for the garrison exists then the garrison will continue.

However, there is a worst-case scenario which has been avoided up to now but cannot be wholly discounted in the future. This requires Argentina to lose patience with the diplomatic approach and opt for a policy of raising the ante, short of outright attack. An aggressive policy of feint and/or incursion falling short of invasion (which the present garrison could render at least problematic) would massively increase garrisoning costs with virtually no military risk to Argentina. Even very-low-intensity actions of a harassing rather than hostile nature would require at least a doubling or more of the current deployment and its costs. To date Argentina has not taken up this option – the few incidents in 1983 hardly count and may not have been the result of considered policy in any event – but it is one which remains open to them in the future.

Conclusion

There are no signs that this dispute is anywhere near resolution. Both sides profess their reasonableness. Thus Argentina claims that it merely wishes to discuss but not to prejudge sovereignty. For its part, Britain argues that the restoration of friendly relations should be the main goal, a policy seen by Argentina merely as a device to forestall the sovereignty issue altogether, for once relations are restored Britain would be under no pressure to go further. This in turn is seen by the British as evidence of the fact that Argentina would not be content simply to discuss sovereignty.

For Argentina the present impasse is unfortunate but it is relatively costless. Even for Britain the costs are not unbearable. Annual embarrassment in the UN whenever the matter is debated and admonitions from the USA and the EC do not amount to irresistible pressure. Even Britain's relations with Latin America (almost exclusively economic) have not been seriously damaged. Britain's commitment to the islands is undoubtedly less than Argentina's but for so long as Mrs Thatcher remains at the helm there is unlikely to be any movement. Moreover, whoever succeeds her is likely to find that the search for a compromise will be arduous and politically costly.

Technical solutions to the dispute abound – involving internationalisation, delay, splitting up sovereignty, etc. – but until the will to embrace them exists they remain mere speculation. The Falklands is a poignant reminder of the dragons' teeth sown by colonialism and the dilemmas of small peoples in a world of nation states.

References and Further Reading

For general accounts of the dispute see Hastings, M. and Jenkins, S. (1983) *The Battle for the Falklands*, Michael Joseph; Sunday Times Insight Team (1982) *The*

Falklands War, Sphere; and Coll, A.R. and Arend, A.C. (eds) (1985) *The Falklands War: Lessons for Strategy, Diplomacy and International Law*, Allen & Unwin. For an Argentine perspective see Cardoso, O.R. *et al.* (1987) *Falklands: The Secret Plot*, Preston Editions; and Gamba, V. (1987) *The Falklands/Malvinas War: A Model for North–South Crisis Prevention*, Allen & Unwin. The most informative account of the evolution of British policy prior to 1982 can be found in Lord Franks' *Falkland Islands Review* (1983) Cmnd 8787, HMSO.

Foreign Affairs Committee (1982–3) *Falkland Islands*, HC31.

Goebel, J. (1982) *The Struggle for the Falkland Islands*, Yale.

Sanders, D. *et al.* (1987) 'Government popularity and the Falklands War: a reassessment', *British Journal of Political Science*, vol. 17, part 3.

CHAPTER 8

Defence Policy

PETER BYRD

Since 1979 defence has assumed far greater political salience than has been normal in Britain since the Second World War. This politicisation of defence, though encouraged by the government, has not been entirely to its advantage. While, on the one hand, government has emphasised ideological positions – anti-Communism, the community of ties with the United States and a rather crude version of nationalism – on the other hand defence demands massive public expenditures, difficult choices between competing programmes, and quasi-corporatist relationships between state and economy that, in other policy sectors, the government has sought to minimise. Policy difficulties have contributed to a high degree of ministerial instability. One Defence Secretary, Michael Heseltine, and a junior minister, Keith Speed, resigned over policy issues and another Defence Secretary, John Nott, resigned from public life after receiving great public and official criticism of his conduct.

The higher political profile of defence policy can be ascribed partially to developments already in train by 1979 when the new Conservative government took office: the dispute within Nato about the neutron bomb; the shifts in American strategy towards counterforce or, according to its opponents, first-strike doctrines; Nato policies for conventional and nuclear rearmament; above all the breakdown of détente between the superpowers. These factors were largely beyond the control of the government. Two major policy issues were inherited by the government: replacement of Polaris by a new strategic nuclear force, and modernisation of Nato's Intermediate-range Nuclear Forces (INF). In both cases the Callaghan government had not yet come to firm decisions (in the case of INF Nato was still finalising its internal consultations) but the direction of policy was clear – the Labour government was tending strongly towards Trident and towards modernisation of INF. In 1977 it had almost doubled the number of American F1-11 nuclear bombers based in Britain as an interim INF measure. These marked elements of continuity did not prevent defence from becoming an issue in the 1979 election, as the Conservatives pressed home the internal divisions within the Labour party. In 1983 and 1987 the Conservatives capitalised on the advantages presented by Labour's divisions and by its shift of policy towards unilateral nuclear disarmament and what were represented as anti-Nato policies. Although in the period up to the election of 1979, and perhaps beyond to the replacement of Callaghan by Foot and the adoption by Labour of an overtly unilateralist policy, there had been a high degree of bipartisanship on defence; Labour had never seen defence as a major electoral issue. To stress defence overmuch risked exposing the internal opposition to the policies of the Labour leadership and the failure of Labour governments in 1964 and 1974 to implement unilateralist pledges in the election manifesto. The Conservatives felt no such inhibitions and in all three of their election successes sought to maximise the importance of defence as an issue distinguishing themselves from the other parties.

The emphasis in this chapter is on defence as a *policy sector* rather than as a *political arena*. This approach naturally stresses the problems of policy which have confronted the government and the elements of continuity with the pre-1979 period, while playing down the political controversies which would be emphasised if, for instance, one studied the fortunes during this period of the peace movement (Byrd 1985).

Three main issues have dominated the defence policy agenda since 1979: Polaris replacement; relations with Nato allies, and in particular the United States, over the INF issue; and the difficulties of financing defence and meeting a wide range of commitments within a limited budget. These are each studied in turn.

Polaris Replacement

The Polaris force of four (originally to be five) submarines, each firing sixteen missiles, was agreed at the Nassau summit of December 1962 between Macmillan and Kennedy and implemented by the Macmillan, Home and Wilson governments. As early as 1967 preliminary consideration was given to the modernisation of the missiles' warheads. A major programme, codenamed Chevaline, was agreed by the Heath government, implemented in great secrecy and at an alarmingly escalating cost (about £1 billion) by the Wilson and Callaghan governments and was practically completed when the Thatcher government came to power (Committee of Public Accounts 1982). By 1979 the Callaghan government was giving serious attention to the replacement of Polaris/Chevaline, and purchase of the American Trident system was emerging as the best alternative. Trident involved building new submarines, buying the missiles, and developing new warheads and new command and control systems. The election manifestos of 1979 revealed the political problems: while Labour's manifesto obscured the whole issue the Conservatives' emphasised the need for maintaining a national deterrent force. In July 1980 the government announced agreement with President Carter for supply of the Trident C4 (Trident 1) under terms similar to those of the Nassau agreement. Compared with Polaris, Trident offered greater range and hence both more targets in the Soviet Union and, more importantly, a greater area of ocean in which to ensure invulnerability. Trident also offered greater accuracy than Polaris and increased penetration — Trident carried eight warheads per missile compared with the two on the Polaris/Chevaline warhead. The cost was estimated at about £5 billion with a force of four or five submarines.

In 1982 the government amended its policy. It had become clear that the American government saw Trident C4 as a purely interim weapon to be deployed until a weapon of greater range, accuracy and payload, Trident D5 (Trident 2), was available later in the 1980s. Trident 2 offered Britain advantages deriving from deploying the same system as the Americans rather than relying, as had happened with Polaris, on a system no longer deployed by the Americans and for which there were no longer American production lines. The government frankly admitted that the greater range of Trident, its greater accuracy (necessary for American counterforce strategy) and increased striking power (Trident 2 would carry fourteen warheads for the American navy) were irrelevant to Britain's more modest need for a national nuclear force targetted against Soviet cities and in particular Moscow. Similarity of missile equipment with the Americans was the key factor, although the warheads would continue to be produced in Britain. Britain's contribution to the research and development costs was nominal and the only condition attached to the contract was a continuing commitment by the RAF to defend American air bases in Britain with the Rapier short-range ground-to-air missiles (Ministry of Defence 1982). Beyond the stipulations of the contract, purchase of Trident 2 implied a continuing strategic alignment with the United States for the ensuing decades, not only in the narrow military sense – the government decided for instance that it was more economical to rely on America to service the missiles rather than to maintain independent servicing facilities – but also in the broader political–strategic sense.

What were the reasons underlying the government's decision to continue with a nuclear capability, and with Trident in particular? The question of abandoning a nuclear capability appears simply not to have arisen. Since 1947 it has been, in effect, a 'non issue' for all governments. However, whereas governments before 1979 had defended the policy in rather broad terms including national status, world role and responsibility for the disarmament process, since 1979 nuclear capability has been justified in much narrower national security terms. In contrast to earlier broader rationales of the policy by Labour and Conservative governments this has tended to polarise the issue and to weaken the possibility of consensus.

The defence case was threefold. First, that nuclear weapons under national control were the only last-resort deterrent against all-out attack on the British homeland in a situation in which Nato had failed to deter. Secondly, that nuclear weapons were the only effective response against possible Soviet nuclear blackmail intended to coerce a Nato surrender when Nato forces were successfully repelling a conventional attack – a consideration of particular significance given the deployment in forward positions in Germany of the best units of the army and air force. Thirdly, that nuclear weapons deployed by Britain increased Soviet uncertainty about possible Western nuclear response in the event of war. This 'second centre of decision-making argument' was given particular emphasis by the government. It neatly side-stepped awkward questions about whether British nuclear forces implied British uncertainty about the American nuclear guarantee – the existence of any such doubts being strenuously denied – by emphasising instead *Soviet* perceptions of Western behaviour.

Two further general arguments in favour of maintaining a nuclear capability were stated. The first was a belief in the economy of nuclear weapons as a deterrent (an argument going back to its most perfect expression in the Sandys defence statement of 1957) and in particular the proposition that marginal costs strongly favoured nuclear weapons. Which would produce the greater deterrent effect from expenditure of an additional £x billion? Four Trident submarines or twenty additional frigates or a further armoured division in Germany? The answer was self-evident to the government. A second general argument was that a nuclear capability should be maintained to meet any possible future uncertainties and to keep open future options, an argument given powerful inertia by past commitment by the military and bureaucracy to a nuclear capability. While the first of these arguments was taken by the government to point strongly to Trident as the most cost-effective weapons system, the second argument did not. It could be held, for instance, by politicians or military and bureaucratic leaders who, while doubtful about Trident, were reluctant to get out of the whole nuclear business.

The case for Trident as the preferred weapons system nevertheless followed the general case to remain nuclear. Quite simply, no other weapons system was available which met the two key criteria of *survivability* (best met by submarine-based rather than aircraft or surface-ship systems) and *penetration* (best met by ballistic missiles rather than by slower-flying cruise missiles or aircraft). The more the government emphasised these two criteria, the more emphasis it implicitly gave to Trident as a purely national system to meet national needs and the less emphasis it gave to Trident as a British contribution to Nato's need for INF systems. However, there seems little doubt that it was national rather than Nato concerns which dominated the government's thinking.

Trident 1 would have been a more than adequate replacement for Polaris because Trident 2 was unnecessarily sophisticated. The British government has stated, however, that it will not use the full potential of warheads in Trident 2 but confine itself to the level offered by Trident 1 (Ministry of Defence 1987, p. 41). The alternatives to Trident were never serious runners, although a number were canvassed. One was a British-built replacement for the Polaris missiles which maintained a similar level of striking power and range within replacement submarines. The government appears to have concluded that, even if such a system could be built, it could not be produced as quickly or as cheaply as the American product. A second option was an Anglo-French force developed jointly by the two states and making use of their respective strengths. This option had been considered by Edward Heath in the early 1970s and was canvassed by the Alliance in 1986–7. The government thought it politically and technologically unrealistic, although it gave much serious consideration to more modest forms of nuclear collaboration (which are discussed below).

Two further suggested alternatives failed the government's tests of cost-effectiveness, survivability and penetration. One involved a new heavy bomber aircraft which could deploy air-launched cruise missiles, and hence constitute a credible national deterrent force in the way that the shorter-range and lighter, though nuclear-capable, Tornado could not. A second alternative involved cruise missiles deployed from either submarines or surface ships. Such a system raised many questions about survivability and penetration and was discarded.

The government concluded that there was no realistic alternative to Trident 2 and in 1982 a formal agreement was reached with the Americans. The idea of a fifth submarine was quietly dropped and economies were sought by arranging for servicing of the missiles to be carried out in the United States. Trident 2 increased the total estimated cost of the programme, which was then further inflated by the weakness of the pound against the dollar until by 1985 the estimated cost had stabilised at about £10 billion. Trident 2 carried the short-term advantage of postponing investment, pushing the main expenditures back to the late 1980s and early 1990s, but it increased the domestic political risk of cancellation after the next election by which time little money would have been spent. The risk was not completely avoidable, however, in that for the programme to come to fruition the government would need to win that election. With Trident 2 the programme would be far from complete even by the following election.

Trident has thus been a supremely politicised procurement

programme, gradually absorbing more of the defence-equipment budget through the mid-1980s against a background of sustained opposition until the 1987 election from Labour and the Alliance. As a proportion of the equipment budget, Trident has been no more expensive than, for instance, the Tornado programme at its peak. But it places particular demands on scientific resources and has been vulnerable to fluctuations in exchange rates, a process which in fact favoured Trident as the pound grew in strength against the dollar after hitting a nadir in 1984/5. However, while the defence budgetary problem was eased through the early 1980s by sustained growth of about 3 per cent a year, in 1986 this expansion ceased (see the section on finance below) and the completion of the programme remains slightly problematical. In 1988/9 the running costs of Polaris and the greater procurement costs for Trident absorbed about 6 per cent of the defence budget (Ministry of Defence 1987, volume 2, p. 10).

The government's case for Trident after 1980 was not completely unconditional. While the defence of the project was certainly robust, and the difficulties of the opposition parties maximised, government statements accepted that external circumstances could change in a way that would lead to reconsideration. By the summer of 1987, indeed, such external change appeared possible as the two superpowers moved close to agreement on eliminating land-based INF missiles and reducing strategic weapons by 50 per cent. During the negotiations on INF from 1981 to 1987 the Americans successfully resisted all Soviet attempts to include British (and also French) nuclear forces within the INF framework. However, a Soviet attempt to include such forces within a strategic arms treaty might be more difficult to resist, particularly given that Trident was a frontline American system. Trident would be at risk either from direct pressure on the United States by the Soviet Union or, were the United States to resist such pressure and thereby threaten agreement with the Soviet Union, from Britain's continental allies who might interpret British insistence on Trident as undermining the prospect of an important international security agreement with the Soviet Union. The unwelcome prospect thus arose of Trident being targetted not merely by the peace movements but also by allied governments as an impediment to a treaty.

Having coped successfully by the 1987 election with the domestic problems of Trident, the external dimensions loomed larger. The programme raised awkward questions about its impact on the broader strategic and arms control framework. British governments have always been anxious to avoid the sensitive questions posed by its strategic nuclear weapons for continental allies, particularly the Federal Republic, if such weapons either threatened to reduce Britain's conventional force contributions to the alliance or damaged broader security arrangements with the Soviet Union. The Thatcher governments successfully avoided or parried these issues through the INF negotiations and generally satisfied allies that Trident would not be purchased at the expense of conventional force levels. A treaty on strategic arms risked reopening this issue. The government sought to dampen down expectations of major arms reductions urging a general caution for the whole negotiating procedure and arguing that the impact of an INF treaty should be thoroughly digested before more radical measures were taken. When this tactic failed it shifted tack. Having urged general caution the government went on to stress that Trident as a national *minimum* nuclear force was quite separate from the negotiations for a 50 per cent reduction in strategic forces and finally, in September 1987, made an unprecedented commitment to Trident as an unconditional minimum and non-negotiable force. This probably represented only a change of presentation, in that neither the government nor its predecessors had seriously expected a treaty between the superpowers that might seriously threaten Trident (or Polaris before it). The move succeeded. At the Washington summit in December 1987 the Soviets appeared to exclude British and French nuclear forces from the scope of an agreement on strategic arms.

By the end of 1987 Trident had survived seven anxious years and looked much more secure. Financial costs had been brought under control and domestic opposition was subsiding. CND was in decline and, following the INF agreement, in disarray. Even the parliamentary leadership of the Labour party was anxious to revise the policy of unilateral nuclear disarmament, perhaps even to the point of accepting Trident as a factor to be thrown into the negotiating ring as part of a distant phase of strategic arms cuts after the expected 50 per cent reduction.

Nato, the United States and the INF Issue

The Thatcher government has consistently stressed that Nato is the cornerstone of British defence policy. In this respect, as with Polaris/

Trident, there are strong elements of continuity with preceding governments. Within Nato the key issue in the 1980s has been the 'double-track' policy, the origins of which go back to the mid-1970s when European governments, led by Callaghan and Chancellor Schmidt, became concerned about the possible 'decoupling' of American and European security in the context of strategic parity between the superpowers. In October 1977 Nato established its High Level Group to examine the issue and in December 1979, after the Callaghan government had left office, Nato adopted the double-track policy. This sought to reinvigorate Nato's policy of flexible response by the modernisation of its INF capability through installation in Europe of a new generation of land-based missiles capable of hitting targets within the Soviet Union and of bridging an alleged gap between short-range nuclear systems and American strategic forces. By being land-based and spread through five European states (including Britain) they would demonstrate a shared alliance readiness to maintain deterrents. A second track of the policy offered the possibility of obviating the need for these missiles by a major reduction in the Soviet Union's INF capability, particularly its growing numbers of SS-20 missiles. The SS-20 was a military threat to Nato's military capabilities but, more importantly, justified Nato's rearmament within flexible response. An INF agreement was not only unlikely, given the Soviet Union's emphasis on its own INF systems since the 1950s, but would not, in itself, meet the fears about decoupling and the weakening of flexible response which had so alarmed Callaghan and Schmidt.

When the talks between the superpowers on INF began in November 1981, the Thatcher government strongly supported the American 'zero' solution of no new Western deployments in return for Soviet abandonment of all its INF systems. Such an outcome appeared extremely remote but was used by the government to meet the criticisms of the rapidly growing peace movements. Secretary of State for Defence Michael Heseltine devoted his department's main political energies to meeting the challenge from the peace movement which peaked at about the end of 1982. The double-track policy was consistently unpopular with public opinion in Britain and Western Europe, was orchestrated by CND and the peace movements, and threatened the implementation of Nato's rearmament strategy. Heseltine challenged CND head-on by emphasising the government's commitment to the zero solution, since a European-wide removal of nuclear weapons was CND's declared objective.

While public opinion was also hostile to the Trident programme, at this time no significant expenditures were yet being incurred and opposition to Trident was combined with consistent public support in favour of some British nuclear capability. Moreover there was also a 'Gaullist' factor in public opinion which distinguished between British nuclear weapons under national control and American nuclear weapons deployed in Britain over which the government had no absolute control. In 1982–3, therefore, the most important aspect of defence policy was public presentation of the double-track policy and here Heseltine enjoyed surprising success. Although public opposition to the Nato missile deployments persisted until the INF agreement of 1987, he maximised the internal differences on defence within the Labour party and emphasised the general need to support Nato, using Labour's opposition to the double-track policy to indicate its general opposition or indifference to Nato. By the 1983 election, despite the continuing unpopularity of the impending missile deployments, the Conservatives enjoyed a massive 67 per cent lead over Labour on defence – the largest lead ever enjoyed on any political issue.

The INF talks themselves did not directly involve the British government. The Americans negotiated on behalf of the alliance and the chief British concern was to ensure that British nuclear forces were kept safely out of the bargaining process. The Soviet Union did not at first raise the issue but, in 1982 and 1983, as it became clear that the Americans were determined to carry through the rearmament, the Soviet Union introduced the British and French national nuclear forces into the equation. The Americans stoutly resisted, if only because the Soviet tactic was designed to prevent any new Western deployments, the legitimacy of which they continued to challenge. The talks failed to progress as the Soviets continued to oppose all Western deployments and at the end of 1983 the first cruise missiles were flown in to Greenham Common by the Americans. By this time CND was probably in decline and the government congratulated itself on having kept its nerve through a period when both internal and external forces had threatened to knock it off course.

In 1985 the INF talks resumed within a tripartite package including offensive strategic forces and strategic defences, in particular the Americans' 'Star Wars' programme. At the two superpower summits in Geneva 1985 and Reykjavik 1986 the prospect of a zero solution for INF forces emerged, though its relationship to the other two elements of the package remained uncertain as the Soviets continued to stress the necessity of an agreement on strategic defence. Nevertheless, the INF agreement loomed large enough by the autumn of 1986 to alarm the Thatcher government, especially when General Bernard Rogers, Nato's Supreme Commander, denounced such an agreement as undermining the flexible response strategy. But the American insistence on separating an INF agreement from agreement on strategic defence rendered a treaty unlikely. The British government, supported by the Labour party, argued that INF and strategic defence were logically distinct, despite the Soviets' unconditional linkage since the resumption of talks in 1985. In the spring of 1987 the Soviet leader Mikhail Gorbachev produced, step by step, a string of concessions in the INF negotiations which revealed how uncertain had been the British government's commitment to the zero solution. Gorbachev agreed to the removal of the residual 100 INF warheads (confined to Alaska and Soviet Asia) which he had insisted on at Reykjavik. He accepted the most stringent American demands for on-site inspection and verification. He agreed to decouple the INF package from both strategic defence and *modernisation* of the British and French national nuclear forces – a condition that the Soviets had emphasised intermittently since conceding that the *existing* British and French nuclear forces would not be accepted by the Western powers within an INF treaty.

The British government then raised as further objections to a treaty military imbalance arising from Soviet conventional and chemical superiority, but it later abandoned these objections which had not figured in the INF negotiations and threatened to isolate the government within Nato. Mrs Thatcher and Chancellor Kohl then raised the more plausible objection of the massive Soviet superiority in nuclear systems below the INF threshold of 1,000 kilometres, where the Soviets not only enjoyed a clear numerical advantage but had also reinforced their position as a countermove to the Western deployments since 1983. The Soviets then agreed to extend the agreement to include missiles in the range 500–1000 kilometres, in what became known as short-range intermediate nuclear forces (SRINF) in the so-called 'double-zero' solution. During the 1987 election campaign the Thatcher government quietly and without great enthusiasm accepted an agreement on this basis.

The INF agreement that finally emerged in the autumn of 1987 offered the British government everything and more than they had argued for since 1979. The agreement was represented as a victory for multilateral negotiation from strength, in contrast to Labour's policy which would have left all the Soviet missiles intact. Nevertheless the triumph was muted. Two reasons account for this. First, the agreement, and even more the increasing prospect of a strategic arms agreement, raised the difficult questions about the stability of the Trident programme (see above). Secondly, the treaty also raised difficult questions about flexible response following the removal of the American INF missiles. Compensatory measures were placed high on the agenda of the government and of the Nato council. The most pressing concern here was to insist that the process of nuclear disarmament in Europe had gone far enough. Any further reductions into the area of very-short-range battlefield nuclear weapons would raise the spectre of 'denuclearisation', the objective of the peace movements, completely destroy the strategy of flexible response and decouple European defence from the American strategic deterrent forces. In March 1988 the first Nato summit for over two decades recommitted the alliance to maintaining flexible response, but failed to secure clear agreement on British and American demands for modernising the very-short-range nuclear system permitted under the treaty, the German government having called into question its whole nuclear strategy now that all Nato's remaining ground-based missile systems were either based on or targetted on to its territory.

Within the context of Anglo-American defence relations, INF and to a lesser extent Trident were the dominant issues. However three other matters deserve brief mention. The first is the Libyan episode in April 1986. The American bombing raid fell outside the Nato framework and some European allies refused co-operation to the Americans. The British government was consulted by the Americans but was given only very short notice and did not consider that refusal was a serious option. The Americans' use of their British bases did not violate the treaties governing their use and it was clear to the British government that the involvement of forces based in Britain was as much political as military – the Americans wished to implicate Britain in the raid and to stress, so far as was possible, allied solidarity. The incident is a reminder that after the INF treaty has been implemented the Americans will retain in Britain powerful forces capable of striking at the Soviet homeland with nuclear weapons – indeed that as a result of the treaty such forces might be expanded.

The second issue is the British response to President Reagan's Strategic Defense Initiative of March 1983. SDI, or 'Star Wars', aimed to erect a defensive shield against Soviet missile attack by means of an extremely elaborate set of space-based weapons. The first British reaction was one of incredulity at the proposed technology, but the Americans persisted against the opposition of the Soviet Union and the doubts of many American scientists. The proposal caused difficulties for the British government because SDI represented, theoretically at least, a rejection of nuclear *deterrence*, the basis of British defence policy, in favour of a system of *defence*. In her meeting with President Reagan at Camp David in December 1984 Mrs Thatcher sought to soften his doctrinal opposition to nuclear deterrence and an agreed statement committed both powers to a policy of balance between East and West, rather than Western superiority, and to an enhancement rather than a rejection of deterrence. In addition the British pressed the Americans on the question of deployment of space-based weapons systems which, they held, would constitute a violation of the 1972 Anti-Ballistic Missile Treaty. Hence the two powers agreed that, while research and development could continue, in view of treaty obligations deployment would have to be negotiated with the Soviet Union. In March 1985 Foreign Secretary Geoffrey Howe went considerably further in a speech to the Royal United Services Institute. Howe not only emphasised that the 1972 treaty, while permitting research, excluded development and testing of weapons, but he also questioned the whole rationale for the programme. Would a security system based on defence be as stable as one based on deterrence, particularly if there was a mixture of defence and deterrence? Would the technology work? Would defensive systems provoke new instabilities and new arms races? Would arms control be undermined? Howe was also alarmed at the potential impact of a United States defensive system on the cohesion of Nato: 'the security of Nato territory is indivisible. Otherwise the twin pillars of the Alliance might begin to fall apart.' (*Arms Control and Disarmament Newsletter* 1985). Howe's speech, which has been generally interpreted as representing fundamental British doubts about the whole SDI programme, did not prevent the government later that year concluding an agreement with the Americans to allow British companies and researchers to participate in the programme. The contracts concluded under the agreement have, however, proved extremely modest and it is doubtful whether there is British participation in the most scientifically advanced areas of SDI research.

The third area, the most long term and perhaps speculative, is the continuing primacy of the American security relationship. However in the 1980s the British government, together with its European allies, has given attention to ideas about a strategic recasting of Western defence in which European co-operation would be enhanced and the American relationship downgraded. The idea is not new but it has gained in prominence and been given some institutional substance by the revival in June 1984 of the Western European Union, a grouping of the Brussels Treaty powers of 1948 (Britain, France and the three Benelux countries), together with the Federal Republic and Italy. The government, however, is not keen on giving too institutional or firm a basis to these developments out of fear for damaging the American relationship. The prospect of an INF treaty led in 1987 to increased bilateral collaboration between France, the Federal Republic and Britain. In particular George Younger initiated discussions in Paris on Anglo-French nuclear co-operation, including the possibility of collaboration on new intermediate range forces to compensate for the departing American missiles. The government was interested in modernising its tactical nuclear forces by replacing nuclear bombs deployed by Tornado strike aircraft with a new air-launched cruise missile to be developed with France or possibly the United States.

It is not clear how far these trends will go but, as in the 1970s, it is likely that détente between the two superpowers will press the West European powers towards closer co-operation. However, while the Foreign and Commonwealth Office is now thoroughly 'Europeanised', the Ministry of Defence has always been strongly aligned towards the United States, and it is possible that a complex process will develop in which differential rates of progress are made in different sectors of policy. Mrs Thatcher herself would also be reluctant to see European co-operation displace the primacy of the American connection.

Defence Costs

The British defence budget is both large and very hard-pressed. After the Second World War defence spending reached a peak of about 11 per cent of GDP at the height of the Korean War and then gradually fell, to about 7 per cent at the end of the Macmillan–Home era and 6 per cent by the end of the second Wilson government in 1970. The third Wilson government undertook a review in 1974 which reduced expenditure and further cuts were imposed following the 1976 sterling crisis. Defence dipped to a low of 4.7 per cent of GDP in 1978/9 but then began to climb again. In May 1977 the government agreed to a Nato plan, implemented from 1979, to increase expenditures by 3 per cent a year in order to produce long-term improvements in Nato's capability.

The Conservative government thus inherited an expanding budget. The 3 per cent improvement programme was difficult to sustain, especially in the early 1980s when the economy was contracting and the government's emphasis on reducing public expenditure was frustrated by the rapidly increasing cost of social security payments as unemployment escalated rapidly to over three million. Defence expenditure rose to about 5.4 per cent of GDP in 1983/4 and by the end of the 3 per cent expansion in 1985/6 was one of the few Nato members to have achieved the target. After 1985/6 expenditure began to fall in real terms and is likely to fall by 5 per cent by 1989/90. In 1986/7 defence absorbed only 4.7 per cent of GDP, the lowest level since the IMF cuts under Callaghan, and the figure for 1988/9 is certain to be even lower, though of course this decline is exaggerated by a continuing increase in GDP (Ministry of Defence 1988, volume 2, p. 5).

In absolute terms – and allowing for the difficulties of comparison caused by fluctuating exchange rates and reliance on professional forces rather than conscription – Britain was spending about as much as France and Germany. But as a proportion of GDP Britain was spending much more – France about 4 per cent and Germany about 3.3 per cent. Thus to achieve a similar effect Britain has spent a much higher proportion of her much smaller economy. In a general Nato comparison Britain has consistently been third-highest proportional spender after the United States and Greece (whose defence budget is shaped more by her conflict with Turkey than by Nato requirements).

Despite its high level, the defence budget is also severely stretched, partly because the rate of inflation in the defence area is higher than in the civilian economy, but primarily because the British defence effort is very complex and involves the maintenance of a number of quite distinct roles. In small scale, British defence policy mirrors that of America and is distinct from that of all the European members of the alliance. Five separate roles are sustained:

- a *continental commitment*, involving an army corps in Germany with a peacetime strength of about 55,000 men together with a tactical air force of about 17,000 men, each of them requiring the most sophisticated new equipments and constituting major elements in Nato's Northern Army Group under British command (this commitment absorbs the largest single identifiable share of the defence budget);
- a *maritime commitment* in the eastern Atlantic and the seas around Britain, involving surface and submarine ships and shore- and carrier-based aircraft;
- the *defence of the United Kingdom itself*, primarily by means of a major air defence capability;
- the *national nuclear deterrent*, now being modernised after a period in which it was a minor element of the defence budget;
- a range of *'out of area'* commitments, including Hong Kong, Belize, the Arabian Sea and Gulf and 'Fortress Falklands'.

Since 1979 a range of issues have arisen under the general heading of the management of defence costs.

The Rationalisation of the Defence Effort

In June 1981 the government's second defence statement proposed a major review of the defence effort because 'even the increased resources we plan to allocate cannot fund all the force structures and all the plans for improvements we now have' (Ministry of Defence 1982). John Nott, the Secretary of State for Defence proposed that primacy be given to the nuclear role which, he argued (like Duncan Sandys before him in the famous defence review of 1957), represented the best value for money in producing a deterrent effect. Alongside the nuclear deterrent, Nott emphasised the commitment of forces to the central front in Germany and the need for their re-equipment. To meet these two priorities, Nott proposed a major reduction in the navy's surface fleet. The navy's chief role of denying the seas to Soviet naval forces could, he argued, be carried out by shore-based aircraft and submarines with less reliance on surface ships. The general-purpose fleet of frigates and destroyers would decline from about 50 to about 40. Even worse so far as the admirals were concerned, Nott was hostile to the concept of carrier-borne aircraft operating in the north Atlantic, arguing that carriers, and indeed other surface ships, were both expensive and extremely vulnerable to Soviet attacks, while maritime aircraft could be deployed as effectively from shore bases.

Nott, a Thatcher loyalist who had only just replaced Francis Pym as Defence Secretary, ran into an immediate political storm. His most contentious proposal was the downgrading of the navy's new fleet of carriers, termed anti-submarine-warfare cruisers, which represented the Admiralty's surprising re-entry into sea-based airpower after its virtual abandonment in the 1960s. The Callaghan government had committed itself to a fleet of three new ships, which were just coming into service in the early 1980s. Nott proposed selling one of the new ships and the last of the old generation of carriers. A capability based on only two new ships would be so affected by refitting cycles that, the admirals feared, it would prove vulnerable to future cost-cutting.

Nott's plan provoked the resignation of the junior minister with responsibility for the navy, Keith Speed, and led to a tacit unholy alliance between the admirals and the Labour party which condemned the run-down of the surface fleet and defended the capability offered by the aircraft carriers (as the cruisers inevitably became known) for operations outside of the Nato area. Nott's strategy was accepted by the government but within a year the Falklands War had rendered his strategy politically untenable. Twenty-three frigates and destroyers and two carriers (an old and a new) were deployed. Nott could reasonably claim that the war revealed the vulnerability of large surface ships: four major naval vessels were lost and eight damaged, and two support vessels were lost and two damaged. On the other hand the operation, which would hardly have proved possible after his cuts had been implemented, greatly increased the political clout of the navy. The government decided to retain the three new carriers and replace the four surface ships lost with the type-22 frigate which had proved successful against air attack. Nott's strategy was partially abandoned and in 1983 he resigned from government and Parliament.

Nevertheless, the surface fleet inherited by the government in

1979 inexorably declined in size. The government could not sustain the required rate of ordering of type-22s, about three a year, and the introduction of a cheaper ship, the type-23, failed to remedy the situation. Until 1988 the surface fleet of about 50 ships survived but was bound to decline unless either the building programme was increased (and the planned budgets did not provide for this) or the age of ships was allowed to rise to unacceptable levels.

Airborne Radar Systems

In 1976 the Callaghan government decided to develop a new airborne radar system to replace the obsolete Shackleton aircraft. The government preferred a British radar system based on the Nimrod maritime aircraft (itself based on the 1950s Comet airframe) to the alternative Boeing 'AWACS' system already in service with the Americans and selected by Nato as the basis of a new West European radar system. Nimrod would be the British contribution to that European system. The development of the aircraft proved relatively easy but the new radars, entrusted to GEC, proved extremely expensive and unreliable. In 1987 Defence Secretary George Younger advised the government to abandon Nimrod in favour of Boeing. Six aircraft were ordered with a further one added later. Although the Labour party argued for GEC to be given more time, the RAF had always preferred Boeing and had completely lost confidence in Nimrod. The episode revealed the weakness of British industry in offering a base for a national procurement policy in the high-technology area and also the difficulty of maintaining an efficient procurement procedure when, in practice, payments to contractors for research and development were bound to be in the nature of a blank cheque.

Managerial Efficiency

The government has attempted since 1979 to introduce greater discipline and market forces into the management of defence in general and defence procurement in particular. Some success was enjoyed: the share of the budget devoted to equipment increased from just under 40 per cent to over 45 per cent, though it then fell back as the budget contracted. The government placed more contracts by competitive tender and contracted out (privatised) the provision of some services. It is difficult to evaluate the success of this policy, though there was a major shift from 'cost-plus' contracts towards competitive tendering. However in some areas competitive tendering is hardly possible and the Select Committee on Defence has remained sceptical about the success of the policy. In addition to privatising some services there was also a major programme of privatising industry: the Royal Ordnance was sold to Vickers, the remaining holding in British Aerospace was also sold and the management of the Royal Dockyards was privatised.

Under Michael Heseltine there was a series of reforms to rationalise the decision-making structures within the Ministry of Defence on both the civilian side, particularly with the establishment of a single Procurement Executive, and on the military side. Here Heseltine continued the reforms of successive secretaries of state in centralising the top-level military structure. He succeeded in establishing a much stronger post of Chief of the Defence Staff, responsible for advising the government on strategic policy, with the roles of the chiefs of the three services downgraded to administrative and command functions. The objective was to achieve clearer and more unified advice on policy. Through the ministry itself Heseltine introduced management changes designed to give clearer information for decision making, most notably the Ministerial Information Systems or MINIS.

These changes, with the exception of privatisation, were essentially evolutionary and designed partly to avoid the need for a fundamental review of defence policy itself, following the problems that confronted the Nott review. In other words, the aim was to continue to try to squeeze a quartful of commitments and roles into the pint pot of resources allocated by Cabinet. Radical realignment was not the objective and the defence budget remained under intensive pressure, especially after the reductions from the peak year of 1985/6. The 1986 statement referred to the need for 'hard decisions' and the 1987 statement to 'difficult choices to be made between relative priorities in our forward plans' (Ministry of Defence 1987, para. 603). One example will illustrate the problem. The government plans to maintain the role of the Royal Marines in reinforcing the northern flank in Norway. This requires two large assault ships which were successfully deployed in the Falklands but are now due for renewal. The government has continued to postpone a decision about their replacement, the large cost of which would seriously undermine the already inadequate programme of replacing frigates.

Fortress Falklands

After the Falklands War the defence budget received additional appropriations to replace lost equipments and to meet the new commitment of defending the Falklands against the possibility of Argentine attack. After the initial postwar period, force levels on the islands were greatly reduced and the government concentrated resources into a major reinforcement capability, primarily by means of a new airfield. By 1987 the Falklands no longer represented a major drain on the budget – costs had been cut back to a relatively modest £250 million – but they nevertheless had to be squeezed into a declining budget.

Arabian Sea and the Gulf

Britain withdrew from a permanent role in the Indian Ocean in the early 1970s, although there were frequent naval visits. From the outbreak of the Iran–Iraq War in 1980 the government established a permanent naval presence – the Armilla Patrol – in the Arabian Sea and the Straits of Hormuz at the entrance to the Gulf. Two frigates and a supply ship were on station, plus a very small land presence in Oman, with which Britain had long enjoyed a special relationship.

In 1987 the escalation of the Gulf War led the government to increase by an additional frigate the size of the naval force escorting British shipping as it entered the Gulf. The American government pressed Britain to join in a joint-convoying strategy, involving the reflagging under American and British flags of oil tankers serving America and Britain. The British government refused. However, the naval presence was increased in August 1987 by the despatch of a fleet of minehunters when the threat to shipping from mines appeared to be increasing. However, formal convoying was not adopted and the frigates continued to accompany British shipping within a more restricted area than the Americans, whose ships sailed to the head of the Gulf. The British commitment to the area had increased considerably, but the open-ended involvement desired by the Americans and specifically directed at the Iranians was avoided. The British government did not directly collaborate with the large

American fleet though there was some co-operation with the other European governments which followed Britain in despatching minehunters.

Collaborative Projects

Collaboration between Nato members in production of new equipment was a well-established trend by 1979. On the other hand the experience of collaboration was mixed and many of the more ambitious projects had failed to get off the ground at all (such as the 1970s schemes for a new Nato main battle tank), had been abandoned or had run into severe financial or strategic problems. Collaboration on smaller equipment nevertheless continued and was developed under the Conservatives. The most contentious areas involved aircraft, both fixed wing and helicopter. The government inherited the Tornado project to provide both a new strike aircraft (jointly developed with Germany and Italy) and a new air-defence plane (a version of Tornado developed and deployed only by Britain). Tornados of both varieties were brought into service but the air-defence version which became operational in 1987 has suffered severe problems with its new British radars.

After 1980 chief interest in the collaborative area turned to a new aircraft to replace the ageing American Phantoms and Lightnings for air defence and the Anglo-French Jaguars for battlefield support. This project, the European Fighter Aircraft, proved contentious and the French withdrew. During 1986 and 1987 two parallel sets of negotiations proceeded, discretely linked but nevertheless ostensibly independent. The British government, pressed by the RAF, was in negotiation with the other governments – Germany, Spain and Italy – about development costs, share of research and production, and production orders, while British Aerospace negotiated directly with its collaborative partners. British Aerospace, recently national-ised but heavily dependent on government for orders, also led a purely national and speculative project, the Experimental Aircraft Programme. In 1988 the government committed itself firmly to development of the European Fighter Aircraft.

The greatest procurement crisis involved helicopters. The only British supplier is Westland, which has engaged in European collaborative projects but is primarily dependent on American technology, especially from Sikorski. In the autumn of 1985

Westland ran into severe financial difficulties. The Department of
Industry favoured a takeover by Sikorski as the most stable long-
term solution of Westland's problems. Heseltine favoured a
European grouping, arguing that from a secure European base it
would be possible to mount a more effective challenge to American
supremacy in the market and, perhaps less convincingly, that from a
basis of greater American–European parity, more effective collaboration within Nato between Americans and Europeans would become
possible. To some extent the requirements of defence policy
appeared to conflict with those of industrial policy. The issue
became increasingly involved, with the management of Westland
strongly favouring the American option. For Heseltine it eventually
became an issue of confidence in the Cabinet's management of public
policy. In January 1986 he resigned from the government, closely
followed by his adversary in the affair, Leon Brittan, the Secretary of
State for Industry (Freedman 1987).

Conclusion

On two of the issues confronting the government in 1979, namely
Polaris renewal and the implementation of the INF modernisation
programme, the government could claim considerable success by
1987. However, both issues had politicised and polarised defence
policy, and ended a national consensus, though the government
could reasonably claim that it was Labour that had abandoned
previously consensual policies in its shift towards unilateral nuclear
disarmament. This politicisation of defence, though remarkable in
the light of the post-1945 British consensus, is much less striking
when set in the European context of a massive anti-nuclear
movement between the late-1970s and the mid-1980s.

INF raised no financial questions and Trident finally stabilised
itself at a level that the government clearly regarded as affordable. In
the third area discussed in this chapter, the problem of managing
defence costs, the government has been less successful. Difficult
questions were avoided or postponed in favour of an emphasis on
ideologically attractive ideas, such as privatisation and managerial
efficiency, which were simply inadequate to resolve the structural
problems within the defence budget. In 1988 the defence budget
appears to be in need of either a massive injection of funds or a

serious review of commitments. The government has rejected the first and refuses to contemplate the second. The relative successes of the first two Thatcher governments in defence are therefore likely in the third term to be succeeded by severe financial problems which may eventually demand a fundamental review of the whole shape of the defence effort and a radical reduction in the number of commitments presently sustained.

References and Further Reading

Arms Control and Disarmament Newsletter, 23, 1985. This contains the text of Howe's speech on SDI.

Baylis, J. (1984) *Anglo-American Defence Relations 1939–84, the Special Relationship*, Macmillan.

Byrd, P. (1985) 'The development of the peace movement in Britain' in Kaltefleiter, W. and Pfaltzgraff, R.L. (eds) *The Peace Movements in Britain and the United States*, Croom Helm.

Committee of Public Accounts (1982) *Ministry of Defence: Chevaline Improvement to the Polaris Missile System*, House of Commons 269, 1981–2.

Duke, S. (1986) *US Defence Bases in the United Kingdom*, Macmillan.

Freedman, L. (1986–7) 'The case of Westland and the bias to Europe', *International Affairs*, vol. 63, no. 1.

McInnes, C. (1986) *Trident: the only option?*, Brasseys.

Ministry of Defence (1980) *Defence in the 1980s: Statement on the Defence Estimates 1980*, Cmnd 7826 I.

Ministry of Defence (1981) *The UK Defence Programme: the Way Ahead*, Cmnd 8517 I.

Ministry of Defence (1982) *The United Kingdom Trident Programme*, Defence Open Government Document 82/1.

Ministry of Defence (1986) *Statement on the Defence Estimates 1986*, Cmnd 9763 I and II.

Ministry of Defence (1987) *Statement on the Defence Estimates 1987*, Cmnd 101 I and II.

Ministry of Defence (1988) *Statement on the Defence Estimates 1988*, Cm. 344 I and II.

See also the regular reports of the House of Commons Select Committee on Defence.

CHAPTER 9

Rational Politicians and Conservative Statecraft in the Open Polity

JIM BULPITT

> In making their decisions, the parties proceed from the objectives of their domestic and economic policies. Foreign policy is in their eyes only a means to their domestic ends.
>
> E. Kehr, *Economic Interest, Militarism and Foreign Policy*, 1977

> A state's involvement in an international network of states is a basis for potential autonomy of action over and against groups and economic arrangements within its jurisdiction – even including the dominant class and existing relations of production.
>
> T. Skocpol, *States and Social Revolution*, 1979

Let us start with a question: what is there about 'British Foreign Policy under Thatcher' which is worthy of our investigation and assessment? The other contributors to this volume have provided one set of answers. They have examined the subject in terms of area, function and crisis. In other words, they have considered the Conservative government's policies towards particular areas of the world, the defence function, and a major externally generated crisis, namely the Falklands War.

A moment's reflection (perhaps more) suggests another dimension to the subject, one concerned with the general linkages between external affairs and British domestic politics in the 1980s. This perspective can be pursued in a variety of ways. The one adopted here is best explained by posing another question: in what ways, and for what reasons, did the first two Thatcher-led administrations seek to manage the impact of external forces on the domestic political scene such that their general interests were either positively promoted or not adversely affected? This chapter will attempt some answers to that question. It is by no means a full investigation. It is best viewed as a preliminary intellectual probe. Hopefully the overall package, both methodology and message, may be of some interest.

Some Problems of Analysis

However brief the exercise, a consideration of some of the analytical obstacles encountered is a necessary preliminary requirement.

A major problem stems from one of the more curious characteristics of British political science. This has always professed an interest in the general subject of government, but it has been markedly reluctant to develop any enthusiasm about the study of particular governments. That task has usually been hived off to historians and memoir mongers. The consequence is that we possess very little by way of systematic and agreed tools of analysis to assist us in understanding the macro behaviour of politicians in office during specified time periods.

The literature on external affairs analysis provokes similar comments (for an excellent survey, see Gourevitch 1978). Traditionally, the subject was concerned with interstate diplomatic relations. Within that framework foreign policy was what was done to foreigners, more specifically their governments: foreign policy involved the pursuit of the national interest and the export of national values. Domestic politics 'stopped at the water's edge': it had no great impact on the content and style of diplomatic relations (for British examples, see Vital 1968 and Nailor 1983).

The last two decades have witnessed the rise of another approach, the interdependence thesis. As its label suggests, this stresses the advent of a 'global village', a world in which both states and societies are tightly bound together by a mass of economic, political and cultural linkages (Rosenau 1966, Morse 1976, Keohane and Nye 1977, Wallace 1986). Chernobyl, Aids, drug traffickers, football supporters, international currency speculators, terrorists and tourists are all examples of this new interdependence. States are no longer the sole actors on the world stage and their old sovereignty has declined considerably. In this scenario, domestic politics and politicians are relatively unimportant: they merely react to pressures from the external environment.

There is, however, a third approach to external-affairs analysis which makes a more positive connection between foreign policy and domestic politics. We can call this the 'primacy of domestic politics' school (after Kehr 1965). For the most part this has been concerned to isolate the principal domestic influences on the content of foreign policy (Allison 1971, Wallace 1975, Dallin 1981, Alt 1987). Historians have sometimes gone further and investigated the ways in which particular governments or regimes have used foreign policy to support their domestic strategies (Cowling 1975, Kehr 1977, Skocpol 1979, Kennedy 1981, Swartz 1985). But this approach has never been particularly popular in Britain, above all for the analysis of contemporary governments. Thus, once again, the sort of exercise this chapter is interested in receives remarkably little assistance from the specialist literature.

Finally, we need to note the existence of a trio of little difficulties which confront, more or less, all social science analysis but are particularly troublesome in the present context. The first concerns the designation of the principal actor whose behaviour is to be evaluated (Singer 1961, Frey 1985). Is it the state, the government, the foreign and defence policy community, or particular individuals? The choice is clearly significant and needs to be made explicit. The second revolves round the interests of the particular actor designated. The analysis of interests is acknowledged to be a very difficult and contentious aspect of the social sciences (Balbus 1971, Krasner 1978, Saunders 1980). Do political actors merely reflect the interests of other groups, or do they have their own interests? Can these interests be objectively determined? Once again, the response to these questions must be made explicit. The third problem relates to how we go about assessing the behaviour of politicians in the foreign policy sphere over a relatively short period of contemporary time. Much of this behaviour will be hidden from academic investigation. Alternatively, it may take the form of *ad hoc* responses to specific external shocks, or will be analogous to life-insurance policies, designed, hopefully, never to be cashed. Moreover, just what counts as a foreign policy, and whether a particular action can be designated a success, may be open to argument. General assessment in these circumstances will be difficult.

These specific problems are not, of course, insurmountable. The easy way out is to be flexible about principal-actor designation, avoid any serious discussion of interests, and let the story provide the assessment. If challenged, the response can always be that all governance is a cock-up activity and, hence, exhibits no coherent pattern. This escape route will be rejected below. It is safe, but not interesting.

The Approach

The principal methodological assumptions on which the following analysis is based run as follows.

Assumption One

Britain is best regarded as an open polity. For a variety of reasons it is open to penetration by a large number of external forces, some good, some bad and some neutral in their impact on domestic politics.

An open polity is clearly not an insulated sovereign state, which can afford to view the external environment solely in terms of foreign policies to foreigners and the export of national values. But neither is it necessarily a polity whose politicians are completely swamped by the many mechanisms of interdependence. It follows that the external environment and foreign policy are, analytically, integral parts of domestic politics and domestic political management: they cannot be treated as something apart from the mainstream, as mere afterthoughts. This is the same assumption as that underlying open-economy macroeconomics (Begg, Fischer and Dornbusch 1984). Open polities require careful nurture, they demand external support systems; that is to say, foreign policies and domestic political management must both be designed to reduce, as far as possible, the adverse impact of external forces (Bulpitt 1983).

Assumption Two

Principal-actor designation should be granted to the national party leaders in office, to the party in government.

This has a twofold significance. First, it highlights the principal actors rejected, namely the state, the government, key individuals (such as the Prime Minister), the bureaucratic foreign policy community, or the world system/external forces. Secondly, and more positively, the focus is on party government, in the idiosyncratic mode it has taken in Britain. It follows that the connection with domestic politics is, potentially, direct and continuous. We are not dealing with a principal actor which, analytically at least, can be easily divorced from the domestic party-political struggle. National party leaders in office will constantly fight their cause in the political arena and, if forced, may play 'dirty pool'.

Assumption Three

We assume, initially at least, that this ruling party élite will prefer to pursue their own interests and that these may not be the same as the national interest or the interests of powerful domestic and external groups. In short, we postulate a degree of relative autonomy for party leaders in office (Nordlinger 1981, Jessop 1982).

Once again the implications are twofold. The extent and duration of this autonomy – how relative it is – is something to be tested. It may be that it can only be sustained in the short run. In the long run party leaders may be forced to pursue the national interest as generally perceived (Armstrong 1965). But how long is the long run? Moreover, this sort of argument may apply only to foreign policy *per se*, not its domestic presentation and the management of external pressures. The other implication, inherent in this assump-tion, is that the only linkages between the external and domestic environments which require consideration are those perceived to be important by the party leaders in office. Clearly these perceptions may not always be easy to monitor. On the other hand, this approach does have the advantage that it reduces the scope of the enquiry. We do not have to trawl the world, or British politics, searching for all potentially important linkages. In short, it is a relatively parsimonious approach to the subject.

Assumption Four

Party leaders in office operate within a structural framework which, in terms of the political management of external forces on domestic politics, yields both constraints *and* opportunities.

These constraints and opportunities emerge from the relevant historical, party-political and external environmental characteristics of the particular polity under investigation. They are probably best labelled 'structural inferences' since their selection will depend on the perceptions of the individual analyst and, on occasions, the line between them and the actual behaviour of politicians may be difficult to trace.

Assumption Five

Whenever possible, party politicians in office will behave rationally. Or, what amounts to a weaker version of this, it is useful to analyse their behaviour *as if* it were rational.

This is a crucial assumption. It is also an analytical can of worms, opening the way to all sorts of problems, confusions and criticisms. The concept of rational behaviour has entered the social sciences via a number of literatures (for general surveys see Riker and Ordeshook 1973, Simon 1978 and 1979 and Dunleavy and O'Leary 1987). Although these handle the idea in different ways, some common general themes are present. Rational behaviour suggests: the achievement of preconceived goals via the most efficient means; that the actors involved will learn from their past mistakes or those of others; and that rationality can apply to procedures or decisions or both. On the other hand, ambiguities persist regarding the basic nature of rationality and the principal actors to be designated as behaving rationally. Moreover, when applied to practical politics most of the examples are taken from the US, the connections with external affairs often avoided (but see Verba 1961, Allison 1971 and Gilpin 1981) and the behaviour of politicians in office between elections persistently neglected.

So why bother to employ the assumption if it is so complex, so ambiguous and, for many people, so implausible? The response runs as follows. First, we can argue that the initial plausibility of an assumption does not matter: what matters is whether it can be used to produce interesting research results (Friedman 1953). Secondly, if the study of political élites in office is not rooted in some concept of rational behaviour, then it is not clear what sort of game analysts are playing. In the absence of such an assumption they will be reduced to moralising, story telling, supplying simple shopping lists of relevant 'factors', or, even worse, a weary and idle cynicism about the incoherence of government. In short, while élite analysis and the rationality assumption need not be married, of necessity they should be constant bedmates. Finally, in Simon's concepts of 'bounded rationality' and 'satisficing' we have a perfectly reasonable, though not especially rigorous, approach to the rational behaviour of politicians in office. His ideas have been neatly described in the following terms: 'Organisations do not search for the best mushroom in the prairies if they have an hour in which to find it: they choose the first mushroom which satisfies their aspiration level' (Dunleavy and O'Leary, 1987, pp. 172–3). As a general principle this is good enough. More important is what actually counts for rational behaviour by politicians in modern Britain.

Assumption Six

In the British polity rational behaviour on the part of politicians in office means the pursuit of party statecraft. This requires some brief explanation.

I have argued elsewhere (Bulpitt 1986a) that statecraft refers generally to that neglected aspect of political science, namely the *means* by which a country is governed. In terms of the behaviour of politicians in office it has four dimensions: party management, political argument hegemony, a governing competence and a winning electoral strategy. Two of these, party management (in this case the Conservative party) and a winning electoral strategy, speak for themselves. Political argument hegemony means a party achieving an easy predominance in debates, in a variety of locations, about political problems, policies and the general stance of the government. It is both a cruder and more comprehensive concept than political ideology or political ideas. It refers to situations in which a party's arguments become more generally acceptable, and its solutions to key problems more plausible, than those of its opponents. A governing competence is concerned with how politicians in office avoid trouble, attempt policy-implementation successes, use those successes to bolster their position, and generally 'screw' the opposition parties and groups. 'Statecraft' has been traditionally employed as part of the vocabulary of diplomatic or international relations. Hence it is symbolically appropriate in this context. Moreover, the plurality of statecraft dimensions makes it clear that rational political behaviour is not simply a matter of election tactics. Consequently, it enables us to investigate that neglected subject, the achievement of a governing rationality between election campaigns.

But why should rational behaviour on the part of politicians in office take this particular form – the pursuit of party statecraft? The answer lies in three interrelated aspects of the British structure of politics, namely the electoral system, the adversarial party system and the peculiar character of institutional pluralism.

The electoral system has a well-known crude logic: it penalises third parties claiming nationwide support; it generously rewards, in terms of seats won, winning parties which have gained only a relatively small percentage of voter support, and, by allowing the leader of the party in office to select the election date, it gives full scope to managing policies to reap electoral rewards. This is not a system which contributes to the peace of mind of party leaders, especially when accompanied by increasing voter volatility. The adversarial party system compounds the problem. It means that between elections there is a continuous and relatively intense political divide regarding party political rhetoric and actions. What the government does and says, the opposition must usually oppose. if only to keep their supporters happy and maintain their distinctive position. It is true that before 1979 these divisions did not always extend to the actual policies pursued by the parties when in office (Rose 1980). Nevertheless, the adversarial system maintains a level of political aggravation between elections in Britain higher than elsewhere. In a very real sense a party's whole term of office (or opposition) is a practice game for the next election campaign. Finally, whilst institutional pluralism undoubtedly exists in Britain, it is, in important respects, more limited than elsewhere – no powerful second chamber, no elected regional level of

government and no authoritative committee system in Parliament.
Moreover, at least before the 1980s, those elements of institutional
pluralism which did exist – local authorities, schools, universities
and nationalised industries – were not regarded as playing any
important role in the lives of parties. Specifically, they were not
seen, even by party leaders, as reservoirs of party power, especially
when out of office at the centre. Political prestige and authority were
confined to SW1: politics was Westminsterised (Bulpitt 1983).

The consequences are as follows. Britain possesses a frenetic,
preoccupied, restless, querulous set of national politicians. Party
leaders must ensure they stay in the major league and must aim to
win general elections simply because the consequences of defeat, for
an increasingly professional political élite, are so awful. Moreover,
election strategy is not simply a matter of a few weeks' election
campaign: it can and does permeate the whole of the governing
cycle. It is for these reasons that political rationality in Britain can
be plausibly linked to the pursuit of party statecraft. No party has
played this game more seriously and successfully than the Conservative
party. More particularly, and historically, no party leadership has
used foreign policy as a weapon in the interparty battle more often
than the Conservatives (Cowling 1975, Swartz 1985, Pugh 1985).
The Conservative party is pre-eminently the party which thinks and
acts in statecraft terms (Bulpitt 1982, 1986a and b).

The Open Polity: an Impending Critical Juncture?

In the 1980s the changing structure of the open polity imposed both
constraints *and* opportunities on Conservative politicians in office.

Between 1945 and the early 1970s the principal features of the
British open polity remained pretty much the same. The major
themes of this *ancien régime* were the relentless relative decline in the
country's international power resources and status, and the necessity, accepted by all parties in practice, that this decline should be
managed in ways which would ensure that it did not adversely affect
domestic political tranquillity. Hence the twofold determination to
preserve as much of the public form of great-power status as possible
and the unwillingness to join any supranational institutions which
would explicitly and continuously penetrate the domestic political
process. This was a difficult hand to play, but in this period those

responsible for foreign policy possessed a number of 'tricks' to promote their cause: the interparty élite consensus on these matters, the special relationship with the economic and military hegemon, the United States, the long Western economic boom, the prestige of the Foreign Office and the development of the Commonwealth, which, along with the House of Windsor, was employed to mask much of the decline. Mistakes, of course, were made – Suez, the early casual attitude to immigration from the Commonwealth, and the too-long-delayed 1967 sterling devaluation were examples. But on the whole, given the difficulties and strange objects of the game, it was played reasonably well. After the early 1970s, however, a number of developments occurred which made this game more difficult to play. By the end of that decade these, in combination, had assumed such an intensity that they suggested an impending critical juncture in the politics of the open polity.

First, there were some awkward developments in the nature of the external environment and Britain's relations with that environment. The most obvious example was Britain's entry into the European Community in 1973 and the subsequent attempt to legitimise that parliamentary decision, the referendum of 1975. The Community was precisely the kind of supranational institution which, hitherto, British policy makers had tried to avoid, and it is an indication of the weakness of the country's position that this strategy had to be dropped. The 1970s also witnessed some unsettling changes in the relations between the superpowers. It was not so much that by the end of the decade détente had clearly failed, it was more the case that in the course of pursuing that strategy US administrations had neglected their allies and dealt increasingly with the Soviet Union directly. The special relationship, already unsettled by Britain's Community membership, appeared to be entering a more difficult and distant phase. Equally important were some changes in the international economic environment: the decline of US economic hegemony, the advent of floating exchange rate systems, the rise of OPEC, world recession and inflation, and Britain's emergence, after 1975, as an oil-producing and then oil-exporting country. These economic developments were not only awkward for Britain's fragile open economy, they were also unsettling because within government the level of expertise to deal with the problems of managing a floating petrocurrency was not, at first, very great.

Secondly, by the end of the 1970s two internally generated and

potentially destabilising forces had emerged to complicate the
politics of the open polity. One concerned the Conservative party's
stance on foreign affairs between 1975 and 1979. Throughout that
period Mrs Thatcher's speeches indicated a new direction in foreign
policy if the Conservatives were returned to office, a new direction in
terms of diplomatic style, hostility to the Soviet bloc and a greater
determination to press British interests abroad (Wapshott and Brock
1983, Rose 1982). On the other hand, it was generally accepted
that Mrs Thatcher lacked experience in external affairs, the party
was divided, and three Shadow Foreign Secretaries in as many years
was an obstacle to continuity and coherence. The eventual team
chosen for the Foreign Office and Defence in 1979 – Carrington,
Gilmour and Pym – were clearly not members of the Thatcherite
clan. Hence the future of Conservative foreign policy after May 1979
was obscure. The other impending problem was that whichever
party was in office in the 1980s was likely to be faced with some
difficult decisions: a replacement for the Polaris nuclear capability,
accepting cruise missiles, Nato's decision for an annual real increase
of 3 per cent in defence expenditure, Britain's European Community
budget contribution, and the response, if any, to the new
Muzorewa-led government in Rhodesia. These were not only
difficult decisions, they were also potential sources of intense party-
political conflict.

Finally, if the assumption is that external affairs and domestic
policies are positively linked, then what can be called the
'Thatcherite domestic project' in government must be considered as
well. Whether in policy terms this was as radical as is often
suggested is a matter of some dispute (Brittan 1983, Riddell 1985,
Crewe and Searing 1986, Kavanagh 1987). We need to note,
however, several specific features of this policy project, namely: the
Medium-Term Financial Strategy (MTFS) of 1980, which committed the Conservatives to certain economic targets by 1983; the
constant rhetorical support given to two operational principles,
'There is No Alternative' (TINA) and 'The Resolute Approach'; the
abandonment of a strict monetarist policy after 1982; and the
increasing attacks on the autonomy of intermediate institutions such
as local authorities. In more general political terms these were
governments which certainly stirred the domestic political pool, not
least in successfully winning two elections with over three million
unemployed.

In combination, these developments indicate that 1980 marked a critical juncture in the development of the open polity. They are usually perceived as imposing further constraints on the autonomy and sovereignty of British governments. But, theoretically, an equally plausible view is that on some occasions they may provide opportunities for politicians in office to increase both their political standing and autonomy from domestic forces. The 1976 sterling crisis certainly provided such opportunities for Mr Callaghan and Mr Healey (Fay and Young 1978, Donoughue 1987). The European Community clouds responsibility for policies, and the management of a floating currency, with all its problems, does allow the semblance of an autonomous monetary policy without the stark and politically difficult devaluation crises of the *ancien régime*. Moreover, developments which enforce new policy decisions from governments require some response from opposition parties and those responses may give politicians in office new weapons to wield in the party-political battle.

Conservative Statecraft and the Open Polity, 1979–87

How did the Conservative leaders in office after 1979 respond to the new issues, constraints and opportunities posed by this critical juncture? This matter will be considered within the fourfold framework of statecraft dimensions outlined in Assumption Six above. These were originally designed to examine the domestic performance of single administrations (Bulpitt 1986a) but they are useful in the present context because they remind us that the primary drive behind them is the rationality of the domestic political cycle – the need to win elections – whereas external forces and shocks often operate independently of British politicians' tactical or strategic preferences concerned with that cycle. Extending the analysis to more than one political cycle – two administrations of the same party leadership – means that we are also in a position to approach cautiously another, and more generally important, question: were the responses of those Conservative party governments to the critical juncture sufficiently innovative to have generated a new open-polity regime?

Conservative Party Management

It is tempting to argue that the Conservative party (back-bench MPs and extra-parliamentary organisations) had little influence on its

leaders' foreign policy preferences and how they managed the impact
of external forces on domestic politics. After all, the party prides
itself on the freedom it grants its leaders in office, the Falklands
victory guaranteed Mrs Thatcher's reputation in the field with the
rank and file and, after 1983, the internal opposition to the
leadership group was mostly muted, fragmented and dejected. For a
number of reasons, however, this thesis must be treated with some
caution.

One reason stems from the circumstances surrounding Mrs
Thatcher's election to the Conservative leadership in 1975. If
politicians learn from the past mistakes of others, as the rationality
assumption suggests, then the new leadership would have understood from that episode the potential of back-benches power and the
necessity not to ignore MPs preferences in ways too obvious (Fisher
1977, Wapshott and Brock 1983). Again, through the 1980s there
were a number of possible fault lines in the party which were
potential sources of trouble: the division between 'wets' and 'dries',
the continued existence of a right-wing tendency, and cleavages
stemming from personality/office-holding interests (amongst which
must be included Conservative members of some of the new
Commons select committees). Moreover, it is often difficult to
identify examples of party influence, particularly if it is one of a
number of factors which determine that a policy is not pursued, or
never considered seriously. The Ministry of Agriculture illustrates
the problem. Until the latter part of the second administration this
pursued policies in relation to the European Community which were
at odds with the government's public stance to that institution. Was
this a party rebellion by the ministers concerned, bureaucratic
politics, or a deviation accepted because it was politically useful in
relation to the farm vote? It is not clear.

It is possible to argue that some policies resulted from manifesto
commitments. That of 1979 was the most explicit: it promised
increased expenditure on service pay, tighter immigration controls
and a British Nationality Act. All were implemented. Other
policies were pursued with the party 'in mind'. Prime examples were
the sending of the Falklands Task Force and the Rhodesia/
Zimbabwe settlement of 1980, though the latter was criticised by
the right wing and made any movement on the Falklands before
April 1982 – always difficult – even more of a problem. Other
policies could also be placed in this category: the determination to

pursue a European Community budgetary settlement, the unwillingness to impose serious sanctions against South Africa and the
decision to renew Britain's nuclear deterrent. In each case the *reverse*
of these policies would have been difficult to sell to many
Conservative MPs and the annual party conference. Nevertheless,
the most serious and publicised party divisions stemmed from
personality- and institution-based conflicts within these administrations. Francis Pym's tenure at both the Ministry of Defence and the
Foreign Office was a cause of conflict. And the Westland affair,
involving Michael Heseltine and Leon Brittan, reflected similar
problems. Smaller, and less public, conflicts occurred in the
Northern Ireland Office concerning James Prior's policies.

Frankly it is difficult to arrive at any positive conclusions
regarding the influence of the Conservative party on its leaders'
external-affairs functions. The subject requires more detailed
treatment than is possible here.

Political Argument Hegemony

This dimension of statecraft assumed considerable importance
during the life of these two Conservative governments. There were
several reasons for this: the final lamentable failure on this count by
the Heath-led party; the fact that the Thatcher leadership group was
so self-consciously radical; the emergence of the Alliance (particularly David Owen) to complicate political argument; Labour's break
with the 1970s interparty élite consensus on European Community
membership, Britain's nuclear weapons and US nuclear bases; and
finally, developments after 1979 involving the superpowers —
concerning Afghanistan, Poland, the Strategic Defense Initiative,
Nicaragua and, above all, the post-Reykjavik move to a new détente
and agreement on intermediate-range missiles in Europe. Changing
external circumstances often forced Conservative leaders to respond
in *ad hoc* ways and with *ad hoc* arguments to new problems as they
arose. But sometimes those responses took on a more permanent
character, for example in the relative softening of the government's
attitude to the Soviet Union which occurred in 1983–4 (Young and
Sloman 1986). Nevertheless, taking the period 1979 to 1987 as a
whole, it is surprising how many themes of Conservative political
argument in this arena were sustained. These related to the message,
method, and recycling of this subject matter.

The message was designed for foreign consumption. In short, it was produced to indicate to foreigners what to expect by way of basic external policy principles from the Conservative governments. This was foreign policy doctrine as traditionally understood. One constant element was the heavy emphasis placed on their determination to halt Britain's decline and their willingness to accept a positive world role. There was to be no retreat, economically or militarily, into a fortress-Britain syndrome. Another was the idea that the world constantly teetered on the verge of a Hobbesian state of nature, where a variety of gangsters were always willing to hold Western nations to ransom or attack their long-term interests. The remedy was interstate co-operation to combat the threat from the Warsaw Pact, to confront state terrorism and to combat drug trafficking. Thirdly, the Conservatives constantly stressed that Britain was now committed to prudent economic, especially financial, management: no longer was the country to be a source of instability in the international economy. Over time it was possible to add another element to this particular message. If the Western world wished to make a full recovery from its recession then the British economic way – close attention to public-spending levels and the pursuit of privatisation – was the route other governments should follow. This was 'There is No Alternative' (TINA) employed on the external front. The final message was that British governments were now fully prepared to stand up for British interests, whatever the cost and whatever annoyance was caused to other states (and to the Foreign Office). It was a message directed at the United Nations, frontline states in Africa, the European Community, world liberal opinion regarding immigration controls, Syria, Libya and, most obviously, Argentina. This was 'The Resolute Approach' applied to the international arena.

The Conservative's determination to gain political argument hegemony in foreign affairs also encompassed a method, or style, of policy making and international negotiating. Development of this theme parallelled Mrs Thatcher's rise to authority in her Cabinet, simply because it involved the personalisation of foreign policy and behaviour in terms of her attitudes, ideas and image. Increasingly, British foreign policy was presented as the policies of one woman, so that in many respects this method became the message. Foreign governments either used this for their own ends or simply accepted it. Thus Mrs Thatcher's role as world stateswoman, hardly a serious thought in 1979, was a very relevant point for both the content and presentation of British foreign policy by 1987. Hence, over time, statecraft resources can change and one obvious cause is simply the investment benefits gained from the constant presence on the world stage of a determined personality where, for a variety of reasons, other leaders fall by the wayside. At this point the link between domestic policies and external affairs becomes even more explicit.

The final item in the Conservatives' bid for political argument hegemony directly concerned the internal politics of the open polity. It involved the constant recycling of both the foreign policy message and method for domestic consumption as weapons in the internal party-political battle. The Conservatives could claim not simply that their external successes entitled them to govern Britain, but that their foreign policy stance indicated the correctness of their domestic strategy as well. The two were merely different sides of the same coin. This was most apparent over the Falklands issue (Crewe 1984; but see Sanders *et al* 1987). By 1987 the general presentation of domestic economic management was intricately bound up with the awkward state of the world economy and foreign imitations of the Conservatives' economic experiments. In addition, on defence Labour's policies (and to a lesser extent those of the Alliance) could be attacked not only on their intrinsic merits and demerits, but also on the basis that any alteration in Britain's stance and leadership would have an adverse impact on her relations with many other countries. Even appeasement, the skeleton in the Conservatives' cupboard, was finally brought out and affixed to Labour's stance, an interesting reversal of the historical legacy. Not surprisingly, opposition leaders found these tactics difficult to combat. Thus in terms of the interparty élite battle the Conservatives won the contest for political argument hegemony. Whether that hegemony extended to the views of the electorate was less clear.

A Governing Competence

Political argument hegemony is a matter of ideas and their presentation in public political debate. A governing competence is concerned not with policy details or long-term goals, but with actions and decisions (or inactions and non-decisions) designed to protect and promote the interests of the party leaders in office. In the present context it denotes the specific tactics employed to minimise the adverse impact of external forces on domestic politics in ways acceptable to the governing party and, in the process, make life difficult for opposition groups. The sum of such tactics may be dignified as the 'medium-term external strategy'. Politicians, of course, will rarely choose to see their operations in this light, hence at this point the *as if* hypothesis, is pulled in to justify the exercise. The discussion is most conveniently advanced by listing some of the more significant tactics, or ploys, pursued.

Conflict 'Resolution'   This is an up-market label for what in plainer English would be called foreign policy successes. But 'success' suggests finality, a positive end to a problem, and if one thing is clear in international relations it is that problems rarely disappear for ever – they tend to re-emerge in some slightly altered form. Moreover, the political memory of the electorate is notoriously short, so that 'success' or 'resolutions' merely contribute to a general image of competence and, perhaps, free politicians, temporarily, to concentrate on other problems. This said, it can be suggested that the Thatcher-led administrations were associated with more specific cases of conflict resolution than many previous British governments. The principal examples were the creation of Zimbabwe, the military victory in the Falklands, the European Community budgetary settlement at the 1984 Fontainebleau summit, and the deal with China over the future of Hong Kong. To this list, perhaps could be added the British Nationality Act, which, within the Conservative party at least, resolved that awkward matter. No doubt other examples could be cited but the main point has emerged. Over eight years there were sufficient presentational successes to be of some benefit in the interparty game.

Rational Inactivity   Sometimes it is rational for governments to do nothing, or at least appear to do nothing, as long as this produces no obvious adverse consequences. The arguments for inactivity are several: the utility of a particular course of action may be unclear; there is a high risk of implementation failure; action may be pre-empted by another power; or it may be feared that a decision may be unpopular in either the domestic or external arena, or both. Perhaps the best example of this particular ploy during the period under review was the unwillingness of the government to allow sterling to join the exchange-rate mechanism of the European Monetary

System. Such a decision was strongly supported, so it was said, by many elements in the Treasury and Bank of England, but was opposed by Mrs Thatcher and some of her advisers, notably Professor Walters. The Prime Minister's objections were on two grounds: sterling's petrocurrency status made the arrangement inappropriate and membership would curtail the government's freedom in monetary policy. Other examples of inactivity were Grenada (pre-empted by United States action) and the troubles in Sri Lanka and Fiji. On the whole the results were satisfactory: the interests of the Conservative leadership did not noticeably suffer. Even the United States' invasion of Grenada and the public humiliation of Sir Geoffrey Howe by Kenneth Kaunda, both initially embarrassing, were soon forgotten.

Deliberate Politicisation   On many occasions governments will seek to establish a specific policy consensus. But British governments are party governments and therefore always liable to attack from their opponents. Perhaps more interesting are those occasions when a government will deliberately seek conflict, will opt to politicise an issue, either to make life awkward for the opposition, or to re-establish, or promote, its own authority. On the evidence available this appears to have been a favourite tactic of these Thatcher administrations. One explanation for the imposition of stricter immigration controls, the opposition to effective sanctions against South Africa, the stress on the threats posed by the Soviet bloc and the general emphasis on the government's defence policies were the benefits to be gained by the Conservatives from politicising these issues. Indeed, Mr Heseltine was sent to the Ministry of Defence in January 1983 precisely because of his abilities to 'rough up' his opponents. We have seen that one aspect of the domestic project was the attack on intermediate institutions which challenged the authority of these governments. A similar tactic was developed in the field of national security. The abolition of trade unions at GCHQ, the numerous conflicts with the BBC over its foreign and defence affairs coverage (including Northern Ireland), the legal actions against leakages of information by civil servants, culminating in the Peter Wright saga, were all examples of these administrations seeking to enhance their own political authority, as well as protect national security and their relations with the US. So, too, was the centralisation of the policy process within the Ministry of Defence.

The Reversal of Assignments   In the course of a speech delivered in 1984, the Chancellor of the Exchequer complained that many critics misunderstood the new rules of economic management (Bulpitt 1986a). It was, he argued, no use complaining that the government's macroeconomic policy did not seek to solve the unemployment problem. Such criticism missed the point: in so far as unemployment could be tackled by the British government, that task was now in the province of micro, or supply-side, management. There had, he said, been a 'reversal of assignments' on this matter between the macro and micro sectors. The argument here is that a similar reversal of assignments occurred in the field of external policy. The results were that some issues formerly in the realm of the domestic policy sector were partially 'put out' to the external sector for settlement and, in the process, the openness of the British polity was increased.

Not surprisingly most examples of this phenomenon involved the economy. Thus the suspension, and then final abolition, of exchange controls, the 'Big Bang' at the Stock Exchange and the varying policies towards sterling all in effect transferred important aspects of domestic policy to the international market economy for determination. Indeed, the more the Treasury, Downing Street and the Bank of England relied, as they did after 1982, on a combination of interest rates and the exchange rate to regulate the economy, the more they relied on foreign 'confidence' in the British economy to assist them in managing that economy. Moreover, when it suited, the Conservatives would argue that a real and permanent solution to the unemployment problem lay not so much with supply-side policies in Britain as with a general upturn in the world economy. Similarly, the passing of the Single European Act indicated the government's willingness to accept much greater interpenetration between the British economy and that of the European Community after 1992, and the whole issue of sanctions against South Africa could be off-loaded on to the European Community and the Commonwealth. One further interesting example of this tactic requires some comment. The Anglo-Irish Agreement of 1985, by granting governments of the Irish Republic a formal advisory status on Northern Ireland affairs, also partially transferred this issue from its UK context to the external sector. No previous British government had dared to do this. Indeed, the public argument had always been that the Province was entirely a domestic issue (Cmnd 9657 1985, Cox 1987, O'Leary 1987).

Britain's Role: the Two Concentric Circles General comment on Conservative foreign policy in the 1980s has stressed two themes: the government's – or Mrs Thatcher's – crude nationalism and the renewed significance of the special relationship with the United States. Both these themes need to be treated with caution. The Washington connection was clearly important. Yet so much stress on this feature perhaps misunderstands both the nature, and the future, of the relationship. The core of the special relationship, at least since 1945, has always been the many connections between the professional defence communities in the two countries. Only if Labour won office on an explicit unilateralist platform would this very special feature of the special relationship be endangered. Otherwise, it is too much a part of the professionals' 'official mind' on both sides of the Atlantic to wither away too easily. In other policy sectors, and at higher levels, however, the special relationship has been much less intense and continuous. Indeed, at the highest level – the relationship between President and Prime Minister – whatever is special about the connection has to be remade every time a change in personnel occurs. In this sense Mrs Thatcher was very fortunate to encounter Ronald Reagan. What can be called the 'Ron and Maggie show' is probably unique: no repeat performances may be possible. Hence the special relationship can provide no firm basis for future British foreign policy. It is reasonable to assume that Conservative politicians, not least Mrs Thatcher, were aware of this. So, what alternatives were available? The obvious one was the European Community, and in many ways the 'efficient secret' of Thatcherite foreign policy was precisely this: the steady and progressive Europeanisation of Britain's role, despite the many public disputes and professed irritations with that organisation (Davidson 1987). By 1987 Britain was more completely a European Community power than ever before. Partly, this was simply the result of the passage of time. Partly, it was the result of the fact that, at root, there was no alternative to the Community. But it may also have resulted from the realisation that within the complex network of Community institutions a British government could obscure responsibility and hide from awkward domestic forces. Whatever the reason, this Europeanisation of Britain's role was achieved without notable party argument or adverse consequences for the Conservatives. Given the history of the issue that was no mean achievement.

A *Winning Electoral Strategy*

One criticism of the statecraft approach is that it imposes a retrospective coherence on the actions of politicians, a coherence which conveniently ignores the mistakes that were made (Layton-Henry 1986). The analytical search for coherence, however, does not preclude miscalculations, that is actions which have adverse consequences for the policies and/or political aims of the party in office. The problem is to assess their overall impact, especially in the context of election victories.

Two of the most significant, because fully publicised, were the series of actions and inactions which led to the Falklands War and the Westland affair. These were more than miscalculations, they produced political crises of the first importance. Both were aspects of the open polity and both, temporarily at least, weakened the Conservatives' position on all the aspects of statecraft discussed so far. Another example, which had a profound impact on Conservative techniques of economic management, was the initial 'hands-off' approach to the appreciation in the value of sterling in 1979 and 1980 (Niehans 1981, Keegan 1984 and 1985, Alt 1987). Whatever the motives behind that policy, the decision to let international market forces determine the exchange rate, during a period of strict domestic monetary controls and the second world oil crisis, had unfortunate repercussions for the fortunes of British industry and employment levels. The reversal of this policy led not only to more flexible monetary controls but, in addition, to the greater reliance on exchange-rate targets bolstered by domestic interest rates as the key tools of macroeconomic management. In other words, the Conservatives accepted that a fully autonomous monetarism in one small country was impossible. That was the logic of the open economy. Henceforth, British economic management was constrained, as always, by international market forces and the behaviour of other governments, particularly those of the three 'motor' economies, the United States, West Germany and Japan. Finally, it should be noted that, despite the Conservatives' considerable interest in the management of public opinion, survey evidence indicates that on a number of key items of their foreign policy stance – the resolute approach, cruise missiles and relations with the United States – the electorate's views were by no means always fully supportive (Crewe and Searing 1986, Kavanagh 1987).

Despite these mistakes and weaknesses, the Conservatives won two notable election victories in 1983 and 1987. Clearly a variety of factors influenced those results. The question here is: what role, if any, did the politics of the open polity play in these successes? The 1987 election campaign will be used to illustrate the point briefly. For the Conservative leaders the preparations for the campaign probably began in the summer of 1986, in the period when the party was still recovering from the embarrassments of the Westland affair and the use by the United States of its British bases to bomb Libya. The main task was to arrange that over the following year the principal domestic economic indicators favoured the government. The role of external affairs in the overall strategy was threefold. The first was the necessity to avoid external shocks, either to the economy or the government's general foreign policy image. Clearly this was, to a great extent, in the lap of the gods. There were constant fears, for example, of an exchange-rate crisis. That one did not occur was the result partly of increasing international co-operation on exchange rates and partly of the Chancellor's very cautious approach to reducing interest rates. The principal shock to emerge came from a totally unexpected quarter: the awkward political fallout from the Reykjavik summit between Reagan and Gorbachev in the autumn of 1986. The implications of a possible superpower deal on intermediate-range missiles in Europe were potentially very embarrassing for the Conservatives' defence policy and its nuclear commitment. In this respect, it was fortunate that the election was held before these implications became fully operational. Secondly, the government needed to arrange foreign policy to boost its domestic image. The tactic here was to emphasise Mrs Thatcher's role as a world leader. Her visit to Moscow in the early spring of 1987 could be counted a success in this respect. It had the added bonus that Mr Kinnock, playing the same game, failed to gain any positive benefit from his American visit. It was also convenient that the Venice World Summit took place during the election campaign. Finally, external affairs provided campaign issues to attack the opposition parties. Here the Conservatives fully exploited the defence issue to highlight the dangers of a Labour victory for the Western Alliance and the divisions within the Alliance camp. Just as interesting were those external issues which were not pressed during the election campaign. The European Community was one. More significant, nearly all discussions on economic policy were premised on the view that Britain was a closed economy, in which domestic politicians had full control over economic management. This undoubtedly simplified matters for politicians and voters, but there is, perhaps, no better illustration of the ultimate primacy of domestic politics in the open polity.

Conclusions

This examination of the methods employed by Conservative politicians in the 1980s to manage the impact of external forces on domestic British politics yields a number of conclusions. First, this is a neglected and difficult area of study which, perhaps, deserves more attention from British academics than it has hitherto received. Secondly, the idea that these governments would pursue their own interests is revealed to be not implausible. Obviously, many of their actions and policies coincided with some perceptions of the national interest, or those of particular domestic groups. But, overall, the assumption that Conservative leaders would perceive their interests in terms of some relative autonomy for themselves is sustainable. Thirdly, the period considered represents a critical juncture in the development of the British open polity. Conservative leaders appear to have learnt one big thing from the experience: it was possible to protect and support the fragile domestic autonomy of British party governments by submerging many of their activities in a complex network of external commitments, institutions and forces. Previous administrations had always considered their insulation from external forces a necessary condition for the success of their domestic designs. The Thatcher-led Conservative governments were more willing to abandon that strategy if it promoted their own domestic autonomy. This argument reflects the Skocpol thesis outlined in one of the epigraphs to this chapter. It was not, of course, the only strategy pursued by these administrations: the more traditional approach continued to survive. Moreover, the general primacy granted to domestic politics was entirely within the customary conventions of British, and especially Conservative, politicians. Nevertheless, this change in the means to that traditional goal was a significant innovation and one ignored by many commentators on British politics in the 1980s. It suggests the beginnings of a new open-polity regime for Britain. It may be, however, that the methodology adopted in this chapter can only generate the messages outlined above. Hence the final conclusion that this whole exercise should be treated with considerable caution is both obvious and necessary.

References and Further Reading

A fuller treatment of this subject will be attempted in my *The Open Polity: External Affairs and British Domestic Politics in the 1980s*, Philip Allan 1989.

Allison, G.T. (1971) *Essence of Decision: Explaining the Cuban Missile Crisis*, Little, Brown.

Alt, J.E. (1987) 'Crude politics: oil and the political economy of unemployment in Britain and Norway, 1970–85', *British Journal of Political Science*, vol. 17, no. 2.

Armstrong, J.A. (1965) 'The domestic roots of Soviet foreign policy', *International Affairs*, vol. 41, no. 1.

Balbus, I. (1971) 'The concept of interest in pluralist and Marxist analysis', *Politics and Society*, vol. 1, no. 2.

Begg, D., Fischer, S. and Dornbusch, R. (1984) *Economics*, McGraw-Hill.

Brittan, S. (1983) *The Role and Limits of Government*, Temple Smith.

Bulpitt, J. (1982) 'Conservatism, unionism and the problem of territorial management' in Madgwick, P. and Rose, R. (eds) *The Territorial Dimension in United Kingdom Politics*, Macmillan.

Bulpitt, J. (1983) *Territory and Power in the United Kingdom*, Manchester University Press.

Bulpitt, J. (1986a) 'The discipline of the new democracy: Mrs Thatcher's domestic statecraft', *Political Studies*, XXXIV, no. 1.

Bulpitt, J. (1986b) 'Continuity, autonomy and peripheralisation: the anatomy of the centre's race statecraft in England' in Layton-Henry, Z. and Rich, P. (eds) *Race, Government and Politics in Britain*, Macmillan.

Cowling, M. (1975) *The Impact of Hitler: British Politics and British Policy 1933–40*, University of Chicago Press.

Cox, W. (1987) 'Managing Northern Ireland intergovernmentally: an appraisal of the Anglo-Irish Agreement', *Parliamentary Affairs*, vol. 40.

Crewe, I. (1984) 'How to win a landslide without really trying: why the Conservatives won in 1983', *Essex Papers in Politics and Government*, No. 1.

Crewe, I. and Searing, D. (1986) 'Thatcherism: its origins, electoral impact and implications for Downs's theory of party strategy', *Essex Papers in Politics and Government*, No. 37.

Dallin, A. (1981) 'The domestic sources of Soviet foreign policy', in Bialer, S. (ed.) *The Domestic Context of Soviet Foreign Policy*, Croom Helm.

Davidson, I. (1987) 'Foreign policy: the unavoidable connection' in *The Thatcher Years*, The Financial Times.

Donoughue, B. (1987) *Prime Minister: The Conduct of Policy Under Harold Wilson and James Callaghan*, Jonathan Cape.

Dunleavy, P. and O'Leary, B. (1987) *Theories of the State*, Macmillan.

Fay, S. and Young, H. (1978) *The Day the Pound Nearly Died*, The Sunday Times.
Fisher, N. (1977) *The Tory Leaders: Their Struggle for Power*, Weidenfeld and Nicolson.
Frey, F.W. (1985) 'The problem of actor designation in political analysis', *Comparative Politics*.
Friedman, M. (1953) *Essays in Positive Economics*, University of Chicago Press.
Gilpin, R. (1981) *War and Change in World Politics*.
Gourevitch, P. (1978) 'The second image reversed: the international sources of domestic politics', *International Organisation*, vol. 32, no. 4.
Jessop, B. (1982) *The Capitalist State*, Martin Robertson.
Kavanagh, D. (1987) *Thatcherism and British Politics, the End of Consensus*, Clarendon Press.
Keegan, W. (1984) *Mrs Thatcher's Economic Experiment*, Allen Lane Press.
Keegan, W. (1985) *Britain Without Oil*, Penguin.
Kehr, E. (1965) *Der Primat der Innenpolitik*, Walter de Gruyter.
Kehr, E. (1977) *Economic Interest, Militarism and Foreign Policy*, University of California Press.
Kennedy, P. (1981) *The Realities Behind Diplomacy*, Fontana.
Keohane, R. and Nye, J. (1977) *Power and Interdependence*, Little, Brown.
Krasner, S. (1978) *Defending the National Interest*, Princeton University Press.
Layton-Henry, Z. (1986) 'Introduction' in Layton-Henry, Z. and Rich, P. (eds) *Race, Government and Politics in Britain*, Macmillan.
Morse, E. (1976) *Modernisation and the Transformation of International Relations*, Free Press.
Nailor, P. (1983) 'Foreign and defence policy', in Druckedr, H. (ed.) *Developments in British Politics*, Macmillan.
Niehans, J. (1981) *The Appreciation of Sterling – Causes, Effects, Policies*. University of Rochester.
Nordlinger, E. (1981) *The Autonomy of the Democratic State*, Harvard University Press.
O'Leary, B. (1987) 'The Anglo–Irish Agreement: folly or statecraft?', *West European Politics*, vol. 10, no. 1.
Pugh, M. (1985) *The Tories and the People*, Blackwell.
Riddell, P. (1985) *The Thatcher Government*, Blackwell.
Riker, W. and Ordeshook, P. (1973) *An Introduction to Positive Political Theory*, Prentice Hall.
Rose, R. (1980) *Do Parties Make A Difference?*, Macmillan.
Rose, R. (1982) 'The British Conservative party' in Morgan, R. and Silvester, S. (eds) *Moderates and Conservatives in Western Europe*, Heinemann.
Rosenau, J. (1966) 'Pre-theories and theories of foreign policy' in Farrell, R.B. (ed.) *Approaches to Comparative and International Politics*, Northwestern University Press.
Sanders, D. *et al.* (1987) 'Government popularity and the Falklands War: a reassessment', *British Journal of Political Science*, vol. 17, no. 3.
Saunders, P. (1980) *Urban Politics*, Penguin Books.
Skocpol, T. (1979) *States and Social Revolution*, Cambridge University Press.
Simon, H. (1979) 'Rational decision making in business organisation', *American Economic Review*, LXIX.

Simon, H. (1987) 'Rationality as process and a product of thought', *American Economic Review*, LXXVII.

Singer, J.D. (1961) 'The level of analysis problem in international relations' in Knorr, K. and Verba, S. (eds) *The International System: Theoretical Essays*, Princeton University Press.

Swartz, M. (1985) *The Politics of British Foreign Policy in the Era of Disraeli and Gladstone*, Macmillan.

Verba, S. (1961) 'Assumptions of rationality and non-rationality in models of the international system' in Knorr, K. and Verba, S. (eds) *The International System: Theoretical Essays*, Princeton University Press.

Vital, D. (1968) *The Making of British Foreign Policy*, Allen & Unwin.

Wallace, W. (1975) *The Foreign Policy Process in Britain*, Chatham House.

Wallace, W. (1986) 'What price independence? Sovereignty and interdependence in British politics', *International Affairs*, vol. 62, no. 3.

Wapshott, N. and Brock, G. (1983) *Thatcher*, Futura.

Young, H. and Sloman, A. (1986) *The Thatcher Phenomenon*, BBC Publications.

Cmnd 9657 (1985) *Agreement between the Government of the United Kingdom and the Government of the Republic of Ireland*, HMSO.

Index